A Nation of Idiots

An In-Your-Face Look at the Underbelly of Public Education

By

Karl Thelen MS Ed.

© 2001, 2003 by Karl E. Thelen. All rights reserved.

No part of this book may be reproduced, stored in a retrieval system, or transmitted by any means, electronic, mechanical, photocopying, recording, or otherwise, without written permission from the author.

ISBN: 1-4033-9508-X (e-book)
ISBN: 1-4033-9509-8 (Paperback)
ISBN: 1-4033-9510-1 (Dustjacket)

Library of Congress Control Number: 2002095792

This book is printed on acid free paper.

Printed in the United States of America
Bloomington, IN

1stBooks - rev. 12/19/02

This book is dedicated to my mother, Virginia Thelen, 82 and still going strong. She deserves this and so much more.

Acknowledgements

I would like to thank the following people who made this book possible: Former students Meredith and Allie Thompson, both honor students of the highest caliber, whose attention to detail and insightful comments gave me a great lesson in the English language; Reva Cousino, June Sargent, Jane Cooper, Mike Corey and Maxine Connor who read many pages of rough draft and kept me honest and on the straight and narrow with their corrections and suggestions; Shane Thelen, my eldest son and a master teacher in his own right, whose diligent proof reading and diverse educational experience proved invaluable; Jason Emmons, another former student, whose unique perspective on life directed me to valuable information regarding the tremendous influence that the great manipulators have on our lives; Jim Ross, my good friend and colleague for the past twenty-three years, for his constant encouragement and interest in what I was doing; My mother, Virginia Thelen who was the first to ask to read what I had written; Dr. Robert Cialdini of Arizona State University for his generous permission to quote from his book, <u>Influence</u>, which every student of the media should read; Justin Axelroth, Jim Helsley and everyone at 1st Books who make dreams come true; and lastly, my wife of thirty-four years, Mary, for being there. She gives me strength and inspiration by her proximity to me.

I also promised to mention former students Ed Cherrier and Steve Audy, so there it is boys. And, oh, yes, Nikki Lee☺

Table of Contents

Acknowledgements v
Chapter 1. An Overview; what you see is what you get 1
    First, a note about Feelgooders 3
    Second, a note about Master Teachers 5
Chapter 2. Those Teachers; those *#%&!!** teachers 17
    Teacher Testing 22
Chapter 3. Administrators; School Boards, Taxpayers and Parents; they all should be spanked 31
Chapter 4. Pharmaceutical Companies; take your medicine, it's good for us 46
Chapter 5. Mass Media Manipulators; purveyors of the ambient light 52
Chapter 6. Mushy Brains and Weapons of Influence; bad touching 72
Chapter 7. Special Education; very little bang for the buck 95
Chapter 8. Effective Teaching: if it's working, don't fix it 116
Chapter 9. Effective Schools, top heavy they're not 130
    Classroom characteristics and practices 138
    School characteristics and practices 152
Chapter 10. A Circle of Assessment; how to get there from here 163
    Standardized Testing 165
    Portfolios 168
    Multiple Intelligences 170
    Hemisphericity 172
    Learning Styles 175
    Memory 177
Chapter 11. Things That I Do; time to toot 183
Chapter 12. In Conclusion; it's all been said before 202
Index 209
Bibliography 215

Chapter one

An Overview; What you see is what you get

We are raising and educating **A Nation of Idiots**. That is my premise, and I will make the case for it in the following pages. I've been teaching for thirty-three years. I'm a parent of four, a taxpayer; I have a master's degree in Administration and Supervision, and was on a school board for seven years. I have all the bases covered. I feel qualified to make the following statements.

Many people won't like what I have to say: teachers, administrators, school board members, parents, taxpayers, special educators, legislators, the American Medical Association, the pharmaceutical industry, the huge mass media complex, college professors and, unfortunately, some of my current colleagues. Most certainly those whom I have come to call Feelgooders, will like me the least.

All of these groups mentioned are guilty of diminishing education in the United States, and creating **A Nation of Idiots**, and the worse thing is they don't even know it. Through ignorance, their own stupidity, incredible greed, indifference, or a desire to right every wrong and make everyone 'feel good,' each group has ignored its responsibility to the future. Each has missed the essence of education in their headlong rush to satisfy their own needs or to prove that they were at least doing **something**.

Ironically, at historical moments, like now, when great decisions have to be made (in this case about education), people who don't know what they're doing tend to agree with each other over mediocrity in hopes that no one will discover that they really don't know what they are doing. So it is in public education in America today.

Too many people involved with education have agreed with each other over the years and made poor decisions regarding the direction of education because no one was really sure what to do, so we wound up with mediocrity. Mediocrity won't cut it in the new millennium. Often these mediocre-maker people are the ones who have a lot of time to be on school committees, which is sad since the committees make all the important decisions. If the committees were made up of master teachers that would be one thing, but, unfortunately, that's usually not the case.

A large part of the book is against what I have come to call in education Feelgoodenism, the desire to have every one feel good about themselves and their education. Feelgoodenism is practiced by Feelgooders. Their ideas, however, are contrary to the discipline needed to get students to a point where learning is valued and the results of hard and persistent work become obvious. You can certainly have respect and concern for the students as human beings, but not if it means lowering expectations for student behavior and academic outcomes.

Thanks to already lowered expectations, many students today are less inclined to spend a lot of time on schoolwork, plagiarism can be called rampant (original thought in this video game age is difficult), common courtesies have just about disappeared, and students react slowly, or not at all, to situations where others need help. Their basic academic skills dwindle each year, and, for most, academic curiosity is almost nonexistent. Many students feel that much of life should be free for the taking, or with minimal effort. They can become abusive and hostile if their minimal efforts aren't rewarded. Their work ethic, not just in school but outside as well, is appalling. One employer said that often the students he's hired don't even call up if they aren't coming in to work. They just don't show up. The ability to think has decreased with the lessening of the need. Computers have taken over many cognitive functions and replaced them with computer functions. It is not a pretty picture that I paint. Feelgooders complicate all aspects of education.

There are huge challenges ahead of us as we wend our way through the new millennium, and we need educated people to see us through those times. Unfortunately, in many instances across America, that education isn't happening. Unless something is done to halt the spread of further idiocy and Feelgoodenism, as I will continue to call it, and the continued reliance by greedy corporate giants and the media on 'mushy brained,' uneducated consumers, the future of our nation as a historical light in the darkness will vanish.

First, a note about Feelgooders

Feelgooders have preempted a large part of education in America. They have caused our academic standards to drop to lows unthinkable just a couple of generations ago, and all under the guise of 'quality education.' Their code words are 'standards,' 'innovation,' 'equality,' and 'political correctness' (which leads directly to the debacle of zero tolerance). The mission of these Feelgooders is to make every student 'feel good' about their educational experience. Inadvertently they tend to lower everyone academically to a standard that, they believe, shows, without question, that these folks, along with the State (where Feelgooders are rampant), know what they are doing when it comes to equality and quality in education. They believe their ideas will eliminate stress caused by learning.

Feelgooders are everywhere. In education in general, in the legislatures, in our bloated Federal educational system, in the large, lumbering out-of-touch teachers' unions, in the media, in special education, on school boards and, thanks to the media, in the general population at large. But, scariest of all, they hide right there in plain sight in many classrooms.

Feelgooders believe that a student needs to 'feel good' about themselves first before they can learn. Once that state of mind is achieved, they will willingly be educated and become good contributing members of society, and in turn, pass that Feelgooderness on to future generations until, extrapolated, we are a complete nation of feeling good people-who, by the way, will be pretty stupid since education will have been the loser way back when.

What Feelgooders fail to understand, is that feeling good about oneself comes through a feeling of success, achieved most often through hard, persistent and consistent work, not a vague feeling inside that was placed there by a Feelgooder who praised a poorly done project as 'a very good effort' in order to make the student feel good. This attitude engenders nothing but a desire to feel good again, usually by producing the same poorly done project as before. No learning took place. There is no educational value in false praise.

Karl E. Thelen

What is of value is honest praise for an honest effort. Feelgooders do our nation a great disservice.

Most students really want to learn, but many have no idea how to do it, since the Feelgood movement doesn't really require thinking. That means the art of studying is being lost. Over the years expectations have been lowered considerably. Emphasis on grammar, punctuation and spelling have been diminished in many elementary schools as too stressful, and any emphasis on working to understand and know the material has been watered down considerably by the Feelgooders who don't believe that there should be any undue stress on students. Stress doesn't feel good. After all, we now have 'spell check' for those who can't spell, and electronic encyclopedias for those who want to do research, and aides to do the reading for those who can't read, and on and on and on.

A Feelgooder once said to me that he would never require his students to do a speech in class (an English class) because he was scared to death to get up and speak in front of people and he would not ask any of his students to experience that awful feeling of pressure. To not have students do speeches in an English class is ironic, especially since speaking well is one of the three main criteria for success in our society along with writing well, and having a good vocabulary. Once the emphasis on these three things is diminished or eliminated, the value of education itself is diminished. Students start doing what they **feel** will benefit them the most, that which would make them 'feel good.' Quite often that choice isn't sufficient to get them the base of knowledge they need in order to reach the higher levels of thinking, which is really what education is all about. The emphasis needs to be on learning, not on feeling good. Feeling good comes from successfully learning something and being able, in turn, to demonstrate that learning.

I recently went into a local KFC and ordered a couple of meals. The bill came to $12.99. I handed a twenty to the cashier. When the girl, who looked to be about thirteen, rang up the bill, where normally the amount of change to give to the customer would be, there were only zeroes. The girl stared at the zeroes for several seconds, clearly not knowing what to do since the machine didn't tell her how much change to give. She waved to another girl, rapidly, trying to get her over to the cash register faster. Panic had set in. They both stared at the zeroes for several more seconds before the second girl got a piece of paper and subtracted 12.99 from 20.00. They both looked at the answer for several more seconds before the second girl whispered, "I'm pretty sure that's right." I have seen this happen often. Casualties, I call them, of the Feelgood movement. It isn't just my experience, it's universal, and the inability to exercise basic skills is going to get worse if the current trends continue.

Another time, in a Stewarts, in a nearby town I needed cash and stopped in to see if they had an ATM. I asked the boy behind the counter if they had an "automatic teller." He said "A what?" I said, "An automatic teller machine." He looked at me a second, then at the girl standing next to him, then back to me before I realized my mistake. "Do you have an ATM machine?" I asked. "Oh, yeah, we do," he said. He looked at me like I was a little off since I apparently didn't know what to call that thing that spits out money.

A case of empty soda bottles that I took to Walmart to get my deposit back didn't have bar codes so they had to be taken to the courtesy desk. I told the person working there (about age 16 or 17) that there was a case. He started to count them. My son who was with me said that there were 24 bottles there. The Walmartian looked at my son for a few seconds and then looked back down and started to count them over again until he got to 24, which he then wrote down on a piece of paper. The ability to do simple math in our heads is disappearing. Memorizing times tables and so on puts a lot of pressure on students. It's easier to just let students get by with being able to explain the process they're going through to get the answer. That always feels so much better than having to come up with the right answer.

Second, a note about Master Teachers

The expression 'master teacher' is used often throughout the book. This means those in education who have an innate ability to teach, to impart information and ideas to their students successfully, and inspire, in some way, many of their students to achieve beyond what they would have otherwise. Master teachers are self-motivated and improve all on their own because they want to. They have a control in their classrooms that is just expected. They are competent and confident in the art and science of teaching. They are effective teachers. Whereas a Feelgooder wouldn't want to put undue pressure

Karl E. Thelen

on a student, a master teacher knows that working under some pressure has considerable advantage.

Madeline Hunter with her work on **Effective Teaching** said that a certain level of frustration is good for students, since that is when they do their best work. If teachers maintained that level of frustration (akin to working under pressure, a point at which so many students and adults say they work best), the results would be proof positive that the concept is sound.

I'll talk more about Effective Teaching when I talk about things that work. Madeline Hunter got a bad rap in the United States because Effective Teaching concepts were shoved down teachers' throats at teacher in-service days, those days free of students when school districts believe, through the workshops and programs the district picks and provides, there will be good coming to all teachers, and therefore, eventually, to all students. This is the educational trickle down theory.

The Effective Schools movement, begun by Dr. Larry Lazotte of Michigan State and the late Ron Edmonds, is worth spending some time on since the ideas espoused are those that allow for teachers to teach and for students to learn. Both of these concepts, Effective Teaching and Effective Schools, are based on good things that good teachers and good schools are already doing.

Master teachers have an intuition that reflects effective teaching techniques and effective schools concepts. They don't have to be told or taught about good teaching and how a school needs to be run for learning to be maximized. Master teachers just do it. Because of this, they should be left alone to teach.

My intent in the following chapters is to expose those elements involved in the education of our children, directly and indirectly, and show how their involvement is detrimental and contrary to what Americans have consistently indicated was a priority issue; education. Education should never be taken lightly. It is of the utmost importance for future economic, political and social survival. Education must be based on sound principles of the art and science of teaching. Although many of the groups I am writing about are entwined regarding their relationship to education, I separate them for the sake of discussion.

First and foremost are the **teachers** currently in the system, from the newbies who do not yet have a clue because college really doesn't prepare anyone to teach, to the oldies, who have successfully avoided being held accountable for the fact that they don't have, and never had, any idea what they are doing. They're easy to spot (As many parents and most students already know), and yet they manage to survive. These teachers are the biggest embarrassment to all of us in education who work hard at what we do. These teachers get an inordinate amount of attention because of the poor job that they do, and take attention away from those teachers who deserve to be recognized for their positive, contributing efforts to improve and maintain quality education.

If you're going to talk about teachers, then you need also to talk about the colleges that put them there. **Colleges**, for all their own hype and fuss over tradition and focus on learning, and being bastions of free speech and educational freedom, need to kick themselves in the seat of their own pants. The dummying of America is certainly seen in microcosm in many of our institutions of higher learning. From their grading policies to their lack of concern for moral values (having moral values would chase students away and, therefore, tuition money and alumni funds), our colleges have fostered a culture of get in, go through, get out, and the hell with any real learning in the process. The degree is the thing, and things like grades shouldn't get in the way. The priority, on the college level, for professors is being published, not on teaching anyone how to teach.

Colleges can also be the forerunners of **A Nation of Idiots**. Many colleges now have remedial courses for students who can't do the work. Apparently the knowledge needed in high school in order to get to college wasn't gained. Where colleges used to be something to work for, many of them now merely extend the high school years a little longer and offer no real challenge. Once these 'college graduates' go forth and take positions reflective of their degree, there is a decrease in the quality of the product, whether it's from a school or factory or delivering the mail, it's a little less than it was before.

Colleges also don't require much of their future education graduates other than to take certain required courses, none of which actually prepares someone to teach. The closest colleges can come to the preparation needed for future teachers is with student teacher programs, which are geared towards students practicing ideas from their college courses but bear little reality with learning how to teach.

Karl E. Thelen

Many professors have never taught in a high school classroom, or taught there twenty years ago, and therefore have very little empirical expertise in how that job is done. It's certainly a lot different teaching in a public school than lecturing to a large group of students and placing the entire burden of learning on the group. Professors are also immune, of course, to the reaches of angry or unruly parents, who can cause great harm to a public school teacher. And unless the colleges are involved in some way with programs that encourage effective mastery teaching, then their program is worthless.

The best thing a college can do to prepare their students for teaching is to turn the job over to master teachers from the very beginning. Similar to the apprentice system, those who are interested in the difficult job of teaching will become immersed early on in the art and science of teaching.

Next are the **administrators**. In this category are many paper pushers and non-disciplinarians who couldn't hack it in the classroom, or just didn't like it in the classroom, and have moved on. They are those whose main agenda is to improve their own position in the educational hierarchy, to move up and over as quickly as they can, and with each move assume more and more responsibility until they run the whole thing. The average life of an administrator in any position is three years. They hide in their offices a lot. When you have a Feelgood administrator there is the potential for real disaster.

Administrators should be Academic Leaders; they should know what's going on in all classrooms; they should be in the halls and know what the environment within the school is. A good administrator doesn't hide in his office. However, good ones are getting harder and harder to find. The job has become prohibitive in what is expected of administrators, much of which takes away from the real purpose of an academic leader.

School board members aren't going to be spared either. Although there are many dedicated people who do a good job in the stewardship of their district's educational responsibility, there are far too many who have no right to be making decisions that are far ranging and affect so many. Many school board members are one-issue candidates and political in nature. That's why instead of having a school board of citizens who, for the most part, have no real understanding of how education works, there should be committees of

A Nation of Idiots

master teachers making the decisions about the direction, future, and expenditures of the school.

Many **taxpayers** should be ashamed of being so stingy when it comes to the most important product produced by any community, the future of their children and the children after them. The ones who should be the most ashamed are those whose children are already out of the local school and believe that they shouldn't have to help pay the bill anymore. The bill is everyone's responsibility. The effort should be directed towards those things that cause the costs to be so high such as fuel, health coverage, and special education legislation.

Many **parents** have abdicated their parental authority. When they find out that their kid who they expected would always act in a positive, polite manner and have a certain level of etiquette, has now become a loud, verbal monster, parents turn their anger on the schools and blame them for what used to be considered family responsibilities. Too many parents have become complaining babies, excusing their kids from all blame or responsibility for their actions.

An overriding attitude among many parents, especially those who expect their kids to always be at the top academically, is that their kid is always right, is smarter than every other kid, and deserves special consideration when they do something wrong. These parents, if their kid is involved, are also the first to complain about an unfair grading policy, overly harsh discipline in regards to drugs, violence, and outright crimes against humanity and commonsense. They expect the schools to be baby sitter, cook, grandmother, maid, whipping post, moral educator, and righter of all social and biological wrongs. There are many categories of parents, some of which will be included here.

All State **legislators** should be brought out in a public forum and whipped. Once the hand of government gets on the designing of educational programs or raising or lowering expectations, watch out. Here comes something destined to go wrong. The last people any community should want touching their education is a large group of men and women who have different political dogmas, different beliefs as to what makes good education, and a wide, disparate range of educational experiences, many of which are powering their own particular bias for or against how schools should be run. God help us all. Unless the government is going to pay for its bright ideas, it shouldn't get into it, because every time it does, taxes go up and the quality of education goes down.

Karl E. Thelen

Corporations are not immune to guilt. For decades, aided by legislation and making use of the mass media, corporations, solely for marketing purposes, have been subtly helping to turn the minds of Americans to mush. Since the advent of television and mass marketing, there is an unbroken chain from child to parent to grandparent of mushy brained consumers. With profits as their motivation, and a lack of concern for learning, companies have been misspelling words, changing how and when words are capitalized, cheapening expectations by making products planned for obsolescence, and chipping away at our future brain trust by making use of a variety of media tricks and con games to do a massive head job on America and its youth.

Secondly, it's a crime what many large corporations continue to do to both our nation's elderly, whose only choice in this fast paced technological age is to agree and go along or be left behind, and to all those gullible baby boomers raised and nurtured by early TV. In a nation where liver and soup bones used to be free, it's obscene when credit card companies, banks, insurance companies, the medical profession, and a horde of others have as their sole intent only to extract as much money out of their 'clientele' as they can before the good host dies. Each of these entities relies on **A Nation of Idiots** to peddle their wares, using the means offered by the vast mass media, whose **only** concern, ironically, is to also shake as much money from the public as quickly as they can before the mushy brained masses get enough crust on their brain and catch on to what's being done to them.

I also blame the **medical profession** and **pharmaceutical companies** for many of our educational ills. They keep the costs of health care extremely high by over prescribing, over x-raying, over medicating, and over emphasizing minor aches and pains in order to put up costly fences against the onslaught of malpractice suits (another effect of having **A Nation of Idiots**). They also need to keep the gravy train of health-care payments coming, and to keep a line of people moving in and out of the offices on a regular, controlled basis. The pharmaceutical companies charge exorbitant prices for designer drugs that cost them pennies to manufacture, because the health care conglomerates will just pay it since, at the other end, premiums can simply be raised.

A jump in health care premiums causes a sharp rise in local educational costs which forces school districts to either raise taxes or cut costs by limiting resources, hiring less experienced teachers or not filling positions at all because the fringe benefits, which are needed to attract quality people, are too costly. It's a vicious cycle that's hard to break.

The **mass media** should be whipped right out there alongside the corporate heads for their ineptitude when it comes to covering education. The lack of concern for the truth by all segments of the media is unconscionable and the tricks they use to get everyone to want what they are selling or to believe what they are saying is despicable. There is no effort to find out what is really going on with education, only a desire to get a scoop, some exciting story where there is good video, a winning sound bite, and a lot of wall papering in the background to draw in the viewer or reader.

If the media wants to help education then they can start by not printing SAT scores or standardized test scores, for schools or a multitude of other scores that the media use to rate how well or poorly a school is doing. These scores, usually in large headlines, are all meaningless for purposes of comparison. Groups of students come through in cycles. There is an ebb and flow to how smart or capable, in general, any particular group of students is. For this reason alone, the test scores should never be used to say whether a particular group is doing better than or worse than any other group. Don't get me wrong, there are always capable students in every class, but using the whole group as a barometer, the cycles can be traced up and down, followed by stories in the media about success or failure.

The fact of the matter is, these scores don't mean a heck of a lot about the particular school district since there are too many variables, which need to be considered before such a judgment can be made. Not all students take the SAT's. If all the students in a particular school took the SAT's then the scores would go down, indicating, that that school has dropped in ability. As a reaction, programs will be instituted to fix the problem; in-service programs to train teachers, professional days for teachers to visit places where the idea is working, and on and on, the cost of which is passed on to the taxpayers.

If any school wants their scores to go up, they should limit who can take the test to the top five or ten percent of the student body.

Karl E. Thelen

That school will look pretty good in the headlines compared to the year before.

A recent article in our local paper said that New York SAT scores had risen among college sophomores. The gist was that something good must have been going on. At the same time, a mailer to all residents from my current school showed the standardized test scores for our students and compared them to the state average and recent years. In both instances, the numbers were used to show progress or lack of it, but the numbers are meaningless in terms of student success in their chosen careers. What the numbers do do, is institute change of some kind, either to raise the scores and do better, or to duplicate the apparent success. Conclusions and actions taken based on those test results are of no real value to education.

The instituted changes, however, whether district or state mandated, have the potential for doing more harm than good since they were designed to change something that may not have needed changing. This will be the result, eventually, of President Bush's 'Leave No Child Behind' legislation that will test students in all grades from third to eighth. The test results will be tied directly to a funding formula, but since the results will fluctuate due to human nature, many schools will become psychotic trying to keep their Federal Aid.

The media tend to be superficial in their reporting of, and concern for, education. What they are concerned about, however, is the profit to be made from an uneducated population, or at least one uneducated to the manipulative ways of the mass media and what their real concerns are. The mass media depend on a compliant population that can be mesmerized by the ambient light of the TV, the colorful graphics, misleading headlines and short, to-the-point articles found in many newspapers, like USA Today, designed for 'fast news,' or McNews as it's being called. Slick layouts and a lot of skin in most magazines on the stands sell everything from car parts to carrot sticks. The new slogan for CNN's Headline News is 'Real News, Real Fast.' At least we get to see all those distracting people walking around in the background.

The media are also blind to the legislative fallout when laws regarding education are passed, and they fail to comprehend the slightest bit when it comes to explaining the effects of the legislation to the public. Act 60 in Vermont, designed to reform education, is an excellent example of that type of legislative ignorance. Only now, several years after its passage, are people seeing what the bill was all about and many people don't like what they see; higher taxes, less local control, and mandates by the State for standards to be in place with no means of funding the legislation.

The United States is often compared in the media, usually in large headlines, to other countries, especially the Japanese, when it comes to how our students are doing academically. The media pick up on the fact that, on paper, the Japanese students do so much better than American kids. This, then, creates frenzy among many American educators and politicians as to why we are so deficient when compared to other countries.

What the media fail to mention is that different cultures with different academic and social expectations have different reasons for doing what they do or living how they live. These demographic facts are never clearly defined to the readers or viewers. Disparities in population size between the United States and other countries, and the diversity within those populations (or, in Japan, as well as many European countries, the lack of diversity) need to be considered as well. However, the media mention only the disparity in scores.

There are, as people may know, many programs in public education that drain money away from quality education. Aside from the large number of unqualified teachers, the largest drain for the least gain is **special education**. If ever there was a legal rip off of local tax dollars, this is it. Special education sucks more money out of the local taxpayers than any other aspect of education (currently two and one half times more than the cost of regular education students), and yet delivers the least results for the investment. It is equivalent to a voracious omnivore that stops at nothing to satisfy its needs. Federal and State legislation mandate that all wrongs be righted, which is ridiculous since it can't be done, in an attempt to guarantee the rights of all students for their lives as students. It is the goal of all **Feelgoodintended** people to make every student as equally successful as every other student; to level the playing field so everyone can play, whether they really can or not.

Sometime in the future, no doubt, after the newest Federal special education, all-inclusive, equal opportunity, mandated legislation (with no comparable funds to pay for the mandate), is passed and ALL people in America are legally obligated to be no better than the next person, the playing field will finally be leveled and no one ever again will need to feel less than anyone else. If there are people, found through some form of standardized testing, who are smarter, or more capable than others, then a unique system of mandated equalization will be put into place to correct the defect. This will be overseen by many offices of the special ed. dynasty, backed by the power, might and money of the Federal government. As far-fetched as this may seem, actual case scenarios can be even more so.

On the other side of the coin, the unique aspects of the special educator's job tend to eventually burn out the most experienced teacher. Not only are the student loads often beyond reasonable (they **are** dealing with less motivated, more problematic types of students who require a much different approach than the regular classroom teacher), the added paper work demanded by the district, State and Federal governments can be prohibitive. Add in the pressure of having to deal with advocates, unreasonable parents, supervision of support staff, and a legal system taken over by Feelgooders and the job can become overwhelming.

There are good things about education, and the hope for the future. **Effective Teaching** research is one of them. Effective Teaching ideas got a bum rap some years ago because, as with many fads in education, it was shoved down teachers' throats at in-services and then the universal dark humor took over and buried the ideas. Consequently, many teachers made fun of Effective Teaching literature when it first came out. Even today I hear teachers speak negatively about Effective Teaching, but when asked to be specific, they can't. It's just one more vague concept. But if any teacher wants to know what has been working for thousands of master teachers and effective schools over the years, here's one place to look.

It will be repeated that the terminology used to describe the concepts is not the important focus, but the concepts themselves. The worst thing for education is for all teachers in all schools to all do the same thing in the same way. Each school or teacher should be encouraged to come up with their own words to describe their teaching and what works for them. Identity is important. All master teachers have one.

Along with Effective Teaching research, there is a large body of material on **Effective Schools** that a lot of districts overlook. As with Effective Teaching, the information for Effective Schools comes from

A Nation of Idiots

looking at successful schools and noting what they were doing that other schools weren't. It seems so simple, yet apparently is difficult for many of our nation's schools to understand. Or perhaps they are unwilling to understand because it may shake things up and move them away from the norm or status quo, even though the status quo isn't working.

Effective Schools' ideas should appeal to many teachers because the basic concept is for decisions to be made from the bottom up, by the teachers, which is the way it should be. If the final decisions on curriculum and other aspects of teaching are those handed down by the school board or a superintendent, then there is no effective school.

In trying to keep with the adage that if you don't have a solution, then don't create the problem, **testing** in the United States is included and what would be the best route to follow in order to evaluate our students so that they truly know what their abilities are and what they would be most suited for in life. I call this vision **A Circle of Assessment**. It involves not only knowing about the usual **standardized tests** or **portfolio** assessments sweeping the country, but also about many other types of testing as well as aspects of learning such as **Multiple Intelligences**, **Hemisphericity**, **Learning Styles**, and **Memory**.

I've included a chapter called **What I Do**, things I've picked up over the years that work to some degree, not with every student, but with a large number. Some of it's right from effective teaching and effective schools, some I've stolen from other teachers or borrowed from students. I came up with much of it on my own while doing solo excursions into why something didn't work and what I could do to fix it, and how I can make those things that did work even better.

When I first began teaching in 1970 I didn't have a lot of collegial help or support. The small, rural school I began my teaching in was still a decade back in time. This is why I had to delve into many aspects of education on my own, and discovered many things that I could do to increase the students' attention on the task at hand. I also had the luxury of being able to experiment a lot since I was never observed for the first six years of my teaching.

In Conclusion, I'll sum everything up and reinforce one last time what can be done to save us from becoming any more of **A Nation of Idiots**. The erosion of discipline, hiring of poor teachers, the trend toward mediocrity of the student population, and the promotion of

Karl E. Thelen

ineffective administrators needs to end. Diluted grades, the struggle to keep all your own students above average, the need to raise standardized test scores, the push for portfolios, the lack of information and understanding on the part of many parents, and the constant assault by the media and corporate America all contribute to the current state of education. Consequently, there is a frustrated outcry heard everywhere of 'What's wrong with education?' Well, what's wrong with education is we've become **A Nation of Idiots**.

Chapter two

Those Teachers; Those *#%&!!** teachers

I'm embarrassed to say that over the last thirty-three years, at least half of all the teachers I have known weren't qualified to be in the profession. Some of them were just plain out and out **ignorant** of a lot that teachers should know, lacked the basics of their own discipline, and missed many elements of others, such as the ability to spell, write coherent sentences, and use punctuation correctly. There's no place for illiterate teachers in education. I'm not talking about the occasional mistakes we all make, but the on-going inability to function as a literate, educated person in a field that demands literacy and education.

All teachers should be able to spell and write intelligibly. The number of teachers who consistently misspell words on homework assignments, notices, notes to parents, and a long list of other written items is appalling.

It should be incumbent upon not only the English teachers to expect students to write well, spell correctly or use their language correctly, but on every teacher in the building. If my students do a term paper for another class, that teacher should know that the students have already learned how to write a paper and should expect them to use that knowledge. Students shouldn't be allowed to forget what they know just because they've changed classes. They need to be held accountable for their learning. Many students don't make the connections between their different courses. They learn about writing term papers in English, but don't apply that knowledge on a science paper. Students can't be allowed to forget their grammar, spelling and sentence structure as soon as they walk out of the English class.

Any teacher who assigns written work should be able to correct everything about it, not just grade the content. Once this is achieved and students know they'll be held accountable for learning everywhere in the building, their level of competency in all areas will rise considerably. All teachers need to be schooled in correcting papers for language. I know that it would add to the considerable number of things that teachers have to do every school day, but the academic results would far outweigh any inconvenience to teachers not used to looking for punctuation, spelling, sentence structure, and so on. These are not hard concepts, they just take time and effort and a trained eye to spot these types of errors quickly. But it's important that all teachers do it. It's important to hold everyone, teachers and students, accountable.

This concept, being held accountable for doing your job, goes to the heart of quality teaching. This concept is also one of the biggest problems in public education. How can any school survive academically if a percentage of their teachers are unqualified? How can a teacher continue to teach and be unqualified, without someone in the administration knowing about that teacher's lack of qualifications? Therein lies a secondary problem. In order to discover poor teaching, the school district needs to have qualified administrators. If many administrators rise up from the ranks of poor teachers, then you have the blind evaluating the blind. Accountability goes by the wayside.

It's also important for teachers to know their content area. This sounds like a no-brainer, but the large number of teachers who really don't know what they're talking about is scary. Results from teacher tests around the United States attest to that.

In the faculty lounge where I used to teach, a fourth grade teacher sat at a table correcting papers. She sighed off and on for several minutes, shaking her head at the papers she was working on. She turned to me after a while and said, completely exasperated, "Why can't these kids write a perfect sentence?" I asked her what she meant by a perfect sentence. She sat there for a moment and then said, "Well, I don't know." I asked her if she didn't know, then how could she expect the kids to know? Teachers need to know what they are asking of their students and be able to explain why they are doing it in case someone should ever ask. An ignorant teacher, if they remain so, is unqualified to be in the profession.

Under the current educational situation, I would, if I had the authority, eliminate many teachers from the profession. Some of these

A Nation of Idiots

people aren't qualified because they are **punishers,** usually through cruelty towards their students. Punishers revel in the pain they cause. They enjoy the power being a teacher gives over the lives of others, and misuse the trust that the job of teaching bestows. Often their cruelty is subtle; they may play mind games with grades, homework and detentions. All are weapons that can be used to bend a student to the teacher's point of view.

One teacher in particular, early in my career, bragged about how he had instigated a fight between two students in his class, one white, and the other black, by alleging racial slurs on the part of the white student. None of it was true, and the teacher laughed when he explained how he used that instance to show what happens to students who cause trouble in his classroom. Cruelty should not be allowed in education.

Some teachers punish students with grades. This one is harder to prove than some of the other types of punishment. Grading can be very subtle, but a point here, a point there and soon the deed is accomplished. Some teachers have certain students graded before they even come in the room and therefore have to have the student's work match that grade. They can also punish by loading up the homework and class work so it's way beyond a reasonable frustration level. This is usually reserved for punishing the whole class. The grading punisher is probably the most sinister.

Another segment of the teaching population should be dismissed because of their **inability to keep track** of the work the students have done or to even know who is in attendance. All teachers need to keep a rank book, the book that attendance and grades are kept in. Any student at any time should be able to ask any teacher how they are doing in the class and the teacher should be able to produce that information easily and quickly. Students who know their grades on a regular basis do better in school. They have the chance to use the information to make corrections in their behavior. In these instances this means better grades.

It's also a law in many states that **attendance** must be kept. Whether it's too confusing for some teachers to figure out which students are present at any given time or it's just too much work for some is beyond me. The inability to keep track of students and their grades should be grounds for dismissal.

Karl E. Thelen

The **need to plan** for what will be taught and an understanding of how that will be accomplished is a must, and any one who can't sit down and plot their course, no pun intended, should seek employment elsewhere. If you know where you're going, it's easier to get there.

Others I would dismiss for **not being in control** of their classroom. To not have any expectations for student behavior, or any expectations for student achievement, is unacceptable, and yet it's being accepted and tolerated around the nation. Many teachers I have known were actually afraid of their students and therefore never expected them to rise to acceptable behavior, the least of which is to be quiet and pay attention, respectfully, so that the teacher can teach and the students can learn. Without that starting point, learning won't take place since no one is listening.

Being in control doesn't apply only to the classroom. It applies to all corners of the school. Study halls especially need control if they are to be places where study can take place. In a meeting at our school, for example, regarding unruliness in the study halls, the study hall monitor asked the administration not to do anything that would interfere with her rapport with the students. She had become their friend (Feelgooder alert). The students wouldn't listen to her when she asked them to be quiet and study, but she still didn't want to lose the rapport.

A true rapport with students comes from holding them accountable and having them succeed. Once the students know that it was being held accountable that made them do the work, that teacher will have a rapport. And the rapport will be positive and effective in terms of education, which is why we're all there to begin with.

It's the desire to be friends, prevalent especially in new teachers, which leads to the next category, **the enabler**. The enabler is that teacher who, through their inability to control or maintain any semblance of expectations, allows students to behave in a manner opposite that which is conducive to learning. Some teachers' expectations are so low, that any effort is accepted. These teachers, in fact, enable students to fail by never holding them accountable.

I also would get rid of the **yellers and the screamers**. I don't mean those who raise their voices on occasion, or who yell at a student who was being totally out of control. At moments like those, teachers need the freedom to respond quickly and firmly. Once a student crosses a certain behavior line, however, they give up all rights to be treated with civility and with the respect most people deserve. I'm talking about those teachers who yell all the time.

My classroom was once next to a screamer. Even through the thick concrete walls, I could hear him yelling at his students, "I told you to shut up. Now be quiet." This went on almost every period of every day.

Once, when a substitute was in for this teacher, the students, ninth graders, were giving her a loud, hard time. I stepped into the room and just stood there. They quieted down immediately. I told them that I realized they were used to being told to shut up in a loud voice, but that I thought they were better than that and that a simple request for their attention should be all that was required. I apologized for them being yelled at all the time and added that I thought they could respond to better treatment. They were quiet for the rest of the period. The sub thanked me afterwards. The teacher, by the way, was not rehired.

Other teachers that would have to go would be those who maintain a **stark, bland, undecorated, uninspiring classroom**. Anyone walking into any classroom should be able to figure out what is taught there by the posters, bulletin boards or other student work that is on display.

I had a middle school student, a student who is not in one of my classes, step into my room and say, "I like coming in here." He was responding to the projects on shelves around the room, posters hanging in every spare space (usually neatly), and the general overall feel of the room. Students need to be visually stimulated and the stimulation should be directly related to what they are learning in that class. Unfortunately, a lot of teachers don't understand this simple concept.

I'd get rid of all the **good ol' boys**, too. These are the ineffective teachers who continue to hang on because they agree with whatever innovations, fads, or edicts are imposed on them just so they can be close to the administration; too close, hopefully, to get fired. The good ol' boys quite often get perks that others don't because the administration, often needing allies, will align with anyone willing to be a buddy. There is strength, or at least comfort, in numbers. An unqualified administrator and his gang of good ol' boys can do a lot of damage in a school system.

Karl E. Thelen

I'd also get rid of anyone who didn't help out with **discipline** around the entire school. This is everyone's job, and no one should pass it off. All teachers are responsible for the educational atmosphere in the building. No one should allow a student to go barreling past them. No teacher should pass by any type of trouble brewing in the hallways. Everyone should say something to the loud and obnoxious students who are having a hard time finding their identity. No adult, especially the teacher, is immune or excused from discipline duty.

Teacher Testing

I realize that a lot of people not in the education field have a concept of teaching and teachers that isn't even close to what the job really entails. Most adults remember their own experience in school as a student and tend to carry that attitude with them for life. To most students, teachers just stand up there and teach. That's all there is to it. But in reality, the teaching job, when done right, is a lot of real work.

There's first the planning that makes a semester or year-long class come together, acquiring all the materials needed to teach the class, and then the actual work of getting the students to understand the concepts and have them be able to apply those concepts.

There's also considerable assessing, which must be done, to show whether the teaching was effective or not. Good teachers want to know if what they are doing is having an affect. Poor teachers go through the year just to get through it. This should not be an option. If the teaching isn't working, then it needs to be changed.

Lastly, there's the mindless, but necessary, paper work that goes into making the whole program work; grades, attendance sheets, progress reports, assessment forms, cut slips, lesson plans and so on. Teachers don't just stand there and teach.

I'm saying all this because I've often heard people who are not in education say that there should be teacher testing to weed out those who won't do a good job. Their concept of a test for such a situation is based on their own educational experience. There are no tests to see who would be a good teacher or not. Only the experience of being on the job will determine that. This is why there has to be an apprenticeship for would-be teachers rather than the current ineffective course work and student teaching offered in most colleges.

A Nation of Idiots

Currently there are 44 states that have teacher-testing to determine a person's ability to teach. More are considering it. In some of the states, teachers can get only 50% right and still pass. The most common tests are the Praxis I and Praxis II, taken by teacher candidates in 25 states. The Praxis I test used for elementary candidates tests at a tenth grade level, and the test for the high school candidates is only a little higher, according to Katy Haycock of The Education Trust.

In Oregon, a passing grade of 65 is required, while in Georgia future teachers only need to get a 46. Many states have cutoff scores that are embarrassingly low, a lot lower than would be expected of the students these teachers will be teaching. It's scary to think of just whom these tests are eliminating, and just as scary to think of those teachers the tests are still allowing into the profession.

Teacher testing has many critics, and rightly so since the tests don't indicate how good someone will be as a teacher. Passing with a 47% doesn't say much for that person, but the tests do appear to be effective in weeding out the most deficient of future educators. Recently, 20% of Texas teachers couldn't pass their state's simple teacher test. Fifty-nine percent of Massachusetts's prospective teachers couldn't pass the state's teacher exam, which was designed to evaluate the prospective teacher's reading and writing ability along with a subject test in their field.

The most controversial part of the test was a dictation part, where candidates had to listen to a reading from the Federalist Papers and then write down what they heard. It didn't test for remembering facts or anything specific from the reading. It was only used to see if the prospective teachers in Massachusetts could spell, write an intelligent sentence and punctuate and capitalize correctly. Many couldn't.

Massachusetts is the only state that uses the dictation, by the way, which lends itself to the controversy surrounding the 59% who didn't pass it. Critics felt it was unfair to have teachers respond to a dictated passage. Instead of focusing on the critics' arguments, which still don't do anything for teacher effectiveness, we should instead look at the poor results of so many teachers in terms of what the test was testing for; can teachers punctuate, spell and write intelligibly? The results say no and something should be done about it. Regardless of the difficulty of a passage, or the simple nature of easy questions, the spotlight is still on those who are unqualified to trust the future of our children to. All tests test for something, and at their simplest level, all teachers should be able to pass them.

When it comes to content in a specific field, we should be even more focused. Knowing deep content in a chosen field has been shown to be important to student learning. A 1998 Education Trust study, "found that teacher quality was the single most-important factor in student achievement." Education Trust researchers said that the number of students passing the state of North Carolina's competency test could go up by 5% if the passing score on the teacher licensing test was raised by 1 percent. Imagine if the passing score was raised 10 percent. That's the difference good teachers make.

What to do? The task of ensuring effective learning sounds insurmountable, but nothing is ever as hopeless as it seems. The answer is going to be tough, though. Some nice people, who just aren't good teachers, will have to go. The corps of administrators has to be retooled, since they evaluate the teachers, and many nice, but ineffective, administrators will have to go. The position must morph into something that isn't a tool of the school board or superintendent. Administrators have to be, as in the Effective Schools movement, academic leaders. This means they have to come from the ranks of master teachers.

The evaluation process has to be overhauled so that those most experienced in successful classroom management and the art and science of teaching are in charge. Master teachers also need to be in charge of administrating the school's educational goals.

Along with the teachers and administrators, the academic playing field, so to speak, has to be leveled in terms of academic time on task, which Effective Schools' research shows to be important to learning. Any new idea that comes along and puts down time-on-task is suspect (probably the product of Feelgooder thinking). Something must be done about anything that takes students out of their classes; guidance groups, early dismissal for sports, assemblies, field trips, family vacations, shopping and so on.

No advice is any good if there isn't a plan as to how to accomplish it. Starting with the teaching profession, there has to be more attention to several aspects of the art and science of teaching, and the means by which they are achieved.

First, and foremost, because of its importance, the need for discipline cannot be overstressed. And this doesn't mean corporal

A Nation of Idiots

punishment or a harsh 1984 reality, but the ability of a teacher to maintain control of the classroom's educational environment at all times, and to know what's going on in every corner of the room, so learning may take place. This is not some whacked out theory. This is already happening in many classrooms of teachers who either have an innate ability, or have developed the ability, to command attention in a respectful manner. Without discipline, you have nothing, and this is true of every thing in life that has value and meaning.

Teachers need to be aware of effective teaching techniques. They need to be aware of what works and what doesn't. They need to know what others in their profession, who have been identified as being master teachers, are doing that makes them master teachers. I guarantee that there will be a pattern there that should be a model to guide the training, weeding out, and hiring of all teachers.

All teachers should be aware of and be expected to follow effective schools correlates. The evidence is substantial and leaves little room for doubt as to what makes an effective school. This doesn't engender robots, as some have expressed to me, but allows for the teaching and learning environment to be present. Using that which has been shown to work only enhances the educational value.

Teachers need to be aware of how information goes from short-term to long-term memory; in other words, how people learn. There is now a large base of knowledge and information on how the brain works, how memory goes from short to long term memory, how to assist this process in students, and how to reinforce information so the students 'learn' it, rather than just learn it long enough to spit it back on a test and then forget it. In that case, which is prevalent in public education, nothing was learned. What **was** reinforced, however, was that the information given wasn't important, and this is how you deal with it.

Teachers should know that there are many intelligences and that all students possess intelligence. Understanding Gardner's theories on multiple intelligences is valuable, but there also are other means of studying intelligence theories.

The concept of hemisphericity, right and left brain dominance, which fits in so well with Multiple Intelligences, should be stressed. Teachers need to make students aware of their preferences in order to maximize their education.

Karl E. Thelen

There should be an emphasis on future teachers becoming immersed in the profession right from the moment they decide they want to be a teacher, and this includes special emphasis on their particular discipline. As it is now, too many 'student teachers' come into a class with little understanding of the importance of discipline in the classroom and how to get or maintain the needed level of discipline, or without any knowledge of the daily tasks that all teachers do without thinking.

Without understanding these important first steps, what they pick up from the 'student teaching experience' will be disjointed and without real meaning in terms of effective teaching skills. If, however, these students of education were put into classroom settings, with master teachers, much earlier in their college career, they would pick up vital information in the running of a classroom prior to their actual teaching experience.

The key here is to be placed with a master teacher, not just one who volunteers to do it or who is available. The latter two would merely perpetuate the status quo, and probably drive a lot of good future teachers away.

There has to be the expectation that all teachers are knowledgeable in their discipline. English teachers should know how to write and speak and punctuate properly. That makes it easier to teach it to their students. History teachers should have a firm grasp of the important historical markers and information in that discipline that gives them the right to be considered qualified to teach what they know to students. Science teachers should have some practical experience in the field. That should be a starting point. All teachers need to know their content well.

It may sound silly, but teachers also need to **know how** to get students to the point where they **want** to learn. It may sound equally silly, but students first have to be brought to the point where they want to learn before the real learning kicks in. They don't all come to school prepared or equipped to do that, just as not all teachers come into the profession prepared or equipped to teach.

Although this may seem like an overwhelming task, there is already enough research on the art and science of teaching, as well as those components of an effective school, to help straighten the whole mess out. There is already a solid core of master teachers all over the United States who have been doing what it takes for many years.

A Nation of Idiots

These are the teachers who know the job and have spent the years perfecting the art and science of teaching. They get better all the time, on their own. They don't do what they do because the State told them to. They don't do what they do because another deadening in-service was shoved down their throats, and they certainly don't do what they do because some administrator came up with another great idea. These teachers need to be identified. They need be at the center of any real move to stop spitting out **A Nation of Idiots** from our public schools.

Master teachers also should have the largest roles in important aspects of public education. Unfortunately, the group of educated people that should be in charge isn't. According to the Department of Education office of research article called *"Who is in charge – teacher views on control over school policy classroom practices,"* "teachers currently may not play a key role in many school decisions." Most of the important decisions go to the administrators. "Implicit in this call for greater school level implements is the belief that those closest to the children...know best what is needed to improve their schools."[1] Ah, who could that be?

Certainly the impression of control influences the climate of the school. Teachers, who feel powerless or left out of the loop, tend to do less than they could in their jobs. "Overall, teachers did not believe that they had much influence over determining discipline policy or the content of in-service programs, setting policy on grouping students in classes by ability, or establishing curriculum. The following percentages bear this out.

Only 39 percent believe they have considerable influence over determining discipline policy.

Only 37 percent believe they have much influence over establishing curriculum.

Only 33 percent believe they have much influence over determining the content of in-service programs.

Only 29 percent believe they were instrumental in setting the policy and grouping students in classes by ability.[2]

---

[1] "Who is in charge? Teachers' Views on Control Over School Policy and Classroom Practices," Office of Research, Office of Educational Research and Improvement (OERI). Research Report. (August 1994), p. 1
[2] Ibid., p. 1

Karl E. Thelen

The exception was private school teachers. "Out of all of the school policy areas, private school teachers were more likely than public school teachers to believe they had control, but even in private schools teachers did not feel that much control. About half of the private school teachers said they had considerable influence over discipline policy and curriculum, and a minority believe they have much control over in-service programs or ability grouping." Private schools, of course, have generally much more control over everything than public schools, especially in the absence of State or Federal mandates.

The report also pointed out that community types could also determine who has control. For example, "Test studies of public school principals and teachers found that the type of community in which schools are located influence the perception of who made school decisions. Big city schools are more often part of large school districts that exercise central control over decisions. In the small town or rural schools, ...teachers play a larger role in decision-making."[3]

Public school teachers did, however, feel that they had control in the classroom, especially when it came to selecting textbooks or deciding what skills should be taught. "More than half believed they had considerable control over selecting textbooks and other instructional materials, and 62 percent felt they had control over the content, topics, and skills to be taught in the classroom."

On the opposite side of the coin, who do administrators believe run the schools? According to the article "Who runs the schools? The principal's view," administrators believe that they and the district do. Again, the teachers are on the back burner. "Public school principals painted a picture in which they and the school district considerably influence curriculum, hiring teachers, and setting discipline policy. They believe that school district personnel were most likely to establish curriculum, that principals have the greatest responsibility for hiring new full-time teachers and the school district or the principal was most likely to set discipline policy."[4]

The report also said that teachers didn't see themselves as having primary responsibility over any of these areas. "Only 12 percent of

---

[3] Ibid., p. 3
[4] "Who Runs the School? The Principal's view." Department of Education Research Report. (May 1993), p. 1

principals thought that the teachers were primarily responsible for establishing curriculum, and only one percent said that teachers had primary responsibility for hiring new teachers or setting discipline policy."[5]

Demographics rarely show the extent that the environment influences perceptions. The real perceptions should be the reality; that a core of master teachers makes the important decisions on the direction or future of the school district.

A professional and academic atmosphere should be maintained at all times. I'm sorry so many younger teachers don't know this or, if they do, scoff at it; and yet that is exactly that which engenders an academic atmosphere. If the atmosphere, or expectation, is one of quiet, serious attention to academic studies, than this will permeate the classroom. If, however, the atmosphere is loose; carnival-like; then the atmosphere in the classrooms will be also. The latter is not conducive to academic study.

Libraries should be quiet alcoves of studying. They're not meant to be, should not be, centers for adolescent, social exuberance. Yet, many libraries turn into social centers, especially for seniors with senior privileges.

Hallways should be safe and orderly. Students should not be allowed to lay in the hallway floors, congregate in large numbers upon the doorways, play games, or throw footballs in the main lobby.

All employees need to be involved in the disciplinary process.

All students deserve respect; up until certain lines are crossed, at which point that student abdicates all rights and privileges. There's no room for insubordination.

Senior privileges should be earned, kept to a minimum and enforced. The real privilege is being allowed an education.

All students attend classes. Schools exist for academic reasons.

Discipline should be fair, firm, and practiced throughout the building.

If any teacher isn't sure (especially a Feelgooder) when to make a decision regarding student behavior, ask the following questions.

---

[5] "Who is in charge? Teachers' Views on Control Over School Policy and Classroom Practices," Office of Research, Office of Educational Research and Improvement (OERI). Research Report. (August 1994), p. 1

Karl E. Thelen

At what age does someone know that they don't spit on the floor or stairs?

At what age does someone know that you don't hurt someone else?

And at what age does someone know they were supposed to go to class?

If the answer to all these questions is beyond age 18, then excuse them, please, for they know not what they do. If it's not 18, however, if it's at a much younger age, then there are no excuses.

Warnings to students are a waste of time. They give the wrong parameters of acceptable behavior. If students are given three chances, for example, and there are 100 students, then there could be three hundred unacceptable behaviors before any consequences are meted out. Those parameters are too wide.

Students who know where the boundaries of acceptable behavior are and know that they will be enforced, will turn their attention to what is expected of them, which is to study, to learn, to become educated. That's what we want them to pass on to the Next Generation and the ones after that.

Good teachers work hard. They put a lot of time in, in school and at home, because that's what doing the job well demands. To be effective means to be a teacher 24/7. There's no way around it. That's why the average life of a teacher in the United States is about seven years. That's when the frenetic pace, the workload, or the gnawing guilt because the teacher never had a clue and couldn't carry the scam anymore catches up with some. Getting out of teaching for these people is an escape. Had they been trained at **my** school, they would have realized that final truth early (that teaching isn't for them), or developed the skill and experience to overcome that feeling and become a master teacher. After all, the quality of education depends on the quality of the individual teacher.

Chapter three

Administrators, School Boards, Taxpayers and Parents; They All Should Be Spanked

Administrators

I have known a few good administrators over the years. I consider them to be good for several reasons. These reasons are what every administrator should be.

First, they knew what was going on in the school in general and the classrooms specifically. They knew who was teaching well and who wasn't, and why. They knew what was expected of their teachers and expected them to do it. They also knew to allow the teachers the chance to do it. These administrators were, as the Effective Schools literature calls them, academic leaders. They were in the classrooms often. They just popped in, stayed for a few minutes and left for another classroom or engaged in what was going on in class and stayed a while. And no master teacher would object, since there is always something going on.

One administrator I knew even agreed to fire a starter's pistol, representing the assassin's gun, in a media exercise I was conducting in order to duplicate the sounds and images from an actual historical event, the assassination of President John F. Kennedy. Later he showed me the powder burn left on his jacket when he fired from under his folded coat. (The student portraying a secret service agent, by the way, was the only one to correctly identify where the actual shots had come from and chased the principal out of the room and down the stairs, telling him he was under arrest. The administrator had to convince the student that he, the assassin, was supposed to get away).

Secondly, good administrators are free of disciplinary duties. I've spoken to many principals who came into the job with high hopes and

Karl E. Thelen

expectations to make a long lasting contribution to the local education, and then become bogged down with a long, continuous line of students in need of discipline.

If all teachers and adults in the building maintained discipline in terms of student behaviors and academic expectations (and I mean aides, custodians, cafeteria, office, and all other staff), there wouldn't be the lines to the office that are there now and administrators would be free to do the job they should be doing.

Effective Schools' literature says that discipline should be firm, fair, and consistent throughout the building. This gives all students a wall, a known limit, parameters within which they can operate comfortably. All students need and, as many will acknowledge, want an orderly and safe environment conducive to learning.

Thirdly, the good administrators used to be teachers, and I mean teachers who did the job, master teachers, who know what it takes to do the job well. Without this, you'll have someone who doesn't really know what they are looking for when they have to evaluate a teacher, continuing the long line of 'passing them on.' You'll have someone who doesn't appreciate the staff, and that's the end of that honeymoon right there, a disaster waiting to happen. You'll also have someone who doesn't really understand how a school operates. More disaster. And without an appreciation for discipline in every corner of the class and school, there will be a large gap in the school's effectiveness where there shouldn't be any.

Not all administrators are all this involved or concerned. Not all have been teachers. A large part of that has to do with the fluidity of the job, the trend to stay a short while and then move up or over to more responsibility and more pay, usually at another school in another district. The needed continuity at a critical spot in the school's hierarchy is missing.

Not all administrators really want the job. They couldn't hack it in the classroom (it's a lot of work) so they got their degree and moved up, but that turns out to be work, too. These administrators are the ones who exemplify the Peter Principle, where people are promoted eventually to their 'level of incompetence.' Early retirement then looks pretty good.

I've met my share of administrators who were just waiting to retire and had given up even pretending to care. The main problem here is that nothing of importance gets done since most things require an involved principal, one who cares. In one school I was in, over a period of years discipline eroded, academics fell, and a general sense of 'so what?' pervaded parts of the faculty. The lack of leadership, especially academic leadership, will kill any school quickly.

Part of the reason so many administrators don't cut it is, first of all, the special demands the job entails. The drastic change from the classroom to the entire school is eye opening. Where the teacher could isolate himself from the outside world, the principal is exposed. The demands now confronting the principal are seemingly insurmountable, and if the person in charge isn't completely up to the job, the job will never get done.

Elizabeth Hartling in an *Eric Digest* article called, "Retaining Principals," shows what a principal today could be up against; long hours-for most, a 60-to 80-hour week, workload and complexity of job, supervision of evening activities can be unending, minimal pay difference between top teacher and administrator, feeling overwhelmed with very high expectations, State and district mandates that require "mountains" of paperwork, increasingly complex society and social problems." And so they leave.

The administrator also has to be a people person. They will meet with all kinds of people in all stages of intellect and emotion. If they can't deal with that complicated task, they won't be long for the job. They also have to have a psychology background if they're going to deal with the many teacher and parent personalities they are going to encounter.

They have to know how to deal with the new teachers as well as the entrenched, the good and the bad, how to support one and encourage and help the other, or be strong enough to cut them loose. Other burdens for principals include "Complaints from parents on everything from too much to too little homework, busses that arrive late or early, accidents and fights on the playground, pressures from the central office for paperwork, budget deadlines, committee assignments, occasional grievances, and many other demands on the principal may be sources of stress."[6] For these reasons, few principals live up to the job. The position quite often is a way station until some thing (perceived as) better comes along.

---

[6] Lawrence Giandomenico and Lawrence Shulman, *Working With Teachers Effectively* (Springfield: Charles C. Thomas, 1991.)

Karl E. Thelen

Administrators will be further dealt with in the chapters on Effective Teaching and Effective Schools.

School Board Members

I was on a school board for a total of seven years, two years of hell in one term, and then five years of ignorance (not mine) and disbelief (mine) in another. We never discussed anything educational. The main topic was 'what if the boiler blows?'

I have had experience with another school board for twenty-three years and know that, sometimes, things can work. I have also seen that it doesn't take much for a few angry community members to change what once was good to merely mediocre.

The biggest problem with school boards, other than information overload, is, first off, one-issue members. These are people who got hot real quick over a single issue, got a petition to run, ran and won. We had one such member who became upset that his child, who had participated in a 'prank' where they borrowed a rather large, expensive sign in front of the local vocational school, was disciplined by the school. Many people would say the sign was stolen. The father became incensed, got a petition, ran for the school board and won.

Another board member was there, admittedly, to keep his own taxes down. Another's sole purpose in volunteering so much civic time was to weed out the bad teachers, something he found to be a formidable task, first in identifying the poor teachers, (although he thought he knew who they were), and secondly, in starting the dismissal procedure which turns out to be expensive. It's often easier to just pay the teacher a year's salary to leave, with a good recommendation.

The list goes on, but each person who gets elected to a school board for a single issue, or because everyone knows them, soon finds out that the real issues take up all the time. It's a real education for anyone to see just what is involved, from the logistical point of view, in running a school. Most of every school budget is contractual by nature, so those monies can't be touched in terms of 'cutting the budget.' The building needs to be heated. There has to be electricity, or some means of generating power. There has to be toilet paper. Health care is paid even if there isn't a new contract. In the school I used to teach in, the district still pays for health care premiums for all retired teachers. These are paid whether the budget passes or not.

Anyone who gets on a school board in order to trim the budget soon runs into these realities. Only about 20% of any budget can be manipulated to bring down a tax rate, so it's always the supplies, the things that are needed every day in a school, that go. This can be a hard reality for someone who was elected and had plans of shaking the place up. The only shaking that can occur is to create tension among the other board members. Too often the end result is for the board to try and micromanage education in the school or district instead of setting policy, which is their actual role.

Tension between the superintendent and the board can also cause problems. This is especially true when the superintendent is a YUMA (Young Upwardly Mobile Administrator) who has no intention of investing in the district but is merely gaining credentials so they can move on. I've seen many superintendents of this nature and they are always ineffective for the long haul. Unless someone is there for the district and not themselves, they will do more damage than good.

School board members, who often want to do the superintendent's duties in running the district, create tension and cause superintendents to not want to work with school boards. The boards should leave such things as contractual concerns, personnel, and the daily running of the buildings to the superintendents and focus on policy, but they don't. In turn, school board members who are there to work on educational issues, get discouraged because of current board politics that prevent honest educational efforts.

School board members also need to be able to comprehend the larger educational picture so that they have a realistic view of test scores and curriculum and what makes a school and its teachers effective.

The lack of people who might be qualified to be good school board members is national in nature. The teacher shortage is national and the shortage of qualified administrators is national as well. These are not local problems. But they all contribute to the power outage at the top. These folks are also easily manipulated by the media and the constant messages designed to keep people stupid, so that when they do get to the board or superintendent level, they can't think any better than the average mushy brained resident of **A Nation of Idiots.**

Karl E. Thelen

The Taxpayers

Taxpayers are also parents and school board members, so not a lot need be said other than no one really wants to pay the price of education. I'm the first one to admit that it's become expensive and unwieldy. There are reasons which I believe explain a lot of it (special education, health coverage), but the fact remains that we need education, so we need to deal with it rationally, not vote down budgets because we're angry over other things that we have no control over, like insurance premiums, or oil and gasoline prices, or the cost of breathing. These things just keep sucking us dry since that is what they're designed for, and all we can do is take it. But locally, the school taxes are fair game. The school taxes are the only thing residents have any leverage on, and if they become angry, they'll use that leverage to vote the school budget down, even if it's really the State or Federal government they're angry at.

Anyone who is going to legitimately complain about a school's budget needs to know, just as school board members do, about contractual obligations before they vote no. Voting no doesn't change the contractual obligations of a school. Those are the things already mentioned that the school has to have regardless of cost if it is going to remain open: oil, electricity, salaries, bank notes, repairs, and so on. What is most often hurt by the no vote are field trips, extra-curricular activities, busses, and as a last trump card, sports. This is why the burden of the local cost of education has to be transferred to a more stable and reliable source of funding.

Parents

As a teacher, one of the last things I want to hear a parent say is, "There's nothing I can do," when talking about their child. This indicates to me that that parent abdicated his parental authority a long time ago. I would even surmise that they gave it away out of fear that they would cause irreparable harm to the young psyche if the child was disciplined or told no, or was expected to behave in a manner conducive to getting along in a democratic society. This is either poor parenting skills or Feelgoodeness at its best in the general population.

Many parents are afraid to discipline their kids, at first in public, but now even in their own homes. There is plenty of evidence to this end. Many parents also abdicate their parental authority because they're just plain afraid of their children. Along with all sorts of various punishable abuses should be parent abuse, something that's more prevalent than many people are aware.

I've met many concerned parents over the years who were sincere in their efforts to give their children the best education. They appreciated what the schools were doing, under the circumstances, and were supportive in many ways. What the schools lacked, these parents made up for at home. It was, from my point of view, very workable, parents and the school working together. This is when it's a pleasure to communicate with the parents because I knew they cared. They appreciated the grade sheets I sent home every two weeks to be signed and expressed that appreciation in a variety of ways.

On the other hand, many parents don't take much notice of what their child is doing until the teacher or the school contacts them because of a discipline problem or poor grades. Then, it's never their child's fault but the school's, since their child's needs weren't met. Makes sense to me. Feelgoodenism embraces this concept, so now, thanks to Feelgood legislators, congressmen and senators, we now have IEP's, 504 plans, and various diagnosed learning problems that need specific legislated remedies, regardless of the cost. Thanks to poor parenting skills, a new industry has blossomed in every school district in the US of A. Thanks to the alcohol and cigarette industries, every taxpayer gets to participate in the higher cost of 'special needs' education that alcohol and hundreds of other chemicals created.

The parents whose child does no wrong are probably the biggest nemeses to quality education, since they keep everyone off balance through their constant harangue, to the teacher, the administrator, the board, or, as happens often, the local paper. Many in education have been lambasted through the local media because irate letters, like good gossip, generate sales. Most of this educational hate mail is generated by people who never understood their own need for an education let alone now, as adults, the need to pay for the educational present; 'What was bad enough for me should be bad enough for them.'

An elementary teacher I know has had just these kinds of experiences from various parents and specific families over the past few years. One family blamed most of their children's problems on this particular teacher, which would be humorous if the local paper hadn't printed their letter saying so. This teacher was blamed right up

Karl E. Thelen

until the child switched to the high school in another town. Now those teachers are responsible for all of this family's children's bad behavior.

In another situation an irate parent was upset at her daughter's workload; it was too much, the reading assignment too long, and her daughter had five hours of homework each night (homework in that particular class was only incurred if the student didn't finish the class work). She also wanted to know why the school didn't care about her daughter's self-esteem (Uh, oh, Feelgoodenism alert). She said nothing about challenging her daughter, who happens to be one of the brighter students in the school, and getting the most from her daughter's ability. There was also no discussion of what happens at home to help the daughter with her self-esteem or other experiences that would challenge her at home to do her best, especially in reading and writing, which are what prompted the complaint in the first place.

The schools and the teachers should not be expected to take over the complete role of childrearing, nor should they be totally responsible for the intellectual and moral character of the student. Parents need to take more responsibility for what goes on within their own family. They need to exercise their inherent parental authority.

According to an Education Research Report "Parents' Literacy and Their Children's Success in School: Recent Research, Promising Practices, and Research Implications," by L. Ann Benjamin, as part of a series published by the office of Research of the U.S. Department of Education, parents may have more control over how well their children read than the school.

> **"One study of parental involvement, based on a model of children reading to parents, found that children who read to their parents on a regular basis made greater gains than children receiving equivalent amount of extra reading instruction by reading specialists at school (Tizard, Schofield, & Hewison, 1982)."**

The article further states that,

> **"Indirect factors including frequency of children's outings with adults, number of maternal outings, emotional climate of the home, amount of time spent interacting with adults, level of**

financial stress, enrichment activities, and parental involvement with the school had a stronger effect on many aspects of reading and writing than did direct literacy activities, such as help with homework"(Auerbach, 1989).

Under these circumstances, the irate parent should have taken responsibility for her lack of involvement instead of blaming the teacher, or the school in general. On the other hand, ironically, these parents are usually the ones who would be the least capable to come to any sort of intellectual decision based on the various aspects of the problem that they perceive is created by the school or individual teacher.

More parents need to understand that there can't be a big blank, educationally, once their children arrive home. Many students, although they may not readily admit it, would actually prefer to be involved with their parents on just these types of activities. That doesn't mean the parents can wait fifteen years and then all of a sudden want to get involved. It has to be right from the start, before their kids are in school. There's so much that can be done to enrich any child's life, but if the awareness isn't there, it will never happen. It's just easier to blame the school.

As much as it will anger many parents, they also aren't really qualified to determine what should be taught in the school or in the classroom. Too often decisions are made because of the politics involved; who knows whom and whether or not the parents are willing to make a fuss. Some administrators will do anything; even sell out their staff, if they think they can quiet an angry parent.

A few years ago the school district I'm currently in held a community forum where the community members could come in and vent their anger and frustration with all of the perceived ills foisted by the school and the teachers on the students and community. The teachers were asked to attend but not to respond to anything that was said. As the principal said, "Let them get it out and then it'll be done with."

Well, 'done with' is the furthest thing from the reality. By not standing up for programs and activities that were vilified by a handful (5) of community members who actually spoke, the teachers looked stupid, as if they had nothing to say in their defense and the entire district went in to a several year long frenzy of **accountability**.

Karl E. Thelen

We spent a lot of time on rubrics, those neat little packaged formulas for determining if a student's work was an A+, A, A-, B+, B, and so on since one of the complaints was about some teachers' inability to grade papers. Committees were formed and hundreds of hours were spent rewriting every curriculum in the school since some parents thought they weren't clear enough.

So parents can be good and bad. But I'm only going to focus on the bad, because that's really more fun. Over the years I've categorized many different types of parents (some categories I've stolen from other teachers). They are as follows, and none of the categories are exclusive. They can appear in any combination of one, two or more categories in the same set of parents.

The Whiners: These are the most common type of irritating parent. No matter what the school or teacher does, it's wrong; the school is to blame for everything. Whiners don't just complain once in a while. It's constant, never-ending. The grading is wrong, the work is too hard, and the teachers don't care about their child's psyche, (sound familiar?) and on and on. The only defense against a whiner is a strong, academic leader type administrator, who isn't concerned about the local politics. A strong administrator can stop whiners in their tracks by knowing the teachers and their policies and standing up for the staff right then. No administrator should ever cave to parents, especially when they are known to be whiners, and let them get beyond the principal's office. If there is reason for real concern, the academic leader deals with it after the parents are gone. No teacher should be whipped publicly or sacrificed just to get the parents to stop whining.

The Screamers: If this were a movie, the title Screamers would make for an interesting story line, but these screamers can make anyone long for the whiners to come back. Screamers obviously have real issues that go back many years, and they seem to be the only ones who don't know that screaming isn't necessary if the real concern is helping their child. But screamers are never interested in the solution. They only care, can only want, the problem, since that is what sustains their anger and gives them cause to eliminate these childhood fears by screaming. It's heavy stuff, and something that has power. Screamers are always tended to, since it really makes the person being screamed at appear to be the guilty party, especially when the 'guilty' party tries to shush the screamer. These are situations that can snowball quickly. And when there are screamers around, those in proximity always have twenty different versions of what really happened and what precipitated the screaming. I will not meet with known screamers.

The Swearers: The swearers have always intrigued me. I've come to the conclusion that the swearing is the only form of power they have. If it weren't for swearing, they really wouldn't have much to say. And they wait for opportune moments to swear. Usually the swearers are the fathers. They'll sit there quietly for a while and then all of a sudden, boom, it's goddamn this and goddamn that. Those teachers, Those goddamn teachers, and the goddamn school. I've never heard a swearer say 'my goddamn kid.' The sad thing is no one, in any meeting I've ever been in, ever says anything to these people to let them know that this is highly inappropriate. This should be the job of the person who called the meeting. No teacher is ever there, or shouldn't be, to be abused. It's the administrator's job to protect his staff. Period.

The Table Pounders: These are the parents I've enjoyed watching the most over the years. They can make things on the table bounce. I've often wanted to say "Did you go to school to learn that?" but that would only make them pound even harder and I'd be spoken to afterwards for being unprofessional. Table Pounders apparently have discovered that the violence of the action coupled with the volume of the pounding can get results faster than words (maybe they're afraid to scream). I've learned to sit back and enjoy these people because they always wind up either apologizing because they made complete fools of themselves, or are making complete fools of themselves and will never know it.

The Humiliators: These people are on a real trip. They're usually articulate bullies; almost always well educated. It's as if they're saying "I'm so much better than you and I know I can browbeat you and you won't do a thing about it except to try to appease me any way you can to try and get rid of me." It's never ceased to amaze me what Humiliators can get away with without someone saying something to them about how inappropriate their behavior is. Again, it should always be the job of the person who called the meeting to step in before the Humiliator gets up any steam. The sad part is that a lot of teachers won't stand up for themselves. It's as if they either don't realize that they don't have to be spoken to in such a rude manner, or they're afraid of a confrontation. But unless the Humiliators **are** confronted, they will continue to bully anyone they can.

I was in a meeting with a Humiliator who was there with his daughter, a student of mine at the time. The understanding before these meetings was to let the father 'rant' for about a half an hour. At least, I was told, that's usually how long it lasts. I informed the person in charge that if he directed his tirade at me I was leaving. After he was done with his say, which lasted about a half an hour, his daughter turned to him and said, "You're such an asshole." Humiliators don't control everyone.

The Patient Parents: The patient ones always sit patiently through the entire meeting. They say little, appearing to understand and agree with what is being said, nodding occasionally, smiling when someone is humorous, and they take notes no one can see. They can afford to be patient. They know their moment is coming. All they have to do is sit and wait. When they spring, once they are asked what they think, they become business-like, methodical, going through many of the things covered and commenting, from their notes, putting people on the spot better than a good trial lawyer. Slash, slash, slash, cutting away, probing for weak spots. If there's a Feelgooder in the room, they'll be found quickly, through their attempt to get everyone to calm down and feel good, and be skewered before they know it. A seasoned academic leader would know what to say to neutralize the attack. But alas, that seldom happens.

The Litigators: "I'm gonna sue. I'm gonna sue." The last thing any school district wants to hear is "I'm gonna sue." If there's a perception that a certain plan isn't being followed, or the district isn't offering the right courses, or the air isn't right, then all hell breaks loose. The best litigators are parents of kids in special education. They know the language, and they also know something very important, that the louder they get, the quieter the special ed. teachers will try to make it. The louder it gets (short of screaming), the more the likelihood that there will be a lawsuit. No parent should be given that kind of power. Legislators should make it so.

The Absentee Parents: Sad to say, but my experience is that many parents really don't care where their kids are or how they're doing. These parents are never at home when the kids need them. They never go to school events. If they do come in for a meeting, they are always shocked that their kid did anything bad. Since the parents haven't been around, they've missed a lot of formative stuff, and their kid is the one who pays.

The Intellectual Parents: There's nothing worse than parents who try to lord it over you. They are always both well educated, usually at least one of them has a Masters degree, and they think they know as much as any of the teachers in the school. They're also worried about their child's self-esteem and whether the curriculum is challenging enough. They're also the first ones to mention unrealistic goals and objectives, and to anyone not in teaching, they sound pretty good. But they aren't teachers so they're missing a big part of the picture, and that's what's really involved in the job of teaching. It's easy to talk about curriculum, it's another thing to put that curriculum into action. That's where the intellectual parents end it, however. Otherwise they might get their hands dirty.

The Buddy Parents: There's nothing worse than adults trying to be understanding 'friends' of their children. Rather than exercise the burdensome responsibility and make their kid hate them for expecting certain standards in their everyday actions, these parents take the opposite tact. If you're a 'buddy,' then the responsibility is on the one who can least handle it, or should be the one who can least handle it; the kids. That's not to say that later on in life, usually when the kids themselves have kids, that the parents can't be good friends. But adolescents need adults to lean on, whether they know it, or admit it. Buddy parents quite often are the ones who allow their kids to have parties where there is alcohol. Sometimes it's even provided by the parents. That's what buddies do.

The Victim Parents: These parents are usually single moms who can no longer handle their kids. Parent abuse is what it amounts to. I knew one student who would go home with his friends and put his mother in her bedroom and wouldn't let her out until he and his friends were done partying. The mother wouldn't file a complaint and the behavior continued. These are the saddest parents when they come in for meetings because there's a haunting look in their eyes. They shake their head a lot, and utter those deadly words, 'I really don't know what to do with him.'

The Enabler Parents: Parents who allow their kids to use any excuse not to do the best they can in their school work, or life in general, are doing the biggest disservice to their children. The longer parents put off their child's acceptance of life's lumps, and allow them to hide, the more damage they are doing. They are enabling their child to fail. The child in this instance could not successfully fail on their own. Many of these kids would start doing the work if they knew it was also expected at home and that **no** excuses would be accepted. But enablers want excuses; they want reasons other than that they are to blame.

The Badgerer Parents: The badgerers push their kids constantly, always badgering them to do better, always badgering to be number one, to get straight A's, to join all the groups, to take all the challenging courses, to be in the play, to dance, to sing, and with what time is left, to be a part of the family. I knew a student who was badgered his whole life. He was told he would be a doctor, and he worked hard all through school, badgered by his father, also a doctor. The day of graduation the student joined the Navy. He made an instant statement about a life of badgering. Badgering parents tend to put the most pressure on their kids and expect the teachers and the school to do it also.

So parents, chill. Be interested in what your child is doing, keep track of their progress on a daily basis, talk to them about life and its complexities, be a friend, (not a buddy) but don't be so quick to blame the teachers if your sons and daughters aren't turning out right. Much of the foundation of their lives is put in place between the ages of birth to four. There's just as much work to be done at home as there is at school. A parent's responsibility doesn't end once the kids get on the school bus.

The following is from a school's answering service taken from the depths of the Internet. I'm sure it's true.

"Hello! You have reached the automated answering service of your school. In order to assist you in connecting to the right staff member, please listen to all the options before making a selection.

To lie about why your child was absent, press 1.

To make excuses why your child did not do his or her homework, press 2.

To complain about what we do, press 3.

To cuss out staff members, press 4.

To ask why you didn't get information that was mailed to you in your monthly newsletter and in the several bulletins mailed to you, press 5.

If you want us to raise your child, press 6.

If you want to reach out and touch, slap or hit someone, press 7.
To request another teacher for the third time this year, press 8.
To complain about bus transportation, press 9.
To complain about school lunches, press 10.

If you realize this is the real world and your child must be accountable/responsible for his or her own behavior, class work, homework and that it's not the teachers' fault for your child's lack of effort, hang up and have a nice day."

There are times for parents to get involved in what's going on at the school and quite a few acceptable ways to do it. In fact, an effective school depends on parental involvement. This will be pointed out later in chapters nine and ten on effective teaching and effective schools. What isn't needed, however, are whining, screaming, swearing, table-pounding, humiliating, falsely patient, litigating, absentee, intellectually superior, buddy, victim, enabling, badgering parents.

Karl E. Thelen

Chapter four

Pharmaceutical Companies; Take your medicine, it's good for us

When I first mention to people including large pharmaceutical companies in a book on education, I would get strange looks, like 'why?' And so I explain.

I've negotiated for our teachers' association for eleven years. During that time, I've watched healthcare costs skyrocket. Because of this, and since we currently negotiate using the collaborative process, whereby each side considers not their own needs first, but those that would benefit the students, our teachers pay from 5 to 10 percent of the premiums. In some schools this would be higher and others, lower, depending on the individual negotiations. I mention this only to show the first-hand experience with rising health costs. In the year 2000, the premiums for our district health care went up by 26%. It's a growing problem not only in our district, but also all over the United States. Health care can be a budget buster, and quite often is.

Health care is a large 'perk' that is given, one of the 'benefits' of going in to such a low-paying profession. When the benefits are added into the gross salary, all of a sudden teachers look like they're making good money. But as the cost of the premiums rises sharply (health care costs have doubled in the last ten years), the tendency on the part of the school boards, obviously, is to keep costs down. Health care, one of the most important perks in attracting qualified people into teaching, is an easy target. A good tactic for school boards would be to negotiate so teachers pay more on the health care premiums, switch providers, or have the district do it themselves; these plans all work and don't work. These are all temporary measures, of course, and the end result is that you get what you pay for.

There is good and bad in each idea a school board tries. In the meantime, why would someone enter teaching and wind up paying a large chunk of their salary for coverage when they can take a job in private industry and not only make more money, but have better health coverage since private industry knows that a happy, healthy worker is a good worker? Private industry also isn't subject to the whims of the local taxpayers.

In a newspaper article from the March 29th, 2001 issue of the Plattsburgh, New York *Press-Republican* entitled 'Cuts in Store for Peru (New York)' by staff writer Stephen Bartlett, the lead paragraph says, "Facing three years of nearly flat state aid and rising health-care and special education costs, Peru Central School Board members say they can't avoid personnel and program cuts."

"Peru's story," the article goes on, "isn't any different from that of other districts throughout New York. School boards are struggling to draft budgets that reflect the state's forecast of nearly flat aid, for the third year in a row, while coping with the costs of federal and state mandates."

"The cuts largely stem from a 24% increase in special-education costs and about a 15% rise in health-care expenses," the article said. According to one board member there were about $1.5 million in mandates that the district didn't have additional funding for.[7]

This one article is not an isolated case. This is one of thousands all over the United States. Because the costs of health-care, and as you'll see later, special education costs, rise faster than all other costs in education, the quality of education continues to decline. Cuts are usually made to needed programs and, certainly, needed teachers. One of the proposed cuts in the Peru district was for a full-time second grade position, even though studies have shown second grade to be one of the most important for early development and later success.

So on to point two. The fastest growing cost in health care, and really driving up the premiums, are prescription drugs. Not just any prescription drugs, but designer drugs, drugs developed by the industry for specific applications (Viagra, Lipitor, Vioxx, Claritin and Zocor to name a few). Coupled with these designer drugs is one of the largest media campaigns ever in order to get the mushy brained public

---

[7] "Cuts in store for Peru." Stephen Bartlett. Press-Republican. March 29, 2002, pg. A3

to absorb the media mantra into their beings and then request, or demand, the specific designer drugs from their doctors. The pharmaceutical industry spends more money on advertising than it does on research and development (about four to one). It also spends a lot of time in the halls of Congress trying to kill unfavorable prescription drug legislation, and an equal, if not greater, amount of time wooing individual doctors.

According to an article in the March 2002 issue of the AARP magazine *The Nation*, out of every 100 million Americans who see the advertising, 13.2 million say they got the specific drug they asked for. That means that 13.2% of the people who saw the ads got a specific drug that they had seen advertised. It is this 13.2% that the mass media pharmaceutical advertising assault is aimed at. This is their 'target market.' It is this 13.2% that accounts for almost half of the drug companies' profits. It can also be said that this 13.2% is responsible for the giant leaps in health care premiums. It seems that those who are most mushy brained, those who used their education the least, are adversely affecting the quality of education for the future. This is why patients shouldn't be allowed to prescribe for themselves. If doctors really want to be ethical, then they can start by prescribing the least expensive drugs first.

In 2000, the pharmaceutical industry spent around 16 billion dollars promoting their 'golden' drugs. The cost includes giving away free samples ($8 billion) to doctors (this is the retail value; if they put the real value, the actual cost, a lot more people would be upset than are now since the cost is pennies compared to what they charge), as well as considerable promoting to doctors ($4.8 billion). This is called 'detailing,' by the way, one-on-one representatives to "educate" the doctors and hospitals to the benefits of prescribing the better drug.

According to a report by Susan L. Coyle of the Ethics and Human Rights Committee of the American College of Physicians (ACP), the benefits seem to be many; "...free lunches, dinners, tickets to ballgames, skiing trips and fees for giving talks that promote specific drugs". Further costs include consumer advertising ($2.5 billion), that goes directly to the mushy brained consumer who wants what he sees in the commercial and can now pronounce it when he demands it of his doctor because it's been on TV enough times, and advertising in professional journals (less than a billion dollars).

In regard to some of the above, in the year 2000, 83,000 drug representatives made sixty million details. Astra-Zeneca added 1,300 reps just to promote Nexium. There were also over 314,000 pharmaceutical industry sponsored events. Designer drugs were the topics of over three-fourths of these events. [8]

Since 1995, Research and Development staff of U.S. brand name drug companies have decreased by 2%, while marketing staff have increased by 59%. Currently, 22% of staff is employed in research and development, while 39% are in marketing. (PhRMA Industry Profile 2000; percentages calculated by Sager and Socolar).

The American Medical Association (AMA) generates $20 million in annual income by selling detailed personal and professional information on all doctors practicing in the United States to the pharmaceutical industry *(NY Times*, November, 16, 2000).

Everyone, it seems, is going to take the gravy from the health care industry for as long as they can, at least until premiums can't be raised anymore, and Congress steps in, like so many other western countries have already, and limits the costs for prescription drugs. Hopefully, that won't be just after it's too late, and everyone has already been sucked dry, and all the old pharmaceutical executives have retired to foreign lands and managed to take all of their employees' retirement funds with them.

According to the article in *The Nation*, "Sales increases of the 50 most advertised drugs made up almost half of the 21 billion dollar growth in retail spending on prescription drugs from 1999 to 2000." The other half of the sales came from the other 9,850 drugs on the market. This is big money, and everyone is going after it. By advertising the costliest of drugs to a mushy brained society, drug companies can reap profits only imagined a decade ago. And these fifty drugs are going to greatly affect the future quality of teachers and, therefore, education. Unless school districts can get out from under the oppression of these large corporations, little headway will be made, except in the continued direction of **A Nation of Idiots**.

Recently released figures of the Fortune 500 shows the top seven pharmaceutical companies took in more profit than the top seven auto companies, the top seven oil companies, the top seven airline companies and the top seven entertainment or media companies. The

---

[8] Scott-Levin Consulting

median profit for the Fortune Five Hundred, minus the pharmaceutical companies, in 2000 was 5% of revenue. For the pharmaceutical companies, it was 18%.

As a new market ploy (because it works), the pharmaceutical companies began employing celebrities to pitch their newly designed drugs. According to an article in the *Houston Chronicle*, March 7, 1999, "As competition in the drug industry intensifies and pressure mounts on companies to build profits, an increasing number of pharmaceutical companies are employing famous actors, politicians, and sports stars to attract consumer and physician interest." The use of celebrities is the next big way to differentiate a drug, according to the author Phil Galewitz. If it's good enough for Michael (as in Jordan), than it's good enough for me (well, at least that's what my mushy brain tells me).

In July of 1998, thanks in large part to the Food and Drug Administration's loosened restraints on advertising on radio and TV for prescription drugs in 1997, there began a phenomenal increase in drug advertising. In 1996 the drug industry spent around $800 million on advertising. By 2000, that had increased threefold to almost $2.5 billion. Schering-Plough became the first drug company to use celebrities for a designer drug when former Good Morning America anchor Joan Lunden made a pitch for the allergy medicine Claritin. It was then that patients began telling the doctors what they wanted instead of the other way around. Nothing is scarier than a slightly educated, mushy-brained population telling the ones who went to medical school what should be prescribed. Name recognition became important to the drug companies' future.

Worldwide sales of Claritin jumped 35 percent (to $2.3 billion) after the company began advertising. Merck spent $161 million in 2000 to advertise Vioxx, and raked in $1.5 billion. Not bad for a day's work. Viagra sales... Well, anything I say here would be a pun, so I won't, but the point is still the same, sales went up. Drum the name into a mushy brain and a consumer is born. In fact, the research of one early ad man, P.T. Barnum, shows there's one born every minute.

All of these things together: the drug prices, prescription prices, doctor's costs, hospital costs, x-ray costs, bandage costs, advertising costs, all medical costs, add up to higher premiums, and an untenable situation, under the present conditions, for most school districts. It's a vicious cycle; taxes go up, premiums go up, and the American taxpayer takes it bending over because that's the patriotic thing to do; it's the American way. It's good for our National Security.

In our district, at the present, the cost of a family premium is around $9000. Multiply that by 50 to 100, (they aren't all 'family' policies) and the cost just for this one benefit adds up to big money. And ours is not a large district. The answer, then, in most educational cases, is to save where the biggest savings would be, by cutting school staff. Fewer staff means considerably less paid out for health care by the district.

The answer also involves hiring fewer teachers with experience, as well hiring from a large pool of itinerants; teachers who keep moving from school to school because they know they aren't any good and they leave before they're found out. These people won't care what kind of health care they get as long as they get hired.

The answer is not in the government funding prescription drug programs. These are the babies of the pharmaceutical companies; what better child to have than a program which guarantees, with State and Federal money, that their exorbitant prices will remain in effect, and now for all those who previously couldn't afford them. Congress and anyone promoting current legislation to give the elderly discounts on prescription drugs should rethink this one. There are no long-term benefits if the real costs for the drugs remains the same. It simply comes out of the taxpayers' pocket. And the legislation wouldn't even come close to dealing with the pharmaceutical companies' grip on quality education.

The answer to the problem is in regulating the large corporations and their drug deals, as many other industrialized countries do already. If the pharmaceutical giants can't sell their products at fair prices then this is where those with the authority need to step in. Not with discount programs, but with reality programs. Without considerably lowering the cost of health care in America so that quality people can be brought into teaching, education will continue to suffer. Not just from expensive medical coverage, but because the coverage added one more weight to the local taxpayer and history shows us that there is always a breaking point.

Chapter five

Mass Media Manipulators; Purveyors of the ambient light

Much of the blame for **A Nation of Idiots** has to go to the mass media, those large uncaring, global conglomerated purveyors of flashy, flashing images, masses of smooth, silky skin, touched up photos, sleight-of-hand and rapid messages whose only purpose is to get a wide variety of people to all want the same thing, and willingly pay what ever the cost. Americans have mushy brains and people who run the media depend on it.

In show after show, commercial after commercial, Americans are bombarded with a planned assault on their mushy brains. Advertisers know that repetition will slowly mold a mushy brain into a consumer. If the commercial can burrow in and attach itself to the consumer's emotions, then the consumer is hooked for life. Hundreds of tiny tubes hooked up to millions of consumer bodies, go directly into the corporations' pockets; a slow, constant sucking of the consumer dry. The tactics used are tried and true. They work, and the media know it.

Like the cigarette industry's admission that a cigarette is merely a delivery system for nicotine, the media is merely a delivery system for commercials. Without commercials there would be no shows, no magazines, no newspapers. And just as the cigarette industry had, and still has, tactics to get the consumer hooked on their product, even with a warning that basically says their product will kill you, so too the mass media industrial complex has its tactics that hook consumers in broad daylight and with their eyes wide open. Part of that mass media plan is to keep the general populace on a dumb level so they won't see through the con games.

Corporations have to sell if they want to stay in business. That's obvious. To do so, they need buyers, and, again, the dumber the better, and dumber here has nothing to do with intelligence or station in life. There are a lot of 'dumb' consumers who have a Ph.D. To every corporation, the only thing of importance is the '**bottom line**.' Once a mushy brained populace understands that, they begin to see through the glitz and hype and see what advertisers want to do to them. Unfortunately, that takes effort so it doesn't happen often.

One easy way to sell to mushy brained people is to create something that those people would long for, strive for, and eventually, do anything to attain that 'thing.' In the media, the best thing to have all people strive for is an image. An image so tempting, so alluring, so filled with sexual desire, that everyone would work their entire lives to achieve it. The image has to be the perfect woman or the perfect man, always living the perfect life, and always happy. Always.

For the sake of argument, we'll call this image the '**higher image**;' that which epitomizes what we all should be. The neat part about creating this **higher image**, since it can never be attained, is that the general public can be made to feel inferior, or just plain bad, in a relatively short period of time. The best time to start is when they are very young. Even propped in front of the television, mesmerized by the *ambient light* of the TV, they are being prepared for their futures as consumers by corporate America. Television, the 'natural baby sitter,' has many followers, and the roots go deep.

In order to sell the products, by keeping people dumb, many networks and cable channels no longer capitalize the days of the week, the months, or a whole variety of other proper nouns and they quite often don't bother to capitalize the beginnings of sentences or put periods at the end. These things just get in the way; slow things down, dilute the message. Other companies, especially those selling to children, use names like Quik, Kool Aid, Froot Loops, and any number of misspelled product names for kids to see over and over again. These companies, corporations, global media giants, have allowed a wholesale slaughter of the English language, all in the name of profits. Students seeing this repetition internalize a large list of incorrect spellings, punctuation, capitalization, and other intentional grammatical and linguistic errors, and that, in time, becomes who they are, **A Nation of Idiots** unable to make change, unable to explain products they are selling, unable to lead the nation.

Over and over again, flashing out mesmerizingly from the soft, *ambient light* of our baby sitter from so many years ago, lulling us into a warm, trusting relationship, a friend who would never lie or hurt us, the TV reduces educational value. And then the teachers have to deal with it in school. Many students argue when told they are going to correct all the bad things they do in English. "But it's my style. I **want** to spell it that way," or "That's the way I make my letters, no one else cares if I write that way."

Now a Feelgooder would cheer at the individuality of this liberated student, who has style, but in reality, where the work force is, this 'style' wouldn't cut it. A Feelgood teacher would find ways to bend over backwards to accommodate this new educational concept of 'style.' If 'style' makes the student 'feel good' then, hey, it's OK. That way there's no pressure.

A daily watch on any of the ticker tape headlines that run constantly at the bottom of the screen on most 24 hour news shows gives an idea of the depth of the problem. The inability of writers, who know that what they say or write will be seen by millions of people, to spell correctly is frightening. And I'm not talking about the truncated, abbreviated, e-mail words that are used, just the misspellings and incorrect usage. Teachers can't 'do' and then have the media 'undo.' That's not the message we should be sending to kids about what's important. But, then, maybe most people don't know there are errors since they can't spell either. But that's just another example of **A Nation of Idiots.**

For eleven years I've taught a class called TV, Radio, and Print Media. Over those years, having read countless articles about the media, coming up with examples of the concepts being taught, and experiencing some of the media tricks (or 'con games' as they are called in <u>Unreliable Sources</u>) first hand, I've come to be extremely irritated at what I've seen the constant bombardment do to students. It can be seen in behavior and attitudes. Students have become desensitized to a lot in life, especially the threshold of acceptable violence and how to react to it.

The media's impact is replicated in mannerisms, clothing, language, products of all types and a large number of small, almost invisible personality traits that most people wouldn't even notice. In an attempt to be individuals, the media has tricked them into all being the same. The days of good manners seems to have disappeared, ironically just around the time good manners disappeared from television, and advertising in general.

A Nation of Idiots

    The question is often asked, does life imitate art or does art imitate life? In this multi-media day and age, the answer is simple if you have a crust on that mushy brain and can see it. Life imitates what the advertisers want the people to believe. Children on television say what adult writers want them to say. Real children mimic the shows. Bad manners on TV eventually translate into bad manners in general. The choice for our youth is directed. From my point of view it's misdirected. If anyone is truly concerned about the state of education in America, here's one good place to look and to start to do something about it. Until this mindless media frenzy stops jamming garbage images down students' throats through the mindless repetition (which works to move information from short-term to long-term memory) from their early years on, just so the companies can continue to make money, education will not improve.

    The Orwellian future seems to be here. When the **Media Industry** is examined, some scary things become obvious. First is the immense size of the Media Industry, which is no longer a national entity, but a handful of global commercial media conglomerates. Secondly, when you consider the fact that only a handful of media giants control a much too large share of the market, it becomes even scarier.

    In the 1980's, according to an article by **F.A.I.R.** (Fairness and Accuracy In Reporting) called "The Global Media Giants," there was a lot of pressure from the International Monetary Fund, the World Bank, and the U.S. government, to deregulate and privatize media and communications systems. At the same time, satellite and digital technologies were taking off. This created the conditions for the large Media Global Conglomerates, a situation that not too many people could have predicted. The circumstances were right for what HBO president Jeffrey Bewkes called HBO's "Manifest Destiny." [9]

    If these were just large companies, they'd be scary enough. But these large companies have the power, and they use it, to create the **'higher image'** necessary to maintain and increase profits. And now on a global level, much more of the giant media future profits will come from outside the United States.[10] The world is ripe for picking, and it will be a lot easier when it's **A <u>World</u> of Idiots.**

---

[9] Robert McChesney "The Global Media Giants" FAIR (Nov/Dec 1997), p. 3
[10] Ibid., p. 5

Karl E. Thelen

Like the pharmaceutical companies, the media giants have lots of money. They have two rules to govern how to make and keep it. "First, get bigger so you dominate markets and your competition can't buy you out." Firms like Disney and Time Warner (now AOL/Time Warner) the two largest **Media Giants**, almost tripled in size in the past decade.

"Second, have interests in numerous media industries, such as film production, book publishing, music, TV channels and networks, retail stores, amusement parks, magazines, newspapers."[11] (F.A.I.R. 1997), and anything else that can be used to control another's mushy brain to do as the media giants want.

The other giants are Bertelsmann, Viacom, Rupert Murdoch's News Corporation, TCI (largest cable company), General Electric, Sony and Seagram. Each of these companies owns other companies; the tentacles are long and they encircle many.

Time Warner, according to *"The Global Media Giants,"* had as its massive holdings, the following;

> Majority interest in WB, a U.S. television network which reaches 25 % of U.S. households.
> Significant interests in non-U.S. broadcasting joint ventures.
> The largest cable system in the United States, with 22 of the 100 largest markets.
> Several U.S. and global cable channels, including CNN, Headline News, CNNfn, TBS, TNT, Turner Classic Movies, The Cartoon Network, and CNN-SI.
> Partial ownership in Comedy Central and a controlling stake in Court TV.
> HBO and Cinemax cable channels.
> Minority stake in Primestar.
> Warner Brothers and New Line Cinema film studios.
> More than 1,000 movie screens outside the U.S.
> A library of over 6,000 films, 25,000 TV programs, books, music and thousands of cartoons.
> Twenty-four magazines, including *Time*, *People* and *Sports Illustrated*.

---

[11] Ibid., p.1

A Nation of Idiots

Half-owner of DC Comics, publisher of *Superman, Batman* and 60 other titles.

The second largest book-publishing business in the world, including Time-Life books and Book-of-the-Month Club.

Warner Music Group, one of the largest global music businesses.

Six Flags theme park chain.

The Atlanta Hawks and Atlanta Braves.

Retail stores, including over 150 Warner Bros. stores and Turner Retail Group.

Minority interests in toy companies Atari and Hasbro.

Not bad for a local boy. Disney's holdings looks similar;

ABC television and radio networks.

Ten U.S. television stations and 21 radio stations.

U.S. and global cable stations Disney Channel, ESPN, ESPN2, and ESPNews, holdings in Lifetime, A&E and History channels.

Americast, an interactive joint venture with several telephone companies.

Several major film, video and television production studios including Disney, Miramax and Buena Vista.

Magazine and newspaper publishing; Fairchild Publications and Chilton Publications.

Book publishing, including Hyperion Books and Chilton Books.

Several music labels, including Hollywood Records, Mammoth Records and Walt Disney Records.

Theme parks and resorts, including Disneyland, Disney World and stakes in major theme parks in France and Japan.

Disney Cruise Line.

DisneyQuest, a chain of high-tech arcade game stores.

Controlling interests in the NHL Anaheim Ducks and major league baseball's Anaheim Angels.

Consumer products, including more than 550 Disney retail stores worldwide.[12]

---

[12] Ibid., p. 6

Karl E. Thelen

Already these configurations have changed, but that doesn't affect the point being made. The reason for showing all of this is to show the magnitude of the forces against the American people, and therefore against education itself, to keep everyone pliant, receptive, and never able to think long enough to figure it out. The longer large Media Monsters are allowed to grow, gobbling up more radio stations, more TV stations, more newspapers, and more magazines, the narrower becomes the source of information and ideas available on which to make decisions.

Limiting input of information, ideas, and choice, creates a 'dumbing down' atmosphere. Democracy depends on an exchange of ideas and that depends on access to information. This, of course assumes the information is accurate. When information is limited, ideas become limited, and discussion becomes limited to last night's reruns of the currently popular sitcom.

In George Orwell's book 1984, the intent was to limit all thought to only one thought-absolute love for Big Brother, who represents the government. 'Doublethink' was designed to narrow the focus of discussion, to narrow what could be said, to instill limitations from birth, so only that one thought could be achieved.

Today, when only 13 of the top 100 of the world's richest people in the world control most of the media outlets, which means they control most thought, how far away are we from having only ONE thought? The extent of freedom depends on the ability to get the untainted truth. To get the truth we need access to information. What we don't need is for anyone with a few billion dollars to throw around doing everything they can to limit the information we get, making our brains mushier, keeping Americans prisoners in **A Nation of Idiots**.

Limiting ideas also limits identity. As local identity disappears, the mass media's ability to manipulate the masses, as in 1984, becomes much easier. In 1996, following deregulation of ownership laws, one half of all U.S. radio stations were sold, mainly to large media giants who now own hundreds of stations and dominate the market. Democracy depends on a widening of ideas, not a narrowing.

This narrowing of ideas can be seen easily in the sameness of American towns and cities. Every place now has a McDonalds, Burger King, Wendy's, KFC, Walmart, Subway, and so on. Name your favorite place and it's probably there.

The 'sameness' is a sign of tertiary identity loss. America is no longer a vast country of small towns and cities each with their own identity. As sad as it is for our history and the future that won't know variety of lifestyle, this is an environment for the Media Monster to mark his territory and put down roots. It's almost, and I mean ALMOST, to the point where Americans all wear the same clothes, eat the same foods, listen to the same songs, watch the same shows, and shop at the same malls. As individuals, Americans rule.

Further proof is the way that we as a nation think, which has changed, and not necessarily for the better. The days of John Wayne being an American hero are over. The more recent media heroes have been people with names like Homer and Bart Simpson, and found in shows like 'Married With Children', 'Malcolm in the Middle,' and 'Grounded for Life,' where the main characters are generally idiots, and the children all talk back to their parents. When movies called "Dumb and Dumber" and more recently "Jackass," are the rage, then how far behind is quality education?

Thanks to demographics, the media can pick and choose their targets, as well as their target markets. Many people think that they decide many important things in their lives, such as who to vote for, what music to listen to, or what clothes they buy, but in reality, many choices were programmed long ago.

Starting with the commercials from the fifties and sixties, most jobs like cooking, cleaning, shopping, having babies and decorating were female roles, whereas the jobs like war and killing or anything to do with weapons were left to the male species.

This early training of future consumers was in its infancy back then, totally oblivious to the fast paced, computer generated digital future ahead. But it worked, and on this success came that future, a happy future for any one who owns a share of the Mass Media Market.

Today, media techniques are honed by computer generated graphics, digital imagery, and a technology that advances so rapidly that few can keep pace. The cutting edge is the finest in legal mind control, the old brainwashing of the fifties. Now it's legal, and supported by all large corporations who only have America's best interests at heart, providing it doesn't hurt **the bottom line**.

Many of these techniques are worth talking about, since forewarned is forearmed.

Karl E. Thelen

The following is a list of media con games that most citizens need to be aware of. Each con game is designed to manipulate the mushy brains of an unsuspecting public. Those marked by an asterisk came from Unreliable Sources.

1. 15 second commercials
*2. loaded language
*3. headline hanky panky
4. emotional attachment
5. sex and the female image
6. wallpapering
7. sound bites
8. statistics
9. polls
*10. the morgue
*11. buzz words
12. repetition
13. isolate, focus, magnify
14. individuality
*15. The key to manipulation

Commercials used to last 60 seconds. Long enough to go to the bathroom and then go to the kitchen and get a sandwich. As the pace of life increased with the increase in technology (which ironically was supposed to free people up and give us more time to relax), the old 60 seconds became laborious. America was becoming too sophisticated for the old way. The new thirty-second commercial was designed to spellbind the viewer, giving no time for rational thought. The latest research now shows that two different fifteen-second commercials on the same topic, back to back, do even better in manipulating the mushy brained.[13]

My students are always surprised to find out that all the pictures of good looking women are touched up, made to look more perfect, with tiny hairs removed, eyes made the same color, shadows removed, content digitally altered. It's an image game, and the odds are in the favor of the house.

---

[13] "Enhancing the efficacy of split thirty-second television commercials: an encoding variable application." Journal of Advertising. 3/26/99, p. 3

Most commercials, when slowed down and dissected for content, messages (both overt and covert), and visual techniques, show a large number of unrelated images most of which are also unrelated to the product (which shows up eventually, once the flashing is over). It's this stroboscopic effect of images that creates the receptive equanimity of the mushy brain. It's a soothing feeling, a calm in a hectic day, and so easy to understand. So, why not buy the product? We're already humming the jingle. And advertisers were so nice, so thoughtful to make us feel good.

One of the keys to being able to manipulate the mushy brained is the power to label.[14] He who controls the labeling controls the minds of men. By being first to place the label, the labeler gains power. A good example is the abortion issue. The labels are pro-abortion, pro-life, pro-choice, butcher, baby-killer, doctor-killer, and any thing that fits the argument. All labels are designed to set off an emotional response. The media fan this response, and if it turns into violent confrontation, well, then they'll have 'good video,' and everyone can see it on the six o'clock news.

When looked at more closely, however, the labels don't explain the complicated mix of personalities, backgrounds, cultures, beliefs, and so on, nor do they do justice to the truth. Mushy brained people have a hard time separating truth from emotional attachment and that is why manipulation is so successful. If the masses are confused enough, mesmerized enough, and emotionally bonded enough, then they'll run out and do what the labeler programmed them to do. If the labeling comes from large, manipulating corporations out to sell, by flashing those 15-second commercials, then the masses will run out and buy something to make themselves feel better. If the labeler wants America to invade Iraq, then that will happen too.

For instance, in the case of abortion labeling, most abortions are done early in the first trimester when the abortion involves a small amount of tissue and blood. The media image over the years, however, is to go with the more (much more) emotion charged images of pieces of babies (arms, legs, hands, all tiny), lighted and bloodied for the cameras. If the pictures were true, then they would have to be from a very late term abortion, which is rare. To violate the truth to

---

[14] Lee, Martin, Soloman, Norman. <u>Unreliable Sources</u>. Carol Publishing Group: 1992

such a degree merely to shock people into their beliefs should not be the role of the media.

To label anyone is to defile, or at least obfuscate, the truth. However, with no label to identify people or groups of people, the media become confused. It's just easier and, well, convenient to label them and be done with it so reporters can meet their deadline and fill the space. By labeling, the media direct mushy brains to think as the media wishes, and that always cost money.

Labeling leads to another concept from the media mesmerization show, loaded language. I've used this term, as well as most of the others I have listed here, ever since I read it in <u>Unreliable Sources</u>. Loaded language is used to 'get' your enemy, or just to get your friends not to like someone you don't like. It's the language we use to shade the truth, to bend it a little. Everyone does it. It's human nature. But when the media do it, the consequences become ominous. When those who should be most responsible for the public trust misuse that trust, democracy suffers. Access to information suffers.

Journalists, especially, tend to use loaded language in their stories, putting a little slant to it, nudging the direction just enough to fit a premise. One article, before Bill Clinton left office, labeled him as irritated and being angry with the reporters. When I saw the video and heard him speak on the news that evening, there was no hint of irritation in his voice, and his anger at the reporters was not apparent from what he said. More likely, he angered a reporter and that started the loaded language in order to show Clinton as angry and irritated. Loaded language is used to provide bias, to set the viewer or reader up to look for something, and the longer they look, the sooner they'll see it. It works for selling National Security, politics, toilet paper or the cleaning up of the huge Exxon-Valdez oil spill in Alaska.

Conversely, **loaded language** can also be slanted to show the good things. This works well in advertising where all the positive attributes have to be shown. Beer is a social attractant, giver of happiness and babes, and, obviously from the 'language' used, an affluent lifestyle that everyone would want and can achieve if they just drink this beer(The higher image). Not mentioned are the negative aspects of alcohol, the death rate, liver disease, and so on. Loaded language is pure manipulation, and the easiest thing to manipulate is a mushy brain, one kept especially stupid through a lack of education, a model resident of **A Nation of Idiots**.

Headline Hanky Panky is, quite simply, messing around with the headline and the article so the two are quite often unrelated. My favorite says, "The War in Yugoslavia is Over," but the lead paragraph in the article tells about the continued shelling and the number of dead people. Since most people don't read an entire article, and rely on the veracity of headlines to make a determination as to whether they want to read the article or not, newspapers can put any headline on that they want, as long as it gets the attention, and sells the paper. Whether it's true or not doesn't matter once the customer has handed over his money.

Sex sells. The Media know it and pump it out like water from the well. It doesn't matter what the product is, either. That makes sex a potent weapon in the Media arsenal, the ability to make grown men crumple in a whimpering pile at the sight of smooth, silky skin.

A casualty, however, in this mindless digitized assault is the image of women and what the message is in regards to their worth in our modern society. When looked at closely, the use of women and their lack of clothing in commercials and other depictions has a dark side. To the mass media, women become objects, usually to be used and abused by men, since market research has shown that showing men skin is what works. Forgotten in the excitement of so much profit are the consequences in society of the repetition that these commercials will create, thereby creating a cultural truth. Women are second-class citizens and are there to be abused, certainly not to be taken seriously.

Many of these commercials, both on television and in the print media, show women in submissive situations, always with their breasts evident, always with suggestive text. They are usually inviting the sexual encounter and one particular commercial even has the text, for a perfume, that says, "Let him smell the scent that says yes, even as you shake your head no." According to this commercial, even when women say no they really mean yes.[15]

Often, the women are portrayed as innocent girls, luring in those who have a twist of larceny in their soul and will run right out and buy the product that that sexy little girl advertised. Again, women are trivialized; little girl playthings, pouting and sexually enticing.

---

[15] Kilbourne, Jean "Killing us Softly 3" Media Education Foundation, 1999

Madison Avenue, advertising Mecca, manipulates the male psyche and demoralizes and demeans women at the same time.

The last thing the media would want, then, is for a crust to form on any mushy brains. There are too many products to sell, and it's easier to sell to an uneducated, compliant consumer whose brain absorbs whatever is thrown at it or shown to it, most easily if sex is involved. This powerful form of media manipulation should be banned, specifically for males. But since it 'brings home the bacon,' then it will be around as long as there are men.

Women can be seduced just as easily, but it isn't necessarily with skin. It's with image. The images are usually romantic, loving, nurturing, all the things many women in their most open moments reveal they really want. The media give it to them. To men they give sex, to the women love, an ear (with which to be listened to), picnics, warm moments, everlasting faith, family and diamonds forever.

According to the authors of Unreliable Sources, the media's forte is to get a large number of people with varied backgrounds, needs, and desires, to all want the same thing. They need to create some means of reaching deep inside to everyone's sense of individuality and make them believe that by all doing it together, by all being the same, they will have become the true individual they long to be. It sounds wacky, well, it **is** wacky (and it can only happen in **A Nation of Idiots**), but that's what happens.

Creating an **emotional attachment** to any product is the job of the media. By getting a certain cake mix to touch the heartstrings, sales will increase dramatically. By letting consumers know that a certain brand of tire is like a member of the family increases sales. Emotion, too, brings home the bacon. The movie "E.T." increased sales of Reeses Pieces dramatically.

It's the emotion in sex, of course, that makes men drool. That one is obvious. But not every product has a legitimate emotional hook. So some have to be manufactured. They can do it with babies, cute little children, family, the American flag, tragedy. Whatever they have to use to do the job, they'll do it. Nothing is beneath them. Nothing is too undignified. If it increases **the bottom line**, it's good.

A Nation of Idiots

Wallpapering is a term I heard in a Bill Moyers video on "The Public Mind,"[16] a PBS series I've used for many years in class because the content still rings true today. Wallpapering refers to the background on a news story, although obviously it can apply to the print media as well when altering, or setting up, photos.

In the video, the journalist (a well-known, network woman) said that she had made critical remarks concerning Ronald Reagan in her story, but she received a call from Michael Deaver, Reagan's number one front man, thanking her for the story because, even though she was verbally critical, the background was all flags and patriotic themes. That is what the viewers remember most, what they've seen, not what they've heard.

Photos can be manipulated by anyone. A *Calvin and Hobbes* cartoon I use in my media class shows Calvin telling Hobbes to only take his picture on the corner of the bed that he has cleaned off so that people will think he's a clean, neat person. Just before he's ready, Calvin says to Hobbes, "Wait, let me go in and put on a tie and comb my hair." The viewer will see only a neat clean young boy who is well groomed and nicely dressed, those things that are **not** Calvin. What the mushy brain sees is much more important than what the mushy brain's ears hear.

Just as commercials used to be 60 seconds long, the news used to run lengthy quotes from people they were interviewing. It made sense, since the person being interviewed was usually someone with specific knowledge of the topic they were speaking about. When presidential candidates were asked a question, they were allowed to answer. The whole answer, for the most part, aired that night. Now, the thrust of the news brief is the 10-second, or less if it's pithy enough, sound bite.

The sound bite is designed not to give people information, as in the early, less manipulated days of news, but to help shape the story, to put a slant to it. The sound bite is the spice of the story. It's short and to the point. The sad part is that mushy brained viewers still believe that ten seconds is chock full of information, and they feel good at being informed. But news is no longer for the dissemination of information in order for those in a democracy to make informed,

---

[16] Bill Moyers, "The Illusion of News," PBS Documentary Series, "The Public Mind."

Karl E. Thelen

educated decisions on their real National Security; health care, air and water quality, social programs to help the less fortunate. The news is there to entertain. And while they have the mushy brain following the bouncing dollar sign, they drop in a 'brought to you by' and sell you some more from the Media Store. Beware of the non-news.

Statistics are another evil of the media monster. Statistics should show truth. They should represent a breaking down of something, like how the economy is doing, so that it can be understood by the people in terms of the numbers it generates and what those numbers mean. But if numbers are used so that the consumer won't understand how something works, then manipulation is at work. This, along with sources who supply about 70% of the information reporters use (source journalism),[17] is what the media do.

On the best of days, a mushy brain will have trouble with most kinds of math. When it comes to real statistics they're lost, so if the media just tweak the numbers a little bit, it can cause a lot of damage. And tweak they do, the extent of which is determined by whoever is providing the information and numbers to be tweaked, and has a special interest in the outcome desired. It's so much easier to just take information from others who have gone to the trouble of preparing it for publication than to have to dig it up and write it all yourself.

Polls can be made to do what the designer wants, and if that's to create a certain opinion, then so be it, as long as there's money to be made. The **advocacy group**, the one promoting the poll, determines the intent of the poll, how to interpret the results and how best to use the results to their advantage. And there are many advocacy groups.

The important part of a poll is 'setting the table,'[18] that part of the question that sets the reader up to answer a certain way. Lean it to the left and most people vote Democratic; a little to the right and the Republicans are cheering. It works for public policy, gay rights, gray rights, National Security, what foods to eat and how to raise your kids. The polling is incessant, ubiquitous, and highly manipulative. And it works. Now we have instant polls. Obviously the fifteen-second attention span is slipping. We want the results NOW.

---

[17] Lee, Martin A., Soloman, Norman. <u>Unreliable Sources</u>. New York: Carol Publishing Group, 1992

[18] Fred Barnes, "Can You Trust Those Polls?" Readers Digest, July 1995, pg. 49-54

The morgue is a term that refers to where old news articles go. Most people probably think they go in the recycling bin, but they don't. They're saved so they can be used again when some reporter needs to meet a deadline. I've often wondered if other people saw the same paragraphs coming around again and again when numerous stories are being written on a subject in a short period of time

The sad part is, if there are errors in the original story, those errors will be repeated. The media are good at repetition, and if you hear the same mistakes over and over, they eventually become truth. And if the present truth is based on past errors, then the future truth becomes corrupted. It's a vicious cycle and, ironically, education can intervene, but that won't happen as long as we're **A Nation of Idiots**, which is being aided and abetted by the Media for their own selfish reasons.

The media use a lot of words repeatedly; words that convey one message to the public but carry another meaning to those using the words; the word '**cleanup**,' for example. Whenever there is an oil spill, or some other messy accident that is generally toxic in nature and a danger to all life, the media will assure the public it is being cleaned up. The sooner the public feels good about the situation, the sooner the government or large corporation responsible for the situation is out of the spotlight. The 'buzz words' are designed to ameliorate, soothe, pacify, and euphemize the public. Spies become an 'intelligence community,' a 'deterrent' is when we point our missiles at Russia, but an 'aggressive act' is when Russia points their missiles at us. Without knowing what the media is actually saying, a mushy brained society can be manipulated.

Some words that I think make the point best are:

Acting Presidential; This doesn't necessarily mean the president did anything noteworthy. To the public it can instill confidence that our president is doing something good, although most people would be hard put to say what. To the media, it merely means there was some bit of pretending going on and the media liked it. Maybe the president fed the press corps well. If so, he was acting presidential.

Dangerous Drugs; Not killers like alcohol or tobacco. How can something legal be dangerous? And not over-prescribed prescription drugs that are all potentially dangerous and addictive. No, the dangerous drugs are the illegal drugs, and as long as the negative emotional attachment is maintained, the public will be willing to spend almost any amount of money to stop the scourge. Whether

Karl E. Thelen

anyone is actually killed by illegal drugs or not is immaterial. They're illegal and therefore dangerous. Also, because of the emotional attachment, the American people get to have another WAR, plus a Czar; a drug czar, but still a Czar. Ah, the power to label...

Experts; Experts make us feel good because obviously they are knowledgeable in their field and what they say, therefore, must be an accurate and informed opinion. In the real world of Media Magic, however, an expert is whoever they say it is. Quite often the 'expert' is someone who has been chosen because of a known opinion. If that's true, then, why, that's manipulation.

Instability; The American military loves instability. Instability, when it appears on the news, means that the military gets to go in to the unstable area and kick some butt. The US of A likes nothing better than to go into an area of instability and make it right. Panama became unstable, even though prior to that we liked Manuel Noriega the military leader that he was. Once the situation became "unstable," however, Manuel became a military strongman. Now he's in jail. We went in and held all of Panama at bay while we secured our National Security.

Stability; If you're a stable country, don't worry, The US isn't coming in. We like what a stable situation provides for us; a military base, a landing strip, permission to use air space, a bunch of the oil. Areas of stability, as has just been alluded to, are run by Military Leaders, not Military Strongmen.

Military Strongman; I've taken the suspense out of this one, but a Military Strongman is obviously one who would Strong-arm others, and that's not acceptable to the American way of life. The situation needs to change, soon.

Military Leader; Ah, a Military Leader; usually a good friend of ours (for now). Leaders know how to lead, so how can there be anything wrong with that? Americans, after so many years of democracy, appreciate a good Leader.

National Security; The security of the nation is a most important and precious necessity. For a nation to be secure, it should have life, liberty and the pursuit of happiness at the center of its being. And these most precious things are embodied in clean air, clean water, a population whose most basic needs are met, a diverse population that is secure enough in its own identity to be able to accept everyone for what they offer as human beings, not a population torn apart by prejudice, greed, and lack of education.

Nowhere does it enter into the serious consideration of National Security that oil would make us all happier and more secure. It makes large corporations secure, knowing that with plenty of oil they will exist for another generation at least. These same corporations for years soaked up every patent on any form of alternative energy that would have, some time ago, eliminated our nation's need for oil. National Security should be an easy call, but unfortunately there are many who have their own agenda, and lots of money.

Radical; The word radical brings to mind a wild-eyed, red-in-the-face, arm waving, fist-shaking firebomb thrower. It stirs emotions, similar to the days when the good mob would come out to save the taxpayers money and lynch someone for free. Once that emotion is unleashed, it's hard to reel it back in. So if the media point their collective fingers in a certain direction, aided by others in the 'Establishment,' the name tends to stick in every mushy brain out there.

Senior Administrative Official or Someone Close to the President; Almost always the President, but he doesn't want anyone to know it's him, so the media covers it up a bit so he can still talk without us knowing it's him. That way, if we don't like what he said (the media will print it, always), then it wasn't him who said it, and when they find that aide he or she will be fired, or at least moved to another office for a while. Then again, maybe it is someone close to the President and they don't want the President to know it's them.

Terrorism; Terrorism is another good one, because it can have so many different meanings depending on who is doing the labeling. To most Americans, George Washington was the Father of our country. To the King of England he was a terrorist with a price on his head. So, too, old Ben Franklin and Thomas Jefferson and a whole bunch of our historical good guys. But if they had been captured and taken back to England, Ha! Off with their heads! (Well, o.k. Hang by their heads).

Americans, as only an example, have come to view Palestinians, through the media, as terrorists, because they blow things and people up for no apparent reason, while the Israelis, when they blow things and people up, are defending themselves. To many people around the world it's our government that actually sponsors terrorism, but we have better weapons and military leaders to help us out around the globe, 24/7, and better control of the media spin. I'm not trying to make a political statement, just simply pointing out the way the media work. It's all perspective depending on who your friends are.

It never hurts to question, especially in light of the **Con Games** being foisted on the mushy brains of America. Ever vigilant. When a real threat looms over us as a nation, as has happened recently, we rise up and put the hurt to anyone who dares to be our enemy. However, it should be as an educated, well-informed electorate and populace, not as media junkies, being manipulated through our daily fix, glued to the ambient light and believing every word that oozes out day after day. Understanding the terminology gives everyone a defense against overkill, against the **Label** designed to move our emotions to accept anything we're told. That's not in our National Interest.

Special Interests; This has always been a negative label. It identified those who had a personal, greedy reason for getting a vote to go a certain way; large corporations, represented by the well-paid lobbyists knocking on every senatorial and congressional door, the Military, or any large complex that makes its living suckling on Government (oops, our) money.

Now, however, this negative label is applied by the media to mean grassroots supporters, movements that are concerned with clean air, clean water, and keeping the environment free of 'progress.' It also means those who traditionally have less money and little power; minorities, labor unions concerned with the average American, senior citizen groups, etc. These groups care for people on an everyday basis. They are at the hub of humanity, and yet, they are labeled special interests, obviously way outside the mainstream of America.

These aren't all the words the Media use to fool, through sleight of mouth or word, but merely a sampling. The closer you listen, the more you question, the more you think for yourself instead of letting some 'expert' do it for you, the better off you'll be. Education is important. The ability to think freely, and with greater meaning, is important. Don't let anyone, whose interests are not in **your** best interests, manipulate away what is rightfully yours.

Repetition can be used in education to push information from the short-term to long-term memory. In the media business, it's what pushes consumers over the edge of resistance to any and all new products or images that come along to shake the jingle out of their pockets.

The music industry knows it just has to play a song enough times and the tune will get stuck in the collective conscience of an entire nation. The advertising industry knows if they run McDonald's past your nose enough times it will become the dinner table in your house. Repeat the same styles, the same models, and the same features over and over again and soon everyone has to have it in order to retain their individuality.

All of these concepts have the same intent; to drive us like cattle through the chutes and then on to slaughter. Depending on the outcome desired the media could make us dance one way or another. If they want to make us think something is sexy then they'll label it as such, show us skin, load their language with luscious and tantalizing words, wallpaper in red, and get us emotionally involved, and if they can get us to cry, what great video that would be.

If the outcome is to be patriotic, then switch scenes to camouflage, label it as in our national interests and use words like God and country and National Security. Never say the word oil. Wallpaper in American flags all red, white and blue with pictures of Washington, Lincoln and the family in the background, and you'll proudly send your only son off to war.

I could continue on with other concepts such as manliness, womanliness, success, and any number of images that the media want to sell. Get the right mix and the profits will be staggering. The less educated we are, the more dependent we become on the media, and **A Nation of Idiots** is born.

The bottom line (no pun intended) is that the mass media don't give a damn for education since that would work counter to the needs of the advertisers, war makers and image-makers. As with Feelgooders, it's the intention of large corporations and their mediums of manipulation to lower everyone to a common denominator so that no one is any different than anyone else. That way everyone will want the same thing at the same time so money can be made. Commonality is the new individuality. The famous question heard in classrooms all over the country, "does spelling count?" will no longer be heard. Who will there be to ask it?

Karl E. Thelen

Chapter six

Mushy Brains and Weapons of Influence; Bad touching

Another strong argument that manipulation by forces much larger than we is constant and ongoing is presented in a book by Robert B. Cialdini, Ph. D., called <u>Influence</u>. Dr. Cialdini writes that there are six principles that are followed when we are influenced by others to do their bidding, and that whoever knows these principles would have the power to manipulate. These six principles, called weapons of influence, are: Reciprocation, Consistency, Social Proof, Authority, Liking, and Scarcity. These weapons touch us deep in our psyche; in places we don't even know we have.

Some of the weapons of influence include **Trigger Features**, those things inside us that will set off certain predictable responses, called **Fixed Action Patterns**. Fixed action patterns are the responses we always give in certain situations. "They make us terribly vulnerable to anyone who does know how they work."[19] Dr. Cialdini gives several interesting examples of **trigger features**, first from nature and secondly from the mushy-brained kind. The first example was in regards to the mothering instinct of turkey mothers. It seems that the only time that turkey mothers are good mothers is when their baby cheeps. It's this 'trigger' that clues the turkey mother into the fact that she's needed. When the baby doesn't cheep, the turkey mother does nothing. She may even kill the baby.[20]

However, when a natural enemy, in this case a stuffed polecat, emitted a mechanical cheeping, the turkey mother showed it all the

---

[19] Cialdini, Robert B. PH. D. Influence. New York: William Morrow and Company, 1984, p 21

[20] Ibid., p. 16

A Nation of Idiots

same responses that the turkey would have shown to her real baby (covering it with her wings for protection). Once the cheeping was turned off, the turkey mother attacked the stuffed polecat as it would under normal conditions.[21] The trigger feature was manipulated.

One trigger feature in humans, discovered in an experiment by Harvard social psychologist Ellen Langer, is the word 'because.' It seems that when we ask someone to do us a favor, we would get a much greater response by providing a reason. "People simply like to have reasons for what they do."[22]

Three favors that were asked of people waiting in line to use a copier were, "Excuse me, I have five pages. May I use the Xerox machine?" 60% said yes. When a reason was added, "Excuse me, I have five pages. May I use the Xerox machine because I'm in a rush," the response jumped to 94% who said yes. Even if the request was reworded to "Excuse me, I have five pages. May I use the Xerox machine because I have to make some copies," the result was 93% who said yes.[23] They all complied simply because they heard the word 'because.'

In humans, it's almost a crime to know these 'tricks' if you're the manipulative type because they work so well. Two weapons in particular that work well at manipulating the mushy brain are called **Contrast Principles** and **Perceptual Contrast.**

Contrast principles affect the way we see two things presented one after the other. If we want to show that something is attractive, we should first show something unattractive. That, by contrast, will make the second thing shown look better than it otherwise would. "...Studies done on the contrast principle at Arizona State and Montana State Universities suggest that we may be less satisfied with the physical attractiveness of our own mates because of the way the popular media bombard us with examples of unrealistically attractive models."[24] Maybe the media should pay for all the divorces in the U.S., and compensate the children who wind up needing special services, to deal with emotional residue from the divorce. It's one

---

[21] Ibid., p. 16
[22] Ibid., p. 18
[23] Ibid., p. 18
[24] Ibid., p. 25

more example of how the media dangle the **Higher Image** in front of us and make us unhappy. "The same thing can be made to seem very different depending on the nature of the event that preceded it."[25]

Perceptual Contrast is getting many people to see the same thing differently. An example of perceptual contrast is sometimes employed in psychophysics laboratories to have students experience the principle by having each student sit in front of three pails-one cold, one at room temperature, and one hot. After placing one hand in the cold water and one hand in the hot water, the student is told to place both in the lukewarm water at the same time. The obvious contrast of going from hot water to lukewarm will make that water feel cold, and conversely, going from the cold water into the lukewarm will make that water feel hot. Perceptions can be manipulated, and guess who knows it?

Because of these concepts of subtle manipulation, corporate bottom lines can be increased considerably. In retail stores, if customers are shown an expensive item first, they will then be less likely to balk at a less expensive item, even though that item would still be considered expensive, because by contrast the second item is cheaper. In real estate, showing rundown houses at inflated prices first encourages buyers to jump at the house that was intended for them all along.[26]

The mantra in business is 'present the expensive item first.' That way, the influence of the contrast principle will be utilized. To fail to do so is to lose the business. For example, someone may balk at the idea of spending $100 for a sweater, but if he has just bought a $400 suit, a $100 sweater may not seem excessive.

These are just a few of the uses for those who possess the knowledge to persuade and manipulate. On a national scale, the use of such knowledge is reprehensible. On a global scale, especially considering how many countries haven't had years to develop at least minimal protection from such a media-manipulating onslaught, the idea is frightening.

The following concepts are those that cause us to return a favor, donate money, vote as we do, make commitments, determine correct behavior, determine who we like, explain our subservience to

---

[25] Ibid., p. 25
[26] Ibid., p. 27

A Nation of Idiots

authority, and use potential unavailability to make us want whatever is being offered.

Reciprocation, the rule of reciprocity: This is a strong concept, not only in our society, but the world over. "...There is no human society that does not subscribe to the rule."[27] It says that when someone does us a favor, we owe a favor in kind. When we receive a Christmas card, we send one out; we reciprocate. If we are given a present, we will give a present in return; we reciprocate. The reciprocity rule says that we must repay in kind, we are obligated to future indebtedness. There is a psychological burden of debt. And until we repay this favor or kindness, we won't feel comfortable. The author cautions, however, that, "...we will often be 'taken' by individuals who stand to gain from our indebtedness."[28] Extrapolate this on a national or world scale and the profits become staggering.

Amway sales took a giant leap forward when they instituted the BUG concept, a bag of free samples that is left with potential customers so that they may try any or all of the products they wish. By accepting this 'free sample' bag, the customer has fallen prey to the 'reciprocity' rule. First of all, they don't use up all of the sample products, so the BUG can be used again on another customer, but most important of all, this 'free gift' generates tremendous sales. "Even in a company with as excellent a growth record as Amway, the BUG device has created a big stir."[29]

Think of all the other companies that employ the 'reciprocity rule' now that you know what it is; Tupperware, through which a 'hostess' gives many 'free gifts' and makes sure everyone 'wins' something at a Tupperware party. These parties not only sell many products, but the salesperson, with little effort, leaves with a list of other potential hostesses in order to utilize the rule on into the future; getting the first month free from magazines; a 'first month' free premium from an insurance company; free records and books from 'clubs;' 'in-the-clear' weeks from cable channels; free gifts in the mail from any number of companies selling products that they hope you won't be able to live without.

---

[27] Ibid., p. 30
[28] Ibid., p. 30
[29] Ibid., p. 39

There are other aspects of the rule of reciprocity. The rule enforces **uninvited debt**, and triggers **unfair exchanges**. Along with these there is an **obligation to make a concession, mutual concessions, initial concessions**, and the **rejection-then retreat** concept, a "highly effective compliance technique."[30]

The Regan Study, as referred to in <u>Influence</u>, performed by Professor Dennis Regan of Cornell University in the late 1960s, had as an example to show the power of the reciprocity rule the buying of a Coke for one test subject by another (an uninvited gift) and the resulting favor done in return (the buying of raffle tickets). The return favor was, by contrast, a much larger repayment of the reciprocity 'debt.' Not only is this an example of the 'uninvited debt' principle, but it also shows how someone can be manipulated into an 'unfair exchange,' the returning of the gift with something of greater value-a can of Coke versus, on average, two raffle tickets. The largest number of tickets was seven.[31]

Part of the rule of reciprocity also states that there is an obligation to make concessions inherent within the concept. If someone offers something for sale that is priced beyond what we wish to pay, and we refuse the item, they can then drop the offer to something that will cost less, and invoke an unspoken obligation on the part of the buyer to also make a concession and buy the lesser-priced item. This 'mutual concession' is necessary for society to continue working together in an unexploited manner and "...encourages the creation of socially desirable arrangements."[32]

The rejection-then retreat concept is where someone makes a larger request, one likely to be turned down, and then follows that first request with a concession, or retreat, to what was desired all along. This technique, obviously, is what works well during traditional negotiations. The success of this tactic, however, depends on how it is presented. If the initial request is way out of whack, then any concessions will not be viewed as viable. In the hands of professional manipulators, salespeople at every level of society, the

---

[30] Ibid., p. 41-49
[31] Ibid., p. 44
[32] Ibid., p. 48

A Nation of Idiots

duping of innocent shoppers, viewers and consumers, becomes child's play.

There is also the power of connecting the 'reciprocity rule' with the 'perceptual contrast' principle. "In combination, the influences of reciprocity and perceptual contrast can present a fearsomely powerful force. Embodied in the rejection-then retreat sequence, their conjoined energies are capable of genuinely astonishing effects."[33]

One of the examples offered by the author in Influence is worth repeating here because of the national consequences that resulted: the resignation of President Richard M. Nixon. The ridiculous plan of G. Gordan Liddy to break into the offices of the Democratic National Committee chairman, Lawrence O'Brien, offers a prime example of the reciprocity rules mentioned. These offices held no information of any value to Nixon's reelection, an election basically assured since it looked like his opponent would be George McGovern, the Democrat with the least likely chance of winning.

The break-in was actually a 'concession' on the part of those who had the authority to grant Liddy's last request of $250,000. A previous request was for $1,000,000 "…that included (in addition to the bugging of the Watergate) a specially-equipped communications 'chase plane,' break-ins, kidnapping and mugging squads, and a yacht featuring 'high-class call girls' to blackmail Democratic politicians." This was followed by a toned down version for only $500,000.

It was the final plan, for the $250,000 that was approved by John Mitchell, the director for the Committee to Reelect the President (CRP).[34] A classic case of the contrast principle, comparing the first stupid plan to the last stupid plan made the last stupid plan seem not so stupid, and the Perceptual Contrast principle, made the $250,000 price tag seem reasonable when compared to the $1,000,000. The second plan was perceived as a bargain. Liddy employed the rejection-then retreat philosophy well. This invoked the feelings of 'mutual concession' on the part of those involved, and Liddy got his money.

Is it no wonder, then, that an entire nation, world, can be 'duped' into buying, believing, thinking what the great manipulators (the

---

[33] Ibid., p. 53
[34] Ibid., p. 55

media, corporations, medical profession, salespeople, telemarketers, legislators, snake oil salesmen) want us to?

You can protect yourself from all of these preplanned tactics by anyone wishing to manipulate you into a position involving the transfer of your money to them. You merely have to be informed, form a crust on your mushy brain, and refuse to be a citizen of **A Nation of Idiots**. To be forewarned is to be forearmed.

If someone sends you something free in the mail, look at it as a sales ploy, not as a gift. If you're a college student be careful of the free gifts those generous credit card companies are passing out (a new and rapidly growing money sucker). The interest you wind up paying goes way beyond the cost of any gift. If you take a free month of a magazine subscription, look at it as a 'hook' by the company, a trick to get you to respond. I tell my media students that as soon as they hear the words 'free gift,' say 'trick.' If you don't think of them as gifts then you're no longer obligated to the **Reciprocity Rule**. "The rule says that favors are to be met with favors; it does not require that tricks be met with favors."[35]

Commitment and Consistency: The consistency principle basically says that once we commit ourselves, either in writing, publicly, or by making an inner choice, we will make every effort, rightly or wrongly, to maintain that position. It is the "...willingness to believe in the correctness of a difficult choice once made." There is a strong need to keep our thoughts and beliefs consistent with what we have already done. This is not just an individual trait, it is a societal one the world over. Being consistent has a strong attachment to our behavior.

"The drive to be (and look) consistent constitutes a highly potent weapon of social influence, often causing us to act in ways that are clearly contrary to our own best interests... A high degree of consistency is normally associated with personal and intellectual strength. It is at the heart of logic, rationality, stability, and honesty."[36]

The concept of consistency would explain why some people become diehard fans, or political supporters (especially after their candidate is exposed because of some unsavory reason), why we

---

[35] Ibid., p. 64
[36] Ibid., p. 68

A Nation of Idiots

swear by certain products and won't switch, or why we become entrenched in an unrelenting belief. This 'automatic responding' is comfortable since we already know what we need to think in order to maintain a certain position, so there is no need for further thought or time wasted on getting all the information needed in order to have a reasoned response.[37]

Once advertisers get a hold of this (and I think they already have), mushy brained consumers can be manipulated into strongly held beliefs as to which products are the best. Once committed, most consumers will remain consistent with that decision, since consistency is regarded so highly in our society. According to the author, we can see this with toy stores as Christmas nears. By over-advertising a certain toy, so that all children want one (the **Higher Image** of toys), and then undersupplying it to the stores, many parents, who committed themselves to their children to buy that toy for Christmas, are left without being consistent in that commitment. After Christmas, when toy sales tend to slump, the manufacturers then make that toy available so the parents can keep their commitment.[38] The toy store industry is very considerate.

We are a compliant nation, just as the mass media want us to be. Little or no thought on our part is good for business, and if this idea can be inculcated long enough, the consumer will do anything suggested to it. It's the job of advertisers, then, or anyone dedicated to the manipulation of others, to get their foot in the door, to get a commitment of some kind. It's important to get people to take a stand or go on record, the more public the better. "Once a stand is taken (commitment) there is a natural tendency to behave in ways that are stubbornly consistent with the stand."[39]

The idea in business is to start small and build. People in the business of manipulation understand that once their foot is 'in the door,' the chances of getting all the way in are good. Agreeing to something that at the time seems small and trivial can later lead to a much greater commitment. "Such an action has the potential to influence not only [someone's] behavior, but also [their] self-image in

---

[37] Ibid., p. 69
[38] Ibid., p. 74
[39] Ibid., p. 75

ways [they] may not want. And once a person's self-image is altered, all sorts of subtle advantages become available to someone who wants to exploit that new image."[40]

Companies know that if they can get their customers to commit themselves on paper, they will be much more successful in maintaining that customer's 'consistency' in buying the product, so many sponsor essay contests about their products, with nice prizes. Amway encourages all of its salespeople to write their goals down, and then make consistent efforts to achieve those goals.

Psychologically, when we write our goals or whatever it is we wish to achieve on paper, we create a commitment to achieve those goals, which time has shown is accomplished by being consistent in our efforts. "…Something special happens when people personally put their commitments on paper. They live up to what they have written down."[41]

Making a public statement strengthens this commitment. Since consistency is viewed favorably, there will be a greater effort to maintain that public image and appear to be consistent if a lot of other people know about it. Alcoholics Anonymous makes their clients commit to a twelve-step program, part of which involves publicly admitting to a problem, and also requires them to apologize for past transgressions against people they have hurt.

Also, the more **effort** it takes to make the commitment, the stronger the influence on the attitude of the person making the commitment. If it's easy to accomplish and of little consequence, there is no strong attachment, and no strong commitment. If, however, we have to go through a lot to achieve the goal (Dr. Cialdini used an example of pledging a fraternity and the hazing pledges go through, which can sometimes be downright degrading and stressful, just to prove they want to be a member) then the goal will have meaning and we will adapt our behavior to whatever is necessary to be consistent with that goal. "It appears that commitments are most effective in changing a person's self-image and future behavior when they are active, public, and effortful."[42]

---

[40] Ibid., p. 80
[41] Ibid., p. 86
[42] Ibid., p. 96

That, however, which has been found to be most powerful in helping us commit to something is what we tell ourselves on the inside, and once we have convinced our inner selves that it was our decision, and not an outside influence, we become most affected. "Social scientists have determined that we accept inner responsibility for a behavior when we think we have chosen to perform it in the absence of strong outside pressures."[43]

An example of this would be something I discovered many years ago and have since found to be known to many teachers. I had a problem with keeping a showcase near the library in my former school, which was displaying student work, from being vandalized. Nothing big, just parts of projects missing, or pictures torn, annoying things, mindless.

I found out who had been doing it; several boys who tended to be less academically inclined and who, therefore, had to resort to some other means of gaining self-image, ruining someone else's work. I knew that sending them to the office would do no good, and certainly yelling at them would accomplish nothing.

That's when I thought of asking those whose names I had been given to help me put up the next display. They accepted, glad to be 'missing class.' I threw in a few other kids to disguise my ruse. It worked better than I had hoped. They actually did a good job in displaying the student work. Not only did the display stay intact, but also some students told me that those who, before, were responsible for altering the display were now telling others not to touch it. By changing their inner choice, I had changed their behavior, which, in that instance, changed their self-image to one of accomplishment. They had committed themselves to the display, and became consistent in their protection of it.

Mushy brained people can protect themselves from these tactics, but it will take some effort. First, think about what is being presented (there's the effort part). If it demands a foolish, rigid consistency to maintain the commitment, let it go. It's a trick. Even if the thing presented is what you believe at the moment that you want more than anything, take a breath and tell yourself, "Think through the merits of every new action before doing it."[44]

---

[43] Ibid., p. 97
[44] Ibid., p. 108

A last caution would be to watch out for the 'low-ball.' I mention this because I was impressed by its presentation and the fact that, in retrospect, I had been low-balled many times. A good example is the car dealer who offers a good deal to a prospective customer, fills out all the paperwork, and then finds out the deal can't go through as is. By the time the buyer leaves the dealership, he has agreed to pay the original cost of the car, plus more for extras and feels good about it. So, when making a large purchase that started out as a 'deal,' watch for the 'error' or 'miscalculation,' or 'bank refusal' of the original deal. These are all low-ball techniques to get you to make a commitment, and then feel good about fulfilling that commitment even though it costs a lot more money. Forewarned is forearmed. If you watch for it, you'll see it.

Social Proof: This concept indicates that people are swayed in their opinions and actions by a powerful societal force; other people. We often determine what our actions should be based on what we see other people in the same situation doing, and if they are similar to us, then that enhances the likelihood that we'll be impacted by this principle.

Social Proof would account for the large legions of teachers who merely go along with whatever innovation that comes along because they believe everyone else is doing it. I have often said that teachers are like sheep when it comes to making decisions or standing up for themselves. Social Proof is a good indication that that is true.

Since others can manipulate many people easily, consider the possibilities of professional media manipulators making us their marionettes. With the diminished influence of the family over the years, the vacuum of influence has to be filled by others. Today we rely on television, radio, and the print media to show us how to act, dress, eat and think. "95% of the people are imitators and only five percent initiators. People are persuaded more by the actions of others."[45]

The idea of social proof is so strong that, "The greater the number of people who find any idea correct, the more the idea will be correct."[46] It's kind of like repeating erroneous information in the media. Eventually untruth becomes truth.

---

[45] Ibid., p. 119
[46] Ibid., p. 128

A Nation of Idiots

Pluralistic ignorance is when everyone decides on his own that since no one else seems concerned, then they needn't be concerned either. In times of uncertainty, the natural tendency is to look around at the actions of others for clues.[47] This explains why many people witnessing a crime will not offer help. They look around and see that no one else is, so it must not be as serious as they may think.

This scenario of noninvolvement changes, however, depending on how many people are witnessing the need for help. New York based psychology professors Bibb Latane and John Darley, while researching people in need of emergency help, found that when there was a single bystander present, a study participant feigning an epileptic seizure received help 85% of the time. When the crowd grew to five, help was offered only 31% of the time. As the numbers grow, the Social Proof principle kicks in and everyone waits to see what everyone else is going to do. "Because we like to look poised and sophisticated in public, ...we are unlikely to rush to help someone if no one else is."[48]

The idea of similarity is important to the Social Proof theory. It seems that the principle is even stronger when the people we are watching, in order to know how to act, are just like us. This 'similar other' concept has a powerful draw on us, not only consciously, but subconsciously. According to the author, it cannot only affect when we laugh, but when we commit suicide or homicide, what the author calls the "morbid illustration of the principle of social proof."[49]

The idea of morbid proof is founded in something called the "Werther effect." Werther was a character in a book called (in English) The Sorrows of Young Werther, written two centuries ago by Johann von Goethe, in which the main character commits suicide. The book was so popular that, aside from making Goethe famous, "it also sparked a wave of emulative suicides across Europe. So powerful was this effect that authorities in several countries banned the book."[50]

---

[47] Ibid., p. 129
[48] Ibid., p. 135
[49] Ibid., p. 144
[50] Ibid., p. 144

Karl E. Thelen

David Phillips, at the time Dr. Cialdini's book was published, was a sociologist at the University of California at San Diego. He followed this Werther effect into modern times. In a nutshell, Phillips found that whenever there was a news story about a suicide, the number of suicides within that viewing area increased dramatically within a few days, and with a secondary jump a month or so after that. Oftentimes these suicides came in the guise of 'accidents.' "[Phillips] found that within two months after every front page suicide story, an average of fifty-eight more people than usual killed themselves."[51]

The 'similar other' theory also was found to be in effect when these situations arose. "When the newspaper detailed the suicide of a young person, it was young drivers who then piled their cars into trees, poles, and embankments with fatal results; but when the news story concerned an older person's suicide, older drivers died in such crashes. Further research by Phillips showed a correlation between televised acts of violence and homicide rates, as well as an increase in homicide rates following a heavyweight championship fight.[52]

The importance of this information in terms of manipulating mushy brains is scary. If people are so easily influenced by others around them, then how easy is it for everyone to be convinced by the media that they should do as they see others doing, whether in terms of dress, behavior in society, preference for music, and so on?

This also speaks to the issue of violence on TV and in the movies, as well as to episodes like Columbine High School and other copycat scenarios. If others can do mass killings, why not me? By manipulating and tainting our Social Proof, the media has usurped our rights to choose and decide for ourselves without outside interference.

We can defend against this misuse of our 'social proof' principle by, first, watching for the use of false data, that which has been purposefully altered to manipulate us. Things like canned laughter, or actor portrayed testimonials, where the testimonial is scripted. Secondly, we can write letters and complain when a company uses these tactics to sell us their products. Companies don't like negative publicity. Send copies to the newspapers. Lastly, beat the odds by being aware of how influenced we are when we see tragedy on the news. Drive carefully after you hear or read about a suicide in the

---

[51] Ibid., p. 144
[52] Ibid., p. 150

A Nation of Idiots

news. Don't let the subtle influences of Bad Social Evidence affect your behavior. If someone needs help, don't look around to see what others are going to do. They're too busy waiting to see what **you** are going to do. Act.

Liking: It should be no secret that if we like someone we tend to listen to them more than to others. This is part of our nature. If someone in the media wanted to exploit this idea, however, then we'd all be in deep trouble, at least those who hadn't, as yet, formed a crust on their mushy brain.

Tupperware, for example, employs many of the weapons of influence, and does it effortlessly.[53] At a Tupperware party, everyone goes home with a 'gift,' invoking the rule of **Reciprocity**. The guests reciprocate by buying more Tupperware. During the games, "Tupperware" is yelled in place of "Bingo," and public testimony is made to the many wonderful uses of Tupperware. This induces a **Commitment** through **Association** to the product. This also increases sales. When everyone else starts to order, there is **Social Proof** that it's the right thing to do, and the fact that it's **Similar Others** who are doing the ordering, makes the **Influence** even stronger. On top of that, all of the people present should have a **Liking** for the hostess, usually a relatively close friend. This is all done by the Tupperware salesperson without lifting much of a finger, plus the salesperson will leave with future commitments to parties, as well as a list of 'friends' of the hostess to call on for other parties, using the hostesses' name, of course, to get their foot in the door. Tupperware must have read Dr. Cialdini's book.

There are other aspects as to why people we like can manipulate us so easily; **physical attractiveness**, how **similar** they are to us, or appear to be, how **complimentary** they are, the types of **contact and cooperation** we are involved in, and the degree of **conditioning and association** we are exposed to.

In terms of attractiveness, good-looking people have it made. "To good looking individuals we assign favorable traits such as talent, kindness, honesty, intelligence," and yet we are unaware that this is having an affect on us, the effect of which is to be manipulated. The

---

[53] Ibid., p. 164

author called this the "halo effect," where a positive characteristic dominates how one person views another.[54]

In study after study, proof that attractiveness works abounds. Various studies have shown that better-looking people are convicted of crimes less than others and serve less time if convicted. Better-looking women were helped more often when placed in certain situations, even by the same sex. A study of the Canadian elections showed that attractive candidates received two and one half times more votes than candidates considered not so attractive.[55]

"Good looking people enjoy an enormous social advantage in our culture." They are better liked, more persuasive, more frequently helped, and seen as possessing better personality traits and intellectual capacities. We like attractive people and we tend to comply with those we like. "Teachers presume good-looking students to be more intelligent."[56]

This "Halo of Physical Attractiveness," as Dr. Cialdini called the phenomenon of believing that good looking people are smarter, is eerily close to my "Higher Image," that which we all strive to be, whether person or inanimate object, upon which we place all those positive qualities that we admire. If it's a person, then they will be good-looking, intelligent, liked by all, emulated and bronzed. If it's a 'something,' then it's better than anyone else's; it'll work harder, last longer, go faster, and attract the opposite sex. The media rely heavily on this halo of physical attractiveness to do much of their bidding, because it works.

The Mass Media's penchant for lots of sex and good-looking people is a powerful means of manipulating all of the mushy brains into buying products. Our natural tendency to like beauty turns out to be a fatal weakness in the hands of Media Manipulators.

When those doing the manipulating are similar to us, at least in our mind, the manipulation grows in strength. "We like people who are similar to us; opinions, personality traits, backgrounds, lifestyle"[57] In the hands of those people I've already mentioned, this

---

[54] Ibid., p. 166
[55] Ibid., p. 167
[56] Ibid., p. 168
[57] Ibid., p. 169

'tool' carries a lot of torque power, since it's the media's job to get a lot of us with different needs, backgrounds and so on, to all want the same thing.

This 'automatic positive response' to **similar others** increases the chances that we'll be manipulated, through the principles of **liking** and **compliance**, by the **similar** backgrounds. Complimenting us is also a powerful weapon of influence since we all like to hear nice things about ourselves. "We are phenomenal suckers for flattery."[58] In Shakespeare's "*Julius Caesar*," Decius, one of the conspirators, when doubt is raised as to whether Caesar would go the Senate where the conspirators planned to kill him, says

> "Never fear that: if he be so resolved,
> I can o'er sway him; for he loves to hear
> That unicorns may be betray'd with trees,
> And bears with glasses, elephants with holes,
> Lions with toils, and men with flatterers;
> But when I tell him he hates flatterers,
> He says he does, being then most flattered.
> Let me work;
> For I can give his humour the true bent,
> And I will bring him to the Capitol."
> [Act II. sc. I, Li. 202-211]

Decius knows that Caesar can be manipulated through flattery, making good use of the compliment as a weapon of influence.

The scary thing, especially considering the weight the mass media put on us to comply, is that compliments don't have to be true to work, only positive.[59] The best way to give a compliment is to make any negative comments first followed by the positive. This type of compliment increases the **Liking** effect. It seems we can get our frustrations out about someone to their face, but end with **positive comments** and they'll end up liking us more. It's a great weapon in the Media Arsenal.

Contact and **Cooperation** has to do with liking things that are familiar to us. Dr. Cialdini offered the example of someone looking at

---

[58] Ibid., p. 172
[59] Ibid., p. 172

two versions of the same picture of themselves, one regular, and one developed backwards. If the person in the picture and a close friend were asked which picture was better, the friend will pick the regular one, and the person in the picture will pick the one that is reversed. The reason for this is something I have pointed out to students for over twenty years.

The friend sees us, as we really look every day, just as it would appear in the picture. The person, however, sees themselves backwards their whole life in the mirror. They would like the reversed image, which to them looks just like them. Even though the image is reversed, it is familiar and therefore liked. Whenever my own students get their school portraits back, the reaction of almost every person is negative. I tell them to take the picture out, turn it around and hold it up to the light and then ask how it looks now. Most of them will say, "Oh, yeah, that's better." I have to do this with prom portraits that I take. I've actually considered making up a little card to hand out with each package that says to turn the pictures backwards and look at them before deciding if they are good or not.

It's the contact we have every day with people and things that create familiarity. Once we become familiar because of constant contact, we will cooperate much more readily than if the expectation to cooperate had come from a complete stranger. The cooperation can also lead to **Liking**, in which case we're in for a troubled experience by Media Manipulators who are about to pummel us with our own deep-seated psychological needs, whether we know it or not.

It's because of this association and cooperation that the concept of "good cop-bad cop" works so well.[60] Inherent in the act put on by two detectives are several of the weapons of influence. First is the **Perceptual Contrast** principle. The good cop will seem a lot nicer, to the suspect, than he really is when compared to the nasty bad cop. Secondly, the **Reciprocity Rule** kicks in when he intervenes on behalf of the suspect. The suspect now owes the good cop. Now, the suspect, who is feeling more familiar with the good cop, (the good cop even uses the suspect's first name) can begin liking the good cop. This contact will allow the suspect to eventually cooperate with his newfound friend and spill the beans.

---

[60] Ibid., p. 182-184

A Nation of Idiots

The things we are **conditioned** to do through the **associations** we make can have a powerful affect on our mushy brain. On the one side of this concept is 'guilt by association.' It is here that the bearer of bad tidings gets killed. But on the other side, the side where we connect a certain product or idea with things we like, is where the media, and anyone else who wants our money, manipulates us. "In one study, men who saw a new-car ad that included a seductive young woman model rated the car as faster, more appealing, more expensive-looking, and better designed than did men who viewed the same ad without the model. Yet when asked later, the men refused to believe that the presence of the young women had influenced their judgments."[61] Denial is the only way a mushy brain can save face.

Celebrities, therefore, because we are conditioned to **associate** them with **The Higher Image**, have a strong pull when we see them associated with a product. Our **Liking** of them, as long as it's positive, doesn't even have to be logical, which is why sports figures can sell soda or any other product totally unrelated to the sport.[62] This celebrity linkage, which exploits the **association principle**, can also be used effectively in politics, and has a strong attachment to sports and why fans feel so strongly about 'their' team.

The association principle also exploits our fondness for food, since studies have shown that appeals made for money work best during or just after a meal, when the reciprocity principle kicks its hardest.[63]

Once the Media Manipulators get a hold of the principle, however, we become vulnerable as they pull each 'trigger feature' one at a time. Our "reaction to food can be transferred to some other thing through the process of raw association."[64] The **Mass Media** also have the power to connect us not only to **Similar Others**, but also to **Successful Others**, whom we wish, of course, to be like (Our **Higher Image**).

The best way to defend against the factors that lead to **Liking** (**attractiveness, familiarity, association**) is to first let them happen,

---

[61] Ibid., p. 187
[62] Ibid., p. 187
[63] Ibid., p. 189
[64] Ibid., p. 190

and then catch it when this feeling of 'instant' liking of someone or something occurs. It's that **Liking** all of a sudden for some reason we can't quite put a finger on that we need to watch for. "Be alert to a sense of undue liking for a compliance practitioner. The recognition of that feeling can serve as our reminder to separate the dealer from the merits of the deal and to make a decision based on considerations related only to the [merits]."[65]

Authority: The Milgram Experiment, conducted in 1965 by psychology professor Stanley Milgram, can best explain this. The experiment demonstrated a deep-seated sense of duty to authority, a subject's inability to defy the wishes of the boss.[66]

The Milgram Experiment involved subjects, recruited through advertising, who believed they were helping with a memory study. One subject was the student, one the teacher. Each time a student failed to memorize a particular task, or gave a wrong answer, the teacher, who couldn't see the subject, would administer a shock, which became stronger with each incorrect response. "...Participants in the Teacher role were willing to deliver continued, intense, and dangerous levels of shock to a kicking, screeching, and pleading other person."[67] The 'student,' of course, was not really receiving the shocks. The teacher only thought he was. "...The typical Teacher was willing to deliver as much pain as was available to give. Rather than yield to the pleas of the victim, about two thirds of the subjects in Milgram's experiment pulled every one of the thirty shock switches in front of them and continued to engage the last switch (450-volts) until the researcher ended the experiment."[68]

"...Without the researcher's directives to continue, the subjects would have ended the experiment quickly. They hated what they were doing and agonized over their victim's agony. They implored the researcher to let them stop. When he refused, they went on, but in the process they trembled, they perspired, they shook; they stammered protests and additional pleas for the victim's release. Their fingernails dug into their own flesh; they bit their lips until they bled; they held

---

[65] Ibid., p. 202
[66] Ibid., p. 203
[67] Ibid., p. 205
[68] Ibid., p. 206

their heads in their hands; some fell into fits of uncontrollable laughter. As one outside observer to the experiment wrote:

> **'I observed a mature and initially poised businessman enter the laboratory smiling and confident. Within twenty minutes he was reduced to a twitching, stuttering wreck who was rapidly approaching a point of nervous collapse. He constantly pulled at his earlobe and twisted his hands. At one point he pushed his fist into his forehead and muttered: "Oh, God, let's stop it." And yet he continued to respond to every word of the experimenter and obeyed to the end.'**[69]

This would also explain, as I said earlier, why so many teachers are often like sheep and go along with any inane educational innovation or new idea or piece of administrivia that comes their way. It also points out the futility of being on any committee with a strong-willed administrator, one who will impose their own findings and recommendations as those of the committee.

This deep-seated sense of duty to authority can be utilized and manipulated by governments, religions, the medical establishment, and con men. "Information from a recognized authority can provide us a valuable shortcut for deciding how to act in a situation."[70] However, if the authority figures are not real, and the intentions of the manipulators are not in our best interests, then techniques are being used to flip one of our deepest and most easily manipulated switches, the desire to comply with those in authority over us. Using actors to portray doctors in advertisements gives their words more credence. Put a uniform of any kind on someone and the response to his or her requests becomes immediate.

The sad thing about the power of our obedience to authority is that just the appearance of authority is enough to make us comply. We are as vulnerable to the symbols of authority as we are to the substance.[71] It is just this outward sign of authority that can be faked. It is here that con artists are at their best, faking authority. We react to the clothing of authority, the titles of authority, and other 'trappings' of authority

---

[69] Ibid., p. 209
[70] Ibid., p. 211
[71] Ibid., p. 215

such as fine jewelry, expensive cars, and any 'prop' that helps manipulate the minds of others for whatever selfish and sinister reason.

Studies have found that authority affects our perceptions of size and importance. When increases of stature were perceived, the height of the authority figure increased as well. Importance makes things seem larger. Size and status are seen as related.[72]

In one study cited, 95% of nurses complied "unhesitatingly" with a phone-in order, even though it violated hospital policy, from a doctor they had never met or heard of, to give prescription medication, which was on the list of medications not yet authorized by the hospital, for a patient, in a dosage that was considered excessive.[73] They acted against what they knew to be wrong merely because the title of an authority figure, 'doctor,' was used.

We can protect ourselves from the principle of **Authority** by first being aware of the phenomenon. Ask yourself, when confronted with an authority figure, is this 'figure' really an expert on the present situation? Or does he just seem like he knows because of the uniform? Watch out also for those who would begin by arguing against their own interests. It's just a trick to establish that they are basically honest on a minor issue so that they'll be believed later on a larger, more important issue, like how good their product is. Lastly, refuse to listen to authority if it involves injuring in any way another human being. Let the boss push the levers and administer the shock. If you're a teacher, don't be a sheep; don't be timid and shy in the presence of administrators and board members. They're just people, and a title doesn't make them better than you. Teachers know what's best for teaching. Stand up for that.

Scarcity: This is something that shoppers have known for a long time. If there aren't many left, you'll want it all the more. "Opportunities seem more valuable to us when their availability is limited."[74] It's the 'potential unavailability,' the 'limited number,' or 'last chance to order,' or the fact that it's for a limited time only, that

---

[72] Ibid., p. 216
[73] Ibid., p. 218
[74] Ibid., p. 220

causes us to jump into action before they're all gone, whether we need it or not.

The scarcity principle works best when there is competition for scarce resources. There are powerful motivating forces at work when anything becomes scarce, whether it's a closeout sale, bidding at an auction, food, or any other commodity perceived as in danger of disappearing.

It's tough to defend against scarcity, because the instance of scarcity triggers an inability to think of anything except getting what we can't have. It's like being deprived of air. All of a sudden, **that** is the most important thing there is. We also tend to take things for granted until we lose them, and that's when they become most valuable to us. Nothing increases value faster than having had something, and then losing it.

Once again, being aware of the feelings rising inside that there isn't going to be enough of something should be sufficient to sound the alarm to a **Manipulation** going on. It's also important to realize that "scarce items do not taste, or feel, or sound, or ride, or work any better because of their limited availability."[75] Ask yourself why you want the item. If you're not sure, the answer is no. If you only want it because you just found out there isn't going to be any more, but have no need of it, let it go. It's a trick to get your money.

The significance of all of these principles should be obvious by now. If the mass media, slowly being sugared down to only a handful of players, all of whom are very aware of how we think and know how to manipulate us into thinking that way, continue to use this knowledge against us, that puts all of us in a very precarious position. Eventually, if we fail to form a crust on our mushy brains, we will dance to whatever tune the global giants wish us to, and we will buy the new products as they are made available and live our lives in servile, mesmerized splendor, comfortable in our role as **A Nation of Idiots**.

We can be armed against these subtle **weapons of influence**. We can refuse to be taken in, refuse to let strangers touch us in places that they shouldn't touch us. Every time a 'compliance tactic' is employed we should scream NO and run away, and then tell someone. Tell everyone. The more who know what tricks are being employed

---

[75] Ibid., p. 257

Karl E. Thelen

against our will in order to take our money and our souls, the more will be protected. Instead of 'free gift' say 'trick!' It doesn't have to be **A Nation of Idiots**, but it will take effort to change it.

Chapter seven

Special Education; Very little bang for the buck

One of the biggest complaints against special education is the huge amount of money it sucks out of the taxpayers, and the minimal academic results it provides. In all of education, it provides the least bang for the buck. When the byproducts of poor parents and the alcohol and tobacco industries, the affected children, are considered, it becomes powerfully evident that the taxpayers are paying heavily for the crimes of others.

These two huge corporate monsters, alcohol and tobacco, polluting unborn fetuses with alcohol and nicotine, and creating future special-needs students for special ed. to feed on, should be the ones to fund special education in the United States, and any other place where they've helped create a huge educational conundrum. It's a crock and a crime perpetrated upon the taxpayers in every school district when large corporations create a problem and then the Federal government passes legislation that says to the school districts, "Here's what you are obligated to do to fix the problem and here's a little bit of money to get started with." The money is never enough and never lasts for very long, but the legislation is there for life. The next thing you know, property taxes are going up and budgets are being trimmed in order to get the budget past the voters. In 1975 the Federal share of the money provided to help districts keep up with Federal mandates was approximately 60%. Today it's closer to six percent. Guess whoooohooooo pays the rest? It certainly isn't the alcohol or tobacco industry.

In 1975, P.L. 94–142, the Education for all Handicapped Children Act, was passed in order to assure the free, appropriate public education of all children with disabilities. According to the 22nd Annual report to Congress on the implementation of the Individuals with Disabilities Education Act, "No otherwise qualified individual with disabilities in the United States shall, solely by reason of his disability, be excluded from the participation in, be denied the benefits of, or be subjected to discrimination under any program or activity receiving federal financial assistance."

This is what started it all. With this piece of legislation the United States government began the long road to diminishing the quality of education in America. From this act came legions of Feelgooders. They were going to right all the wrongs, eliminate all discriminatory words from our language, eliminate all oppressive acts by teachers, and eventually through the dogma of Feelgoodenism, ensure the feelgood future. Again, unfortunately, reality has a way of making things Aften Gang Agley (Often go wrong).

The Individuals with Disabilities Act was amended in 1997, but its basic intent and nature remains unchanged; a free appropriate public education, an idea first put forth in an annual report to Congress called "Progress Toward a Free Appropriate Public Education (FAPE)." This was preceded by the establishment, in 1966, of the Bureau for Education of the Handicapped by Congress, created under Title VI of the Elementary and Secondary Schools Act. This lead to the Education of the Handicapped Act, P.L., 91-230 passed in 1970. As a result of the legislation, parents began to pursue state laws to force schools to provide services. A new and expensive, bureaucracy was in the making. According the 22nd Annual Report to Congress, "...many children with disabilities remained unserved by public schools." Thus, the obvious remedy would be more Federal legislation. So, as the laws increased, and the search for all children with disabilities (any disability) began in earnest, the future of quality education took a big hit. Now money would need to be funneled away from core programs in order to meet the mandates from the State and Federal governments, or else. Even though over the years school districts had to pick up more of the tab and pass it on to the local taxpayers, the State and Federal governments still held schools accountable through the threat of losing all funding. Too many schools depend on State and Federal aide to bite the hand that mandates.

"By 1975, Congress had determined that millions of American children with disabilities were **still** (my emphasis) not receiving appropriate education, finding that 'More than half of the handicapped children in the United States do not receive appropriate educational services which would enable them to have full equality of opportunity.' Public Law 94-142 was enacted to remedy this situation by **requiring** that all students with disabilities receive FAPE and by providing a funding mechanism to **help defray** the costs of special education programs." (22nd Annual Report to Congress)

Since this time, the number of young Americans who have 'special needs' has increased dramatically. Aside from those students who truly have a deficit that should be helped, many of those designated were done so because of parents who wanted a reason for their child's inability to do the work in school, or because there is a problem socializing, or because special ed., in order to perpetuate its existence, needs bodies. Advocacy groups continually push for more liberal eligibility criteria so more students can be identified as special needs. Vermont has imposed strong restrictions on eligibility criteria. Perhaps the pendulum swings back. This may sound callous to someone who hasn't been in education for many years, and blasphemous to all Feelgooders, but the truth is the truth. Many students should actually be designated LAZY.

Thanks to the rapid growth of special education we now have labels for laziness (defiance to authority), sloth, indolence, apathy, irresponsibility, sneakiness and stupidity, instead of acknowledging that some students and parents are going to milk the system for all it's worth. Changing the box doesn't change what's in it. Changing the label doesn't change the product. An increase in disabilities is justification for increasing special ed. and once it's increased, it has to be fed. It reminds me of "The Little Shop of Horrors" where the tiny plant says, "feed me, I'm hungry," in a tiny voice, and it's actually quite cute. Later, full-grown, it bellows out "FEED ME, I'M HUNGRY!" So goes the hunger of special ed. Feed it, it's hungry.

In the preface of the 22nd Annual Report to Congress on the Implementation of the Individuals with Disabilities Act, the key components of IDEA are listed and explained. The key components are,

>Identification of children with disabilities
>Funding Formula
>Service Provision in the Least Restrictive Environment
>Services to Infants, Toddlers, and Preschoolers

Karl E. Thelen

    Parent Support
    Improving Results
    Personnel
    Transition
    Research
    Conclusions

Identifying children with disabilities came about because Congress (such a vague term) didn't feel that all the students who had disabilities had been identified. This was a direct result of IDEA and amendments that have since been passed, always directed toward identifying more and more disabled students. This was known as 'child find,' and find the children they did. By the 1998-99 school year, 11% of all students ages 6-17 were labeled as 'special ed.' Following current trends, the numbers will continue to grow. Where there are numbers, there's money, and where there's money, can higher numbers be far behind? How long before everyone has a disability? Who will pay for the teachers, the staff, the space once State or Federal money disappears, but the mandates stay? Guess whooohooo?

Speaking of **funding**, it should be pointed out that originally, because finding the children was so important, funding was based on the number of students with a disability in each state. It was, therefore, to each state's advantage to increase the number of special ed. students, which, invariably, increases the size of the special ed. program, which eats up, again, an inordinate amount of the school budget.

The Feds pulled a good one in the 1997 amendments to P.L., 94-142.

    "Starting in Federal Fiscal Year (FFY) 2000, with allocations made available beginning July 1, 2000, the year in which the Federal appropriations for Part B, Section 611 exceeded approximately $4.9 billion, the funding formula changed. States now receive a base allocation consisting of the amount of Section 611 funds that the state received in FFY 1999. Eighty-five of the remaining funds after base allocations are made are distributed to the states based on the relative populations of children ages 3 through 21 who are of the same age as children with disabilities for whom the state ensures the availability of FAPE under IDEA. Fifteen percent of the remaining funds is distributed to states based on the relative populations of children that fall within the age range for which the state ensures the availability of FAPE under IDEA who are living in poverty."(22nd Annual Report to Congress)

It should be noted that approximately 17-20 percent of all American children live below the poverty line. The final numbers of identified special ed. students could be staggering, along with the cost. This amendment is the reason for the movement to limit special ed. eligibility, which in turn dumps all students who have a real need but were no longer eligible, and the increased costs that these students incur onto the local taxpayer. Special ed. costs per students run at approximately two and one-half times the average cost for regular ed. students. These extra costs break many school budgets.

The **service provisions** section is where the famous 'least restrictive environment' is mentioned. Before passage of IDEA, according to the report, the prospects of severely handicapped students receiving any education weren't too good. "This was particularly true for children with **mental retardation** and other **severe developmental disabilities**, many of whom were institutionalized. Today most of those children can expect to live at home, and many receive special education and related services in regular schools. For example, by 1997-98, just eight percent of children with **significant developmental disabilities** were served in separate schools or in residential facilities." (22nd Annual Report to Congress) No mention of the fact that funding dried up under President Reagan, and that that has a lot to do with how many of these students were in which facilities, or none at all. Public education then became the way out, a way to save the government from making really tough choices.

The report added, "Seventy-five percent of the more than 5.5 million 6-21 year olds with disabilities served under IDEA in 1997-98 were educated in regular classrooms with their non-disabled peers." First off, any claim to being 'educated' is just Feelgood talk. Students with 'significant developmental disabilities' do not belong in a public school setting, nor should what is accomplished there be called 'educated.' They need to be in a **truly** least restrictive environment.

A public school academic classroom is actually very restrictive to these students. They need to be where the facilities are specifically suited for significant disabilities. They need to be in special facilities that were built with Federal and Corporate money, and are staffed with well-paid special education personnel who don't have to worry about lawsuits, irate parents, or satisfying any governments with reams of reports verifying and justifying what they are doing. The local taxpayer should not be asked to foot the bill.

An exception to the above, after speaking with special ed. teachers, would be classes such as phys. ed., industrial arts, and art, where the social interaction in a setting where all students can, in many instances, proceed at their own pace, can be beneficial to special needs students.

Services to infants, toddlers, and preschoolers show the extent of the legislation, and how it slowly works its way outward, encompassing more and more. It does, however, make sense to catch any problems early. I have no argument with that, but, first, the concept of finding more and more 'toddlers' with 'special needs' is exactly what a growing bureaucracy needs. Secondly, if there are many problems discovered early, make the large corporations pay for the early intervention. Thirdly, everyone should rail at the following from the report from the 22nd Congress; "In order to continue their eligibility to receive funding under this program, states were **required** (emphasis mine) to make FAPE available to all children ages 3-5 with disabilities by the 1991-92 school year. Today more than 573,000 3-5 year olds with disabilities are served in preschool programs that help them to be successful in school." This is referring to a 1986 amendment to the Education of the Handicapped Act, which established the Early Intervention Program for Infants and Toddlers with Disabilities under what is now Part C of IDEA.

Because of the amendment, "By September 30, 1994, all States and jurisdictions had ensured full implementation of the Early Intervention Program." (22nd Report to Congress) Because of the focus on this age group, many were found. In 1991-92, there were approximately 145,000 infants and toddlers, age's birth through two, served under Part C. In 1998-99 that number had jumped to around 189,000. Add all of that into the cost.

Aside from 'growing' the bureaucracy, the need for bodies is evident. That's where the required part comes in. By requiring the States to do it, bodies will be produced (or no more State aid). If the government is going to do anything positive for special needs students, this is where it should be done, early, so the learning problems don't continue on into the future when the money is gone (although, if the money came from large multi-million and multi-billion dollar corporations, and was spread equally among the states, it might never be gone). At that point in the future, after the Federal money has dried up but the required parts are still there, a lot of people will have to smarten up and figure out a way to pay for it all without killing education all together.

Parent support, according to the report, means the parents are to understand all they can about the disability and its affect on development and to know their rights under IDEA. That way, they can be articulate when they require a district to meet their child's needs. A special ed. teacher I spoke to said the idea of parents knowing enough about the special ed. laws and regulations was silly because she works in the system and doesn't really understand all of it. This is where Advocates come in. Advocates are people who speak for the parents. Many parents are too shy, or can't understand the education laws, or aren't really interested in getting involved, so someone does it for them.

Most advocates, at least in my experience, are loud-mouthed, over-bearing, pushy, know-it-alls who rub everyone the wrong way. They seem to think that if they go on the offensive, and are offensive enough, everyone else will throw up their hands and give the advocate whatever they want. I've seen advocates control meetings and have expectations way outside the range of reason.

Parents understanding about their child's disability is good, knowledge can set you free, but that knowledge should never be used, nor should it be allowed to be used, by anyone; officials in charge or parents; to pummel, demand, intimidate, threaten, or sue a school district. Under the present conditions, most school districts don't have the means to fund the rapidly rising costs of special ed.

In adding to the burgeoning bloat of the special ed. bureaucracy, Congress, in 1986, "required that awards for Parent Training and Information Centers (PTIs) to support parents be made in every state. Now there are 94 PTIs across the country, plus a Technical Assistance

Alliance. In addition, 13 Community Parent Resource Centers work to meet the needs of racially and ethnically diverse communities." (22nd Annual Report to Congress) Before long, special education will be a cabinet position, with the Education Secretary subordinate to the Special Education Czar (and guess whooooohoooooo gets to pay for it?).

In order to be effective, any legislation that involves a student with special needs should require, by law, that the parents are to participate and the student's IEP should reflect the parents' role. Parental support in education is important, and in special ed. it's even more so, since the needs of the student require a more concentrated effort by the parents. Special ed. legislation should include teaching parenting skills and lessen the incentive to 'work the system.'

Improving results is where we get to talk about 'Education Reform.' Education reform is a nice sounding phrase that makes whatever is going on sound positive. It makes people 'feel good.' Besides, everyone knows that education needs to be reformed. The Media tell us that all the time. The Media, by the way, like the buzz word 'reform.'

Under the guise of Education Reform, the Federal government, in the amendments of 1997, pushed the concept of students with special needs to a new level. These amendments "...reaffirmed the strong Federal commitment to the education of children with disabilities and did so within the **context** of education reform." I say it was under the **pretext** of education reform.

A blow to quality education in regards to the rest of the vast student populations is known as Section 612. These amendments contained several new provisions that brought IDEA in line with general education reform efforts. In this section, schools are required to include children with disabilities in State and district wide assessments. Now their scores will be averaged into the mix. The obvious consequence is for the school's average score to drop. This by itself is not significant, and should never be cause for alarm. What is frightening, however, is that it is these scores that the Media, as I have already pointed out, will choose to publish. It's big news when a school's test scores drop, possibly dramatically, depending on the ratio of students with disabilities to those who are not so designated. This, however, is a more complicated question than is addressed here. If scores are looked at in-house more closely, the demographics might show that some special needs students can actually raise the scores since they have alternative assessments and 'ability appropriate' tests as part of their accommodations.

Another aspect of the drop in test scores, even though locally everyone in the building knows why the scores are lower, is the rush to show the public that we in education care and are going to do something about it. This begins a cycle of in-service, retraining, rewriting curriculum, rewriting standards, and attaching them to each breath we take. And where is teaching and learning through all of this? It always takes a back seat until the 'improvements' are done.

The amendments of 1997 also changed the rules governing IEP's, the backbone of special ed., in order to bring them, too, in line with the general education reforms. "The Senate Committee on Labor and Human Resources wrote, 'The majority of children identified as eligible for special education and related services are capable of participating in the general education curriculum to varying degrees with some **adaptations** and **modifications**. This provision is intended to ensure that children's special education and related services are in addition to and are affected by the general education curriculum, not separate from it.'" (22nd Annual Report to Congress)

What the amendments didn't address, however, was the fact that the paperwork for all of these accommodations, as well as the documenting of each student's progress, takes up so much time that little time is left for teaching. Special ed. teachers have to not only evaluate current students, but also prospective students. Each evaluation takes several days to complete. This also doesn't include the time spent in meetings by all the special ed. as well as regular ed. teachers. The amount of time and money wasted because of these amendments is staggering.

In order to facilitate the inclusion of special ed. students into the regular curriculum, "…The 1997 amendments required that the IEP address how a student with disabilities will access the general education curriculum. Similarly, the IEP must include a statement of any individual **accommodations** or **modifications** a student requires in order to participate in State and district wide assessments." This part is the equivalent of educational quicksand. Often no matter what services are provided, they aren't right to someone. It all depends on the type of parent you get.

Karl E. Thelen

The key words in this part of the report are **accommodations** and **modifications**. Savvy students learn quickly how to manipulate the system. They know what words to use and when to use them. They learn early that certain words or phrases get special ed. people's attention. Students know that if there are problems with a class or their grades, or anything else that they know they're promised by Federal law, that it will be the IEP's fault, and a large contingent of special ed. teachers, classroom teachers, administrators, advocates and parents will have to be called in in order to change the IEP to one that works. That involves a lot of time and energy on the part of a lot of busy people.

Feelgooders are, most often, easy to fool by students. A Feelgooder's heartstrings are easily manipulated. The newly hired and inexperienced are also easily fooled by their charges, and high turnover in the profession allows the opportunity for students, as sweet and normal as they are, to manipulate their teachers. Because of these realities, IEP's are sometimes no more than paper, existing merely to satisfy 'the hunger' of special ed., keep lawyers at bay, and to assure the parents that all is well. Once again, the students may not get the actual help they need.

Accommodations and modifications are just buzz words that mean put the bar wherever you need to in order to get them over it, even if that means setting it on the ground or getting rid of the bar altogether. The bar, the challenge, should be for everyone, and if the true intent of the law is to include all students in the regular curriculum, then get out of the way and let the master teachers take care of it. And if the disabilities are severe, then let's admit that there are environments much better suited to that particular student's disability and there's nothing wrong with that. There are, in the true sense of the words, much less restrictive environments than in a classroom where their needs really aren't being met. Most importantly, those teachers trained in special ed. specifically for that purpose should make the curriculum modifications. Since this involves common sense, the Federal government may not allow it.

The amendments also provided for IDEA funds to be used with other Federal money to help to develop school-wide programs under Title I of the Elementary and Secondary Education Act and come up with State Improvement Grants (SIGs) to help States improve education for students with disabilities.

A Nation of Idiots

The **personnel** hired have increased in number consistently over the last twenty years. Each time an amendment was made to IDEA, the expansion of special ed. personnel has been a priority. "...In 1976-77, there were 331,453 teachers and related personnel providing services to children with disabilities; today there are more than 800,000. Personnel preparation efforts supported under IDEA have helped states staff their classrooms with teachers and paraprofessionals trained in special education and related fields and have promoted innovation in teacher preparation." (22nd Annual Report to Congress)

There's also the concern that classroom teachers, many unqualified, demand help with any student with a disability, even if the disability isn't severe. These demands add considerably to the bloat. It's a sad truth that some teachers can accommodate a wide range of students but many can't.

What would be nice is if all of those people hired to help in the special ed. field were qualified. Unfortunately, such is not the case. Many aides don't know the material. Some of them have to study harder than the students, which is ironic, because in so many instances, as the system is flawed, the students weren't going to study anyway. Why should they? They know someone will do it for them.

Having uneducated aides is a cruel joke to play on any special needs student who has to live, eventually, in the real world, especially the many bright learning-disabled students who struggle in writing, or note-taking, or another particular area, but may know the material well. These are the students hurt most noticeably by inexperienced personnel, and, yet, are the ones who could most often be helped by special ed. services.

Part of the reason for hiring inexperienced aides is that local taxes have to make up differences between Federal aid and State aid, so often the salary for paraprofessionals is not much better than minimum wage. That's a lot of work, usually with students who often don't want the help and fight it as best as they can, for little or no real pay.

Transitions from school to adult life can be tough. That's why transition planning was included in the EHA amendments. It mandated that IEP's for anyone over 14 years of age have to include what specific needs need to be addressed for the student to make the transition from school to adult life. This plan has to be updated on a yearly basis. By the age of 16, the idea becomes more complicated. Now there has to be a statement indicating what services will be needed after graduation and what agencies within the special ed. program will need to be accessed. "These transition statements are designed to provide instruction, related services, and community experiences that lead to positive post school results in post secondary education and training, employment, adult services, independent living, and community participation." (22nd Annual Report to Congress)

There's nothing wrong with giving all the help to those who really need it, but in the proper facilities. To have such high expectations for transitioning well-rounded, adaptive, severely handicapped within the present public education system (which is set up to teach larger groups of students with the understanding that there are relatively high expectations and there are time limits that run parallel to being successful in life) is unrealistic and unfair to those severely handicapped. The results, after all the expenditure of money and time, are minimal at best, and can't really be justified in terms of quality education.

In any other business, because of low productivity, the special ed. arm would have been shut down long ago. The proper facilities, those much less restrictive than the local public school building, with properly trained staff, who focus their energies on the particular needs of a particular student, are much better suited for preparing severely handicapped students to live the best lives they can. This is not a harsh social statement, but a realistic look at what public education can and can't do. It would make much more sense to teach life skills to those students who need them, rather than require a term paper from students who can't read or do the most basic of research.

Least restrictive environment should mean that facility which would prepare these students for living in the least restrictive way. Putting truly needy students or severely handicapped in academic classrooms is a sham because public education isn't really doing anything for them. Public education doesn't really prepare them for living after high school. No one follows them around to make sure they're doing what they should. No accommodations are made. When it comes time, how can these students do what they were never taught to do? No one is going to stock the shelves for them, and they really aren't going to work at the local car dealer. This does, however, fulfill

A Nation of Idiots

the law so the funds will keep coming, and it also satisfies the parents who think they're doing the right thing, for whatever reasons.

IDEA has also made grants, called systems change grants, so the States could begin to put in place the service strategies needed for successful transitions. Furthermore, "...the Office of Special Education Programs (OSEP) funded a series of projects in the area of self-determination. These projects have demonstrated to educators, parents, and young people with disabilities how students can take a substantive role in planning for their own future. Rising rates of employment and post secondary enrollment among students with disabilities suggests the importance of transition planning and services for these students." (22nd Annual Report to Congress) The increased pressure on special ed. personnel to get the kids out and into some kind of job is constant.

As for the increased enrollment in post secondary education, it seems to coincide with the dramatic increase in remedial classes at the college level. That does not sound like the rosy assessment of the report, but, then, I could be wrong. When taken in my context, however, there's no way the costs can be justified in terms of paying for special ed. locally. The Federal government just keeps amending the original special ed. law (IDEA) and adding to the ever-increasing cost. The ultimate Federal Feelgooders take no responsibility.

The money has to come from a source more able to pay; my favorites are still the tobacco and alcohol industries and large corporations. They could fund transition programs and then employ the severely handicapped in special work programs, as some do already. A good example of this on the community level is Essex Industries in Mineville, N.Y. They employ exclusively handicapped workers. That's the purpose of the business. The products are real products and sold on the open market. If this can be done on a small, local level, it can be duplicated on an international or global level. If we could just shake loose a small percentage of those huge profits, life for those in the greatest need of help would improve drastically, and the economic picture would improve a lot locally, and the present funding would be more than sufficient to create an effective school.

As far as the **research** goes, I've listed some of the things the Federal government has established in order to keep track of their programs and to see if they are being followed and if the results justify sending more money to the States. Some of the early studies were designed to build a base of knowledge on special ed. in order to make the services students receive better. But also, consider the cost each time the Federal government gets a bright idea.

The National Longitudinal Transition Study (NLTS); This study looked for educational progress and then followed a sample of students in order to "determine their educational, occupational, and independent living status after their exit from special education." (22nd Annual Report to Congress)

The Federal government mandated in the 1986 amendments to study "**special education expenditures**, as well as a series of studies of special populations of children with disabilities. Special populations specifically mentioned in the amendments included American Indian children with disabilities, Native Hawaiian and other native Pacific basin children with disabilities, migrant children with disabilities, children with disabilities living in rural areas, and children with disabilities who had limited English proficiency." (22nd Annual Report to Congress) Those not able to be assimilated and are byproducts of modern western society are out of luck. Ironically, the corporations, in their rush to suck more and more money out of the population, pass these minorities by after making them dependent on our western, commercialized lifestyle.

Established with the 1990 amendments "...**Centers designed to organize**, synthesize, and disseminate current knowledge relating to children with attention deficit disorder." (22nd Annual Report to Congress) There was also an investigation into the early reading problems of those with learning disabilities. "This work pointed out the importance of early attention to phonemic awareness and is now used throughout the country to improve reading instruction for students both with or without disabilities."

- **National Early Intervention Longitudinal Study** (NEILS); This study is designed to follow children who enter early intervention services and see if the interventions are working or need to be modified.
- The **Pre-Elementary Educational Longitudinal Study** (PEELS); This study will follow 3-5 year olds through preschool and into the first years of elementary school.

- The **Special Education Elementary Longitudinal Study** (SEELS); This study will keep track of students who are 6-12 years old when they begin the study, and follow them as they transition from elementary to junior high school, and junior high school to high school.
- The **National Longitudinal Transition Study** (NLTS-2); This is a program for 13-17 year olds, and it will stay with them, checking their progress, until the oldest is twenty-five.
- The **Study of Personnel Needs in Special Education** (SPeNSE); This study deals with the quality and shortage of those who are charged with serving students with special needs. There are nationwide shortages of special ed. people; teachers, aides, paraprofessionals, and qualifications for this growing arm of Education need to be adhered to. "SpeNSE will provide information on the quality of the special education workforce nationally, within each geographic region, and within and across personnel categories. In addition, researchers will explore ways to assess the quality of the workforce based on State and local policies, preservice education, continuing professional development, and working conditions." (22nd Annual Report to Congress)
- **State and Local Implementation of IDEA** (SLIIDEA); The purpose of this study is to see how the 1997 amendments are being put into place by the State and schools. Particular concerns are how students are performing, if they are getting the same curriculum, what type of supports are in place for behavioral concerns, how involved the parents are, and seeing how the transitions from school to life are going.
- **The Special Education Expenditure Project** (SEEP); This project will look in-depth at how the money for special ed. has been spent over the years, something that has never really been done before.

The results of all of these studies and projects will be reported on in the 23rd Annual Report to Congress.

Conclusions; The conclusion to all of this information in the Preface of the 22nd Annual Report to Congress says that, aside from a few changes here and there, the intent of IDEA remains the same.

Karl E. Thelen

It ends by asking some questions about the future of special education. I will answer them.

1. How will we as a nation address the growing shortage of qualified special education teachers and related services personnel, particularly those from culturally and linguistically diverse backgrounds?

The shortage can first be addressed by making the work worth the pay. With the overload (ironically created because of the lack of qualified special ed. personnel), paper work, beatings by the lawyers and the plethora of laws, ever-new amendments, constant changes in expectations, why would anyone **want** the job? From what I've seen, it's akin to running your head into the wall. Until the pay is increased (Come on alcohol industry, tobacco industry, other giant, mega corporations that pollute the air, the water, the souls of our children, cough up. No pun intended.), the megalithic special education leviathan will not have the people to do the business of the law. The law will not go away, so school districts **have** to fill the slots.

2. How will we ensure that special education personnel have the skills they need to effectively serve students with disabilities?

The answer here is in the answer to question one. You ensure that they have the skills by making the job worthwhile. They should be on a pay scale similar to what teachers have so there is a visual understanding of where they can get to in a certain position.

Some schools are doing this already. They just raised the pay for special ed. personnel and stopped trying to save money. It would also help if the personnel were in a facility designed for special ed. purposes. Nurses work better in a hospital. If doctors had to work in the same small room all day, and had the paperwork to do without the benefit of a personal secretary, there wouldn't be many doctors in the U.S.

3. What strategies are most effective in helping students with disabilities to meet higher educational standards?

This is a no-brainer. First, set the bar the same for everyone. No exceptions. By keeping the bar the same for everyone, the goal becomes legitimized. Secondly, have the main strategy be the **attempt** to reach the bar, knowing, as educators, that in the attempt there is quite often more benefit than in the accomplishment. The example of this that I give my students is to add one plus one, then one plus two, and so on. After they have the answers, and they all do, I ask them what they learned. The answer, of course, is nothing. They already knew the answers to the simple problems. So, they accomplished the right answers, but because there was no attempt, no struggle, they learned nothing. This applies to **all** students.

4. What are the most effective models for serving infants and toddlers and their families in natural environments?

I have no expertise in this area, so to answer the question would be silly, other to say that any involvement at this level should be paid for by those I've named earlier. By footing the bill here, and correcting some of their sins, large corporations may save money later on.

5. How can our school systems best respond to the needs of language minority children?

Get them to learn English as fast as possible. If anyone is going to try to adapt to living in society on any level in America, they need to know English. This is our language. I know Feelgooders are jumping up and down right now, but that's too bad. To try to fund a large national program of bi and tri lingual approaches is to delay the inevitable, and drive up the already high cost of education. All students need to speak English.

6. What are the best approaches for increasing the involvement of parents from racial/ethnic minority groups in the education of their children with disabilities?

This could be a tough one. It's just like the Federal government to assume that everyone **needs** to fit in. Some people don't want to. Some people don't have the means. If the government is concerned enough, they can change the circumstances that keeps the numbers of involved minorities low. Parents who don't speak English will be less inclined to go to the school to 'hang out.'

7. How can school districts use assessment data to improve educational opportunities for students with disabilities?

Karl E. Thelen

First, don't let any of the numbers get printed in the media. The data should only be used for internal purposes. It's feedback for that school only. Secondly, there has to be an understanding that the numbers fluctuate from year to year, and that's just part of the mix. There should be no 'retraining' of anyone based on the results, unless there is a multi-year trend.

8. How can the Federal government ensure that all school systems properly implement?

They can't. Not completely, and any attempts, which are going to revolve around money since that is the only leverage the government has, will only get more of the same; a bloated special education program weighted down by tomes of regulations, laws, numbers of different disabilities, many unqualified personnel, and an unfair burden on those teachers who are qualified. It's also hard because when the regular education program and the special education program try to mesh, confusion can often occur slowing results. There's no way the Federal government, in all its incompetence and inability to move quickly or decisively, can keep track of all of the programs it has mandated without the heavy hand of monetary threat. It's the old bull in the china shop.

The Federal government needs to first, under the present circumstances, fund its mandates and then back off. Don't bog the educational institutions down with all the paper proof it would require, or the constant change that the latest amendments engender, nor hold schools accountable if there are aberrations in the results from year to year. This would help ease a lot of the budget blues created by IDEA. Education, and especially special ed., is not a constant, forward motion of improvements. In an area high school, four special educators quit because the State required their old paperwork to reflect the new changes in the law. Lunacy only breeds more of the same.

Secondly, the Federal government needs to make a sincere, concerted effort to get the wealthiest corporations in the United States and the World to pay up. They can't continue to reap in the profits while ignoring the by-product of their manipulations to get mushy brained Americans to buy their products and use them to the point of debility, or to poison people and not accept the eventual responsibility.

A Nation of Idiots

Another area of special education that needs special attention is the propensity to label student debilities. For example, the special ed. concept called disgraphia is a condition whereby the student doesn't write well. For god's sake, half of Americans don't write well. It isn't a condition. It's just the way some things are. Some people do some things well, and others don't. Everyone can improve their writing through practice, although that doesn't mean everyone who practices will become really good at writing. Half of all Americans can't be special ed. (although by today's standards they can be). We haven't the resources-time, money, teachers, and support staff. What used to be just a fact of life, (some people don't write well, speak well, play basketball well), has now become a disability. The insanity has to stop somewhere, soon, before it takes all of education down with it.

If this ill-conceived ploy of the pundits of Feelgoodenism, disguised as caring special ed. bureaucrats, were to be carried to its logical conclusion, where would we be?

We would have people who couldn't play basketball well because they had dishoopia. They would be required by Federal mandate to have someone shoot the ball for them.

Many millions of people would be afflicted with disthinkia because they couldn't think well (as evidenced by their standardized test scores). These people would have several aides, depending on the courses being taken. Various disciplines require different types of thinking.

Many students will be found to have distestia since they can't take tests (studying isn't the answer). Besides, many students, if not most, have a condition that we'll call disworkia, and therefore don't have to do homework. It's the aide's job to do the homework, but many of them are unqualified to perform the task.

Another lunacy that special education requires in many cases is for all special ed. students to be able to take their place in society. Therefore, jobs need to be found where these students can be placed.

We had just such a program at one of the schools I taught at. The instructors were told to find a job for an extremely deficient student. They found a job in a local grocery store stocking shelves. The job itself was a good idea, based on the skills of the student, but the aide who followed the student around in compliance of his special ed. status, his IEP, wound up doing most of the stocking, since the work had to be done for the student to keep the job. Continuous admonitions from the aide for the student to start working had no effect.

I've known many special education teachers over the years. Many of them, including my son Shane who was a special educator for five years, are competent, capable educators who do their job to the best of their abilities. But the realities of the comprehensive legislation, the large volumes of paper work, the large (and growing) number of caseloads, puts enough stumbling blocks in the way that the job becomes almost impossible. Nowhere in education are the expectations for results higher than in special education with less to work with. Consequently, since results are expected, there has to be some way to produce those results, otherwise bad legal things will happen.

Parents of 'special needs' students are the most litigious. So results become extremely important to keep the parents, the advocates, the lawyers, and various social services out of the henhouse.

One way to get the results needed is to let the 'special ed.' kids cheat. This is one reason I personally ask students to stay in my room to take tests. I want to see what they know, and then I can make 'accommodations.' But if they're merely in the special ed. loop so they can pass the class without really doing any work, then what's the point of paying so much money for special education? I can save the district a lot of money and just pass the kid from my class without special ed. That, of course, shouldn't be why we're here.

Instead of helping with strategies to learn, the need for measurable results within a specified time frame (the IEP) pushes the teachers to get the results that will keep the parents or State and Federal governments off the teachers' and schools' backs. Paper results are good enough. If the school can prove the students have improved, or that the plan followed is working, then everyone is happy, they all feel good. It's myopic, but the realities of the situation make it so. A special ed. teacher I know said that one of the teachers he worked with wrote on every IEP, "85% – goal met." There was no proof, no accountability. The paperwork, however, proved that the system was working.

When all the mandates, created by the hundreds of state and federal laws, are considered along with the inherent paper work, time-consuming meetings, referrals, testing, follow-ups, scheduling and so

A Nation of Idiots

on, special ed. has simply grown past the local taxpayer's ability to reasonably pay for it. In a small district, one severely handicapped student moving into the district and requiring the addition of one to several new staff members to meet the new student's federally mandated needs can cause great economic havoc. Since special ed. needs are mandated and academic programs are not, guess where the cuts in the budget will be?

The health concerns created by the tobacco and alcohol industry have to be taken into consideration. Their contribution to the problem foisted on the local taxpayers is considerable. Their premeditated manipulation to get people to use their products is well documented. Not only do they help create future special education students, they are also guilty of driving up the cost of health care by causing diseases that need expensive, long-term care.

Karl E. Thelen

Chapter eight

Effective Teaching; If it's working, don't fix it.

The quality of public education depends on the quality of the individual teacher. If the teacher doesn't have it, learning will not occur. The students' time will have been wasted, and the negative image of public education teachers will be reinforced. There's no excuse for poor teaching or poor teachers, and no excuses should be accepted. It is because of the poor teachers that the media has been able to portray teachers as not being up to the job. What the media don't portray, however, are the ways which teachers can become better, what it takes to be a teacher, and the difficulties inherent in the job.

On February 27th 2001, President George W. Bush jumped into the fray and said in regards to education, "it all depends on the teacher." The president then went on to say "I refuse to leave any child behind in America." The first thing he said was accurate, that it's up to the teacher. The quality of public education does depend on the quality of the individual teacher. It always has and it always will.

In regards to his second, Feelgood statement, I become perplexed. Do we hold up those students who are ready until every student in America catches up? Otherwise, we're going to have to leave some people behind. This is not a war where we're talking about leaving our buddies behind. This is the future of America and we need to go forward with those who are ready and willing to learn.

The media fail to look deep enough to see the real issues. On their own they wouldn't question a statement by the president that on the surface sounds nice and comforting (since no one likes the concept of leaving anyone behind) but in reality would be almost impossible, given the natural state of human nature, to accomplish. Not leaving anyone behind is a Feelgooder concept, one that won't accomplish anything positive in terms of raising the quality of education in America. The recent 'leave no child behind' legislation, where more control goes to the Federal government, is a perfect example of what not to do.

Many states are trying to correct the problem in education by coming up with new standards for all teachers to strive for. Vermont, for example, has their Vermont standards. Vermont standards are designed so the poor teachers will improve their teaching, with the state determining what is important to teach. Once again, the last group of people that any community wants to determine their educational direction is the bureaucrats.

The Vermont standards, simplistic in nature, can be compared to fishing with a mile-long dragline, hoping to catch poor teachers. Unfortunately, they also catch the good teachers. They slow these good teachers down. They get in the way of good programs, interrupt qualified, creative master teachers who know what they're doing, teachers who surpassed the simple standards years ago. I would say to all state legislatures, don't go after the bad teachers by netting everyone. This is done for political reasons. This is done through ignorance. This is done so no fingers will be pointed. Stop handcuffing the good teachers. Administrators are afraid to go after bad teachers, and the teachers' unions protect everyone, qualified or not. That doesn't mean the quality of education should suffer while pusillanimous people pass the buck.

The main problem with the Vermont standards is that they don't go to the heart of the problem, which happens to be unqualified teachers. In fact, poor teachers revel in standards because they are easy to hide behind. No poor teacher can be fired if they have tied their units to the standards as they have been asked to do. They can prove they are doing their job. Since instituting the standards takes a while, a poor teacher can hide for several years. And if they don't do such a good job, so what? "It takes a while to get the hang of it," is an accepted defense.

In Vermont teachers have to be recertified every seven years. The proof of certifiability is a portfolio, put together by the teacher, with certain criteria; proof of nine graduate hours, a seven-year plan proving several areas of educational experience such as Collegiality, Advocacy, and so on, along with any other documented moment in the career of the teacher that can prove worthiness. What looks good on paper doesn't necessarily translate to the classroom.

As long as a poor teacher can document the listed criteria they're certifiable. Any teacher who can come up with three inches of paper proof of their efficacy, and show how their "units" are "standards based," is a good teacher according to the state of Vermont, and also according to our district. If the current trend for American education continues, eventually we will become a third-rate country by default.

The real strength of education, as I have said, is in the strength of the individual teachers who come in and do their job well every day, and continue to strive to be better all on their own; the master teachers. Once the classroom door is closed, if the teacher isn't qualified, nothing is accomplished. Even the poorest of teachers can put a portfolio together or prove on paper that they are teaching to the standards, close their door, and get paid. Only a master teacher gets the job done.

Madeline Hunter wanted to find out if there were things that the good teachers did that others didn't. This was the premise for her research on Effective Teaching. She didn't first come up with a thesis and then set out to prove it. She merely observed hundreds of teachers who were, for one reason or another, considered to be effective teachers. The results came out as the Effective Teaching movement, which was popular for a while, but then, as with so many fads that come along, it faded. Part of the reason was because it was shoved down teachers' throats at in-services all over the country. Instead of focusing on what the results pointed out about good teaching, school districts wanted teachers to start using the same terminology that Hunter used. Ironically, this could also apply to those teachers Hunter observed and now had to change what they were doing to conform to school district edicts.

The focus should have been on the ideas behind the successful teachers. Hunter broke the information down into a number of common attributes, or correlates, those things teachers did that seemed to work. I'm intentionally limiting the use of Madeleine Hunter's terminology, other than to introduce those attributes that were found to work, and speak only to the concept.

For example, Hunter said that the first thing a teacher should do, in terms of planning a lesson, is to have what she called an 'Anticipatory Set,' something that would get the students' attention

A Nation of Idiots

and get them focused for what was coming, so they can 'anticipate' what to do. She found that many good teachers did this, and it worked.

But the point isn't to have every teacher start calling what they do at the beginning of a lesson an 'Anticipatory Set.' Teachers need to feel comfortable in what they are doing. They can't be asked to 'reboot' every time new terminology comes along. The point is to get teachers to start with something that focuses attention on the task at hand. It's mindless to change the style and effectiveness of teachers who already get the students' attention in their own way, using their own terminology. Leave effective teachers alone.

A second concept that proved to be ubiquitous among effective teachers was that they did something rather simple; they told their students what they were going to do and why, before they did it. They simply stated the objective of their lesson. It seems that if students know why they are doing something, they apparently can do it better.

Following that, it was found that if the teacher actually followed their plan and taught to the stated objective, the objective was accomplished much easier (assuming the teacher had mapped out how to get there) and more successfully with a larger number of students. These things seem to be common sense, but most people would be surprised to find that poor teachers don't teach to any objective, and that there's a large spectrum of poor to marginally poor teachers out there.

Good teachers tend to show their students what it is they are talking about. I have always done the first speech in my classes. I tell my students I wouldn't have them do anything that I wasn't willing or able to do, from the speeches to keeping a journal to knowing the vocabulary that I expect them to know. If they have to write an essay, I first show them mine. I show them the process I went through. Modeling correct behavior or learning is beneficial because it works.

The students should also be actively participating in the activities. It's the teacher's job to keep track of who's involved and who isn't. When there is consistent involvement of the student's mind with the learning, learning takes place. If students in a group are just sitting around wasting time, it's the teacher's fault and no learning is taking place.

Active participation seems to be a concept that's hard for many new teachers to understand since they haven't experienced it yet and it isn't long before they're in the trap of calling on the same few students, mainly out of survival since so few students will provide answers or participate in discussions on their own.

What these teachers are missing is a skill that can be readily acquired through practice. Many students fight this part of effective teaching for a variety of reasons, the number one reason being that it takes effort to get the big cog upstairs to start turning sufficiently enough to generate the minimal amount of brain power. Remember, it's the teacher's job to get a student to that point where they want to learn, whether the student wants to or not. You can at least lead a student to knowledge, even though you can't force them to learn.

The reasoning behind the active participation is to check to see if the students are learning anything. Do they understand what you are talking about? I'll quite often change the wording of a question or try to teach it differently if it's obvious some, or all, students have no clue as to what I'm talking about. I'm getting better at these moments, but everyone can improve, even effective teachers. Be honest, recognize the moment, and take the necessary action to reteach what wasn't learned.

Also learn to recognize when they aren't getting it. Hunter called this 'with-it-ness,' knowing what's going on in all corners of the classroom at all times, being in touch with where the students are in terms of getting the material (as well as knowing who's listening and who's not). This is also coupled with 'feeling tone,' the over-all feeling within the classroom, the atmosphere. If it's a good feeling tone, then the students will feel at ease enough to say they don't understand something.

The idea of checking to see if the students understand is a simple idea with many parts. Hunter found there were many ways to not only check to see what they know, but also ways to get the students to maintain the focus and get the material in more depth than is achieved solely through workbooks, lecture, etc.

Effective questioning goes to the heart of teaching because of its effects on the brain. It forces it to work, and once it starts to work (sometimes I tell my students to listen and see if they can hear when the big wheel starts to turn) it doesn't stop. An active mind is a hard thing to slow down.

One of the most important ideas in effective questioning is the idea of giving students time to think. Five seconds of silence while

A Nation of Idiots

everyone thinks of the answer increases class participation considerably. There are many students who get the answer right away, and these are also the students who get called on in most classes. All the other students can be easily left out of a discussion for no reason other than they take a few seconds longer to think of the right answer. Students who know they won't be called on tend to go to sleep.

I call the students who answer right away the Jeopardy students, and I tell the rest that they're probably like me and have to think a bit before getting the answer. It also takes some time to break students from the traditional response to teacher questions. The early volunteers want to shout the answer, and I find, in the beginning, I have to ask them often to hold on to their excitement and wait a few seconds so everyone has an opportunity to come up with the right answer on their own. Both groups will eventually get the answer if the effective questioning directs them there. At first the Jeopardy students get frustrated at not being called on right away and the others, who are used to coasting in classes without ever having to really participate, get angry and often say "Why do you keep calling on me?" I tell them because it's good for them.

Waiting a bit, once everyone gets used to it, does several interesting things. Not only do students who traditionally don't get an opportunity to show what they know have the opportunity to do so, the Jeopardy students, once they put some thought into it, come up with more in-depth answers. I'm not saying this happens every second of every class. Most teachers would know that is impossible. But the instances in which these moments reside can be increased considerably.

Another important aspect of effective questioning is the ability to monitor thought, since it's important to know if the students are getting it or not. By monitoring thought, the teacher can direct it so the student's attention is on the learning at hand. This creates a continual picture of how the lesson is going, and provides the important feedback in order to make mid-course corrections.

Effective questioning also involves dealing with answers that are wrong. How this is handled can determine a lot about successful teaching. The traditional method when dealing with a wrong answer is to say "No, that's not it," or words to that effect. Many of those students won't bother to answer again. I know I never did. It was too embarrassing. There is an effective alternative to the traditional turn off. Hunter called it 'dignifying a wrong answer.' Call it what you will, it works.

Instead of saying an answer is wrong, it's important to point out the question that the student was actually answering. For example, if the question was "How much is 10 x 14?" And the student says 120, the teacher would say, "Had I asked how much was 10 x 12, that would be correct. But I asked, 'How much is 10 x 14?'"

Students who are wrong all the time will stop trying to answer or say, "I don't know" when called on. Dignifying a wrong answer gives the student a chance to retreat from embarrassment and also gives the teacher a chance to point out the soundness of the student's reasoning. When students understand where their answer was in relation to the question asked, by telling them the actual question that they answered, the students can make immediate corrections and bring their thinking in line with the objectives of the lesson. The odds of real learning occurring increase considerably.

Along with the above goes the fact that even with the best of intentions, teachers can get the questions wrong. A good indication of asking the wrong question is when no one is giving you the answer you're looking for. Quite often I'll say to a student "Let me reword the question because I think I worded it poorly since I'm not getting the response I want." Students respect and appreciate directness and honesty. No teacher knows it all and no one knows this faster than the students.

Another technique in effective questioning is letting the students know ahead of time that you'll call on everyone, whether they volunteer or not. This causes more of them to pay attention. Then do it! Keep track of who is called on; draw in as many students as you can. To constantly call only on volunteers, usually those who get the correct answer right away, is to give tacit approval for the rest of the class to go somewhere else. Go back to the same students more than once since it further forces students to pay attention (Don't let them find out that you're only calling on everyone once). If you can direct their thoughts to the lesson at hand, you can almost make them want to learn. And then they'll come back for more.

Another important aspect of effective teaching is called 'Guided Practice.' That's what Hunter called it. But, again, call it what you will. Call it 'Walkabout,' since what good teacher doesn't wander about the room making sure their students understand the work?

A Nation of Idiots

Walking about and seeing how the students are handling the lesson, lets the teacher know right away if the students are able to apply their new knowledge. By intentionally walking about, the teacher also continues to keep the focus on the objectives. The walkabout teacher can immediately correct students heading in the wrong direction, or motivate those who have no direction at all.

Coming to the end of a lesson should be planned. It shouldn't happen by surprise, and it shouldn't be jammed in just as the bell is ringing. The lesson, somehow, should be summed up, and the learning that took place should be emphasized. Just as the teacher told the students ahead of time what they would be learning and why, it's important to say at the end what has been learned and why, and where it's going. Quite often, having several students explain what they have learned will reinforce the lesson for all students.

Another advantage of reviewing the lesson is that the review can be a lead-in to the next lesson or unit. Independent Practice is just that. Practice. It's the opportunity for the student to apply the lessons, or practice the skills, without the immediate help of the teacher. This is quite often called homework. Consequently, the homework **should not** be busy work or lengthy, mind numbing copying or doing fifty of the same problem. The homework, directly related to the class work, should, usually, be short assignments that include drill and practice activities, and can be tied in with prepping the students for the next day.

The homework, by the way, should not be assigned if the students were unable to demonstrate that they could do it. To just give homework, knowing they can't do it, does nothing for learning, except maybe turn kids off. The goal of a teacher should not be to get to a certain point by a certain time. That's often what generates irrelevant homework. Always correct or collect the homework and give it back. If it's truly important and not busy work, they'll need it.

Other concepts that are aligned with effective teaching are the concept of 'covering ground,' knowing the various common sources of wasted time (knowing them helps to avoid them), understanding the need to have various activities ready for students who finish early (or need a larger or deeper challenge), understanding the levels of thinking and knowing how to work the students through them, and understanding hemisphericity and the chalkboard. This is from a notebook called *Design For Effective Instruction*, put together by Dr.

Karl E. Thelen

Lawrence L. Giandomenico of State University of New York at Plattsburgh, the only college professor I ever had who was concerned with his students knowing about effective teaching techniques.

Covering Ground: The following was taken from the *Effective Instruction* notebook in regard to covering ground being the prime goal of a teacher. The original is credited to Pressey, 1959.

> **"One of the most pernicious problems in teaching is the teacher's desire to "cover ground." Many teachers feel that they do not have the time to discover and remedy their pupil's lack of information and skill because they would never be able to "cover" the material called for in the course; So they plunge ahead from a starting point that many of their students never reached, and they proceed to teach the unknown by the incomprehensible. The result is that the student cannot learn effectively and ends the course about where he started."**

It was true in 1959, and it's true today.

Four Sources of Wasted Time: This is also in the *Design For Effective Instruction* notebook.

1. When time and energy are devoted to an unrealistic learning objective, or to an objective that has already been accomplished.

For example, giving students work that is not at their independent level, giving a student who is a remedial reader a math assignment that requires a higher reading level to complete, giving students work that is well below their ability level, which just wastes time and energy.

2. When time and energy is rote and ineffective. When the teacher has a student write spelling words twenty times, or having the students complete a drill of 50-100 math problems of the same type.
3. When time and energy are devoted to unimportant objectives. Memorization of lists of names, dates, capitals, states and so on, unless these things need to be known for a base of knowledge on which further learning will occur, or if the teacher merely has the students copy and recopy material.
4. When student time is wasted from waiting. Waiting for class to settle down to get started, waiting for a group, like reading,

A Nation of Idiots

to gather, waiting to receive papers being passed out, and waiting for dismissal.

The first concern is solved by starting class on time, and not allowing any time to be wasted from the word go.

The second is a little tougher, since you're bucking the tide of human nature, but the problem can be helped considerably by knowing ahead of time how things will proceed and communicating those directions clearly to the students.

As for passing back papers, while I'm doing that, the students are preparing for the entries in their three-ring binders. They have to write the heading in the table of contents, assign a page number, and list that number in the table. They also are given time, while I'm passing back papers, to begin putting corrections from the papers they are receiving onto their correction sheets.

As far as dismissal is concerned, I tell them on the first day that I've never dismissed a class as it was heading towards the door. My plans quite often go right up to the last minute. I don't want them packing up before I'm done. I know other teachers who quit five minutes or more before the end of class and let the students crowd the door so they're ready to leave when it's time to go. That's just sloppy classroom management.

Activities at the Ready: Effective schools literature calls these sponge activities, but, remember, call it what you want. These are merely activities that students can do when they finish the current assignment ahead of others. They aren't busy work. The activities should be designed to review or extend the previous learning, get the student ready for the next learning to happen, and eliminate any discipline problems caused by intelligent, top students who are finished and bored. This also takes planning on the part of the teacher, but once activities are in place, the initial effort need not be duplicated.

Level of Thinking: To understand the levels of thinking, Bloom's Taxonomy has to be explained in more detail. The development of the thought process, according to Bloom, has six levels; knowledge, comprehension, application, analysis, synthesis and evaluation. **Knowledge** is the simplest level, where material is memorized and spit back. No real learning occurs here. Unfortunately 80% of all test questions are at this level. **Comprehension** is what the student understands. There are a lot of comprehension tests around.

Application is the level where learning can be used, applied to the everyday world, or to go to the next educational level. Through application, knowledge and understanding are applied to new situations. **Analysis** allows the mind to take things apart and look at it. Being able to categorize is an important element of analysis. **Synthesis** is where new ideas come from, by taking a bit of science and synthesizing with some history, a new concept is born and lives are saved. This is the level of invention. It is here that creative thinking happens. **Evaluation** is the highest level of cognitive development. On this level judgments are made, usually based on various alternative possibilities. Assumptions can be made from the data.

The journey through the various levels of thinking is a long one, lasting a lifetime, but students who are made aware of the potential and possibilities tend to achieve so much more than those who had it, but never knew it. Working students through the levels involves an understanding of the type of questions and activities that would complement a particular level, and allow students to work their way up as their cognitive ability increases.

When working on the **Knowledge** level, the students should know that they are working with details and information and how easily it can be recalled. Questions on the knowledge level would be 'Who did it?' 'When did it happen?' 'List the things they had,' and any other detail remembered. This might be useful for checking on basic reading, but only on the elementary level.

Comprehension questions ask the student to put things in their own words. They can answer the question 'Why?' and 'What?' They can explain a part of the story in their own words; they can tell what the author's purpose was in a particular scene or paragraph. Comprehension is the ability to translate, to infer, to predict, to understand cause and effect, and to sequence.

Application questions are more involved. Students need to be able to use information in a new situation, so questions are worded to show if a student can use his knowledge. 'Use this **vocabulary word** in a meaning-loaded sentence,' 'What would a character be likely to do if they visited our classroom?'

Analysis is the breaking apart of information for the purpose of examining it. The questions ask the student to compare two events in two stories for similarities, or explain which details support a particular conclusion.

Synthesis is using knowledge from two areas to come up with something new. The student puts previous learning together with new learning and comes up with something new. Questions on this level would ask the student to use the information he has about a character and rewrite the ending to the story, or write a story that uses ten of your vocabulary words correctly.

Evaluation, where the students have to make value judgments where there may not be a right answer, and where the students have to support what they say with reasoning, is the highest level in cognitive development and levels of thinking skills. Questions here would be "which is a better story, and why?" or "who is more honorable in the story and why do you say that?"

Hemisphericity and the chalkboard: A lot of teachers aren't aware that how material is presented on the chalkboard can greatly affect how students perceive it, and therefore affect learning. This occurs because people perceive things and take in information differently depending on which side of the brain they tend to use the most. Briefly, since this is covered later, the left side of the brain processes information sequentially and analytically while the right side is more visual and spatial. When both sides are brought into the learning process, retention increases. The chalkboard is one place where both sides can be engaged.

First, if the teacher says what they're going to put on the board, the students will be looking for it, and can begin processing the information right away.

Secondly, use key words and simple diagrams to make the main ideas stand out. The right side can understand drawings better than the spoken word. Explaining the diagrams while students are looking at them also increases learning and retention.

Thirdly, positioning of material should not be haphazard. The chalkboard should not look like a jumbled mess from the point of view of the students. There should be order with information placed so the students can see the relationships the teacher is trying to point out.

Fourthly, before anything new is introduced, erase what was there. That way the students don't get confused, thinking that the new is part of the old. The habit of writing on the chalkboard wherever there is free space should be eliminated from the teacher's repertoire. Working on the chalkboard should be planned to complement the lesson and draw in as many of the students as possible.

These are not hard concepts, but they work. Staying organized, planning ahead; these are good traits for an effective teacher.

It's important to say, especially to anyone who wants to force all teachers to follow any particular educational fad that happens to be current and cute that these ideas are only tools for teachers to use. Give the good teachers the tools and then get out of their way. That's their job, that's why they get the big bucks. I am a teacher, let me work.

The art of teaching involves many facets other than the actual teaching. Concepts like honesty, anger management, and so on are important. Honesty leads the pack.

I once told a class of seniors that if I seemed angry or upset that it wasn't them, that I had a migraine headache and I felt awful and it was hard to sound pleasant. After class, a student came up to me and thanked me for informing the class that I had a headache. He said it was the first time a teacher had let them know how they felt so the class wouldn't take it personally. It didn't seem like a big deal to me at the time, but I have since realized that honesty at that level always makes things work better.

It's a simple concept, telling the truth, akin to telling the students ahead of time what your goals are for the day or week. If the students know what's expected, they can see it better, get it better, understand it better.

This works especially well, and certainly is a most opportune moment, when the teacher doesn't know something. If you don't know the answer, say so. I've had teachers who were obviously bluffing their way through an answer, or giving out wrong information, and everyone knew it but them.

There's nothing wrong with telling students you don't know. I say it a lot. But I always follow that up with 'but I'll look it up,' and I do ('doing' it is the important part). I also know that modeling the process of looking up an answer is important, and students will pick up on it and do it for themselves the next time. They may also find it easier to admit that they don't know something if the teacher did so already.

Letting your students know that you don't know everything adds to the classroom credibility. It's OK not to know something; it's OK to have a wrong answer. It's good to attempt an answer. It's this process that will lead to the right answer. Often more is learned in the attempt than in the accomplishment. I make a point of telling my students just those things during discussions. It's OK to be wrong, to try an answer. I'm not saying I'm an expert at it, but that's the direction I'm heading in, and I know I have more students join in on discussions or offer answers than the traditional hands that always go up first. Students appreciate honesty.

Heading in a certain direction is important. Once teachers begin going in the direction towards being an effective teacher, they can improve their teaching greatly. Effective teaching isn't a place, but a direction. It isn't something you finally reach. It's a journey. It's ongoing, something to strive for. When someone comes along with a designer fad for education, teachers are expected to stop working on what they believe is important to do what someone, usually an administrator or someone not in the classroom, deems necessary in order to become a 'good' teacher. A good example is a teacher at my current school who once said to me, after we had had much training in 'cooperative learning' that "we are now a cooperative learning school." That's like saying "I'm a Philips head screwdriver mechanic." If everyone is using only a Philips head screwdriver, then only so much can ever be done. Each tool has a purpose, and every teacher should know that. Trust the good teachers to use the right tools, depending on the job that needs to be done. Nothing should be forced on a master teacher. It's the individual spirit of the teacher that makes the difference.

Karl E. Thelen

Chapter nine

Effective Schools; Top heavy they're not. here it's bottoms up

Like Effective Teaching, Effective Schools' research is based on what schools around the nation, considered for one reason or another to be effective, are already doing. Dr. Larry Lazotte, from Michigan State, and the late Ron Edmonds, went to hundreds of these schools and took notes on what was going on, looking for commonalties to explain effective from non-effective. The information they gathered came out as the Effective Schools movement. They found that there **were** common aspects. These were their eleven correlates that seemed to define what made a school effective. They are simple and direct, and to anyone who has been in education for a while, smack of common sense.

The correlates are:

- Positive School Climate
- Planning Process
- Academic Goals
- Clearly Defined Curricula
- Monitoring of Student Progress
- Teacher/Staff Effectiveness
- Administrative Leadership
- Parent and Community Involvement
- Opportunities for Student Responsibility and Participation
- Rewards and Incentives
- Order and Discipline

To the average person this list might represent what every school should be and is expected to be. These are very straightforward. If

A Nation of Idiots

these 'things' are in place, then the school will flourish. What most people don't realize, however, is that very few schools operate this way. What may be common sense on the outside isn't always the way of the world on the inside. There are many reasons for this, but right now I'll focus on that which works and is out there for any school to make use of. Effective Schools concepts and literature should not, however, be shoved down teachers' throats by over-zealous administrators or districts. It is a meal to be partaken of, not used as a threat. Again, as in effective teaching, the terminology is not the focus, but the concept. Everyone doesn't need to be in lock step to be effective, as long as the practices are in place. Many master teachers are already employing the Effective Schools concepts, but don't call the parts by the same names. That's O.K. Leave the master teachers alone. They know what they're doing.

Positive school climate includes many things: a friendly atmosphere that is businesslike, supportive and directed towards learning. The word 'community' is used a lot. One of the most important aspects of having a positive school climate is that ALL people in the building are important to the effectiveness of that school. This includes all secretaries, custodial staff, cafeteria staff, teacher aides, paraprofessionals, bus drivers, student teachers, and members of the community who enter the building. Everyone, not just the teachers and administrators, is responsible for maintaining an atmosphere conducive to teaching and learning, since that's what it's all about, teaching and learning.

Many times I've seen students running down the hall, past custodians, secretaries (although I've seen some good ones nail students dead in their tracks), interns or visitors, or being obnoxious in one of the many ways students have, and no one says anything, so the behavior continues. Even teachers don't say anything; either it's too much trouble, or they just don't know how to stop the behavior or perhaps they're afraid to say anything.

This is unacceptable in an effective school. Everyone in the building needs to at least know what is expected and participate. No one should utter the words "that's not my job." This is a good place to use the word 'community.'

School atmosphere is also reflected on the walls and in the halls. Effective schools always have student work on display, whether literally on the walls or in showcases spotted throughout the school.

Karl E. Thelen

No pictures yellowed by the sun should be allowed. Most elementary schools I've been in do a good job in regards to displaying student work. If that enthusiasm could be maintained through high school, colleges would have to gear up for a great intellectual upsurge. Maybe college remedial classes could even be eliminated.

The second correlate, **Planning Process**, is also directly related to school climate. In Effective Schools, planning doesn't mean dictates from the top down. It means a collaboration of all parties affected so that everyone can buy into the final outcome. By involving everyone, there can be better implementation of expectations. Once again, it isn't something that can be shoved down on people, but something effective teachers have to recognize as viable and want to do. Most will, since most of the effective teachers recognize that which works. Besides teachers, others involved would be other school service professionals, parents, concerned community members, board members, students and administrators.

Having meetings and setting goals means nothing if there is no communication. All the long, hard work would be for naught. Quite often, failure to communicate to everyone will scuttle any hope of being effective before it's even started. All parties, outside as well as inside the building, need to be kept informed. The larger the group, the more personalities will be involved, so involving all parties is good policy and is smart.

Having **academic goals** seems like a no-brainer. It's why we're all here and why we do what we do, but again, it's surprising how many schools have no plan to achieve academic goals. Many pay lip service, but only a relative few actually 'plan' for achievement and, therefore, are effective.

Those that are effective have some things in common. Academic goals are based on a comprehensive, district-wide assessment of the students' needs. This should not be confused, as often is by legislators, parents, board members and others, as being the State's needs. Districts should decide what they want their student to graduate with and focus on that. Effective schools work best when planned for at the local level.

These goals need to be displayed everywhere (part of that communication thing) so all staff, community members and students know what the expectations are. Academic goals should even be displayed throughout the community in businesses and on posters

A Nation of Idiots

along the way. If everyone knows what is expected, then everyone can help in achieving those goals.

For high academics there has to be measurable objectives. It can't rely on 'observation.' If it can't be measured, it doesn't exist. Along with this, of course, are high expectations for student achievement and at the same time, high expectations for staff achievement. Everyone is involved when the expectations involve everyone.

Clearly defined curricula means just that. There's no ambiguity in what the instructional goals and objectives are. These are further identified in order of priority, selected and approved by the staff. If the quality of education rests with the quality of the individual classroom teacher, then it stands to reason that they would be the ones to approve the curriculum. Curriculum should never come from the State. It should not come from a curriculum coordinator. Only the classroom teachers should write and define curriculum.

Along with the planning comes the need to have timelines for implementation. There need to be units and lessons in place in order to aid in student learning, and the planning committee has to identify resources and activities. There is also the expectation that these programs will be funded, a minor point, but an important one. That which is clearly defined can be clearly followed.

Monitoring of student progress is important to maintain the focus on student academics. By knowing, as the year progresses, how the students are progressing, schools can stay on course. Individual teachers need to especially know how their students are doing at any given time. In order to achieve this, there have to be established procedures for student monitoring, a coordination of the various assessments, and a sharing of test results, grade reports, attendance records, and other methods used to determine student performance. This way, academic problem areas are identified and can be corrected. Sometimes one person will see a pattern where others did not. Something so simple could make a huge difference in a student's educational experience. By monitoring progress and identifying weak areas, corrections can be made quickly, either in the instructional program, the teacher's approach or the particular school procedures identified as the problem. Communication, once again, is important.

Teacher/Staff effectiveness should reflect an on-going concern for effective teaching. This is the job of every teacher, as well as every staff member, as has already been mentioned. Since the point of everyone being in the school is to improve academic excellence, then all the training should be geared toward that end. This is called 'staff development' and should be supported by the district. This doesn't mean shoving jargon and terminology down anyone's throat and having in-service training just for the sake of having some training or because some new innovative fad has come along. Staff development should always be directed towards the art and science of teaching, not in an effort to make everyone do the same thing.

In-service should be determined by the classroom teachers involved. Notice I said the 'classroom' teachers. **No one** should decide something as important as in-service for teachers if those making the decisions aren't in the classroom. In-service designed by someone not in the classroom quite often becomes mindless and oppressive for master teachers. Master teachers should not be punished by those unqualified. Many in-service committees are made up mostly of people who are not in the classroom as a teacher. True staff development comes from the heart of master teachers. They're the ones who will use a program or idea and they're the ones who will make it work.

Administrative leadership is important in an effective school. Ironically, this is the one area that falters the most. Finding qualified administrators who don't kow tow to the local deities on the school board or in the community are hard to find. Finding one who is capable of imparting to a staff a vision and a direction to go in is even harder. I've known many principals and superintendents who weren't 'people' oriented, and were unable to communicate anything, let alone a vision.

Administrators also need to have the support of the local power structure so they can move on, hopefully upward, to a new job of equal responsibility and challenge. Therefore, being in-step with the district becomes more important than being an academic leader. How well they implemented district policy becomes a more important indicator of effectiveness than the skills principals really need to succeed.

In an effective school, the administrators need to portray learning as the most important reason for being in school. This becomes exceptionally difficult in today's Feelgood atmosphere, with senior privileges, off-campus rights, and an emphasis on not making students feel bad, all of which contradicts life in general. Most administrators

A Nation of Idiots

are also heavily bogged down with discipline problems, most of which originate because there isn't a clear-cut, fair, yet firm, discipline policy throughout the building.

Administrators also need to know the school's goals and to be able to say them in uncomplicated terms. **Everyone** needs to be able to understand where the school is headed and the administrators need to be able to explain the means by which the goals will be achieved. With so few administrators staying in one district for very long, this becomes an on-going comedy of errors, as each new administrator has to start from scratch in a new school.

As an academic leader, the principal should understand the principles of effective teaching and learning, and be able to identify those traits in his staff. Observations then become empirical tools for determining effectiveness. In the wrong hands, evaluation becomes meaningless. Effective teachers want feedback, and it's best if that feedback comes from someone perceived as being capable and qualified to provide it. Administrators in an effective school need to be themselves models of academic excellence.

Parent and community involvement is a must for a school to be truly effective. Without the support and understanding of the parents and community, the school doesn't really exist. To attain this important link, there has to be something in place to make this happen. Again, communication is important. Parents need to know without question that they are wanted and needed. The home-school connection can be the strongest link in a student's education. There's nothing that works better than keeping tabs on academics not only in school, but at home as well. I'm not saying it takes a whole village to do this, but the more people involved constructively, the more the chances are raised that there will be success at the end of the line.

Opportunities for student responsibility and participation are cited as being important. Student voices need to be heard. They are closest to the action in terms of what they're getting out of their education. Most students, even those doing as little as possible, are honest about their own efforts regarding their learning. The top students know if they're being pushed or not, and the lowest of students knows if the teacher is trying to teach.

Classes in civil responsibilities should be included. Students need to know what their responsibilities are as citizens, and should apply this while they are still in school. Nothing is more damaging than to have a feel good activity like 'senior privileges,' without having a component part called 'senior responsibilities.' Once the responsibility part is met, there then can be room for the next correlate in the Effective Schools lexicon, Rewards and Incentives. Responsible students will act responsibly.

Rewards and incentives are what our society is based on. Whether it should be or not, it is, and there's nothing wrong with finding out that if you do as you're expected and learn the lessons the community has decided are worth learning, then there's a little reward for doing it. I know that works for me. If the reward encourages excellence in learning and excellence in behavior, then that is good.

In order for an incentive to work, it must be based on performance and it must be based on a standard (not ones set by the State), rather than comparison of peers. That way, all students are encouraged to try to be better. All students would be encouraged to learn. All students need to experience the thrill of actually learning something and applying that learning to their lives so that they want to learn some more.

An easy way to instill the concept of learning having its just rewards is to give out awards for achievement, and to start early. Many schools have successful awards programs already, including assemblies and academic recognition nights. Sports have had their sport's award night for many years. It's time academics came up with their own varsity team and be recognized for it.

It's important to mention that there shouldn't be awards for the sake of giving awards. If no one deserves an award, they shouldn't be given one. Students know early whether the award means anything or not. A meaningless award achieves nothing. No teacher should ever be **told** to give an award.

Lastly, and perhaps the most important is **Order and Discipline**. Without discipline there is nothing. Without an orderly environment designed for the highest of expectations, learning will be minimized. I wrote that line on an intern message board in our faculty lounge, 'Without discipline, there is nothing.' Next to it an intern had written, "by whom, Adolf Hitler?"

The new attitude prevalent among many graduates coming out of the teacher schools is indicative of that last comment. There appears to be resistance to expecting the classroom atmosphere to be conducive to learning, which means the students are attentive and focused on the task at hand. Instead, Feelgoodenism takes over and the new teachers want the kids to 'feel good' about their experience in school.

This flies in the face of what has been shown to be an effective school, and creates an environment of educational chaos. It's a lack of discipline, or inability to control the flow of the class so that learning takes place that drives many future teachers out of the business. If this lack of discipline is school-wide, then nothing will work. Learning will not be the primary focus. It will not be, regardless of the rhetoric, an effective school.

In an Effective Schools Consortia Network bulletin on effective school characteristics, the role of the state was mentioned. Remember the people you least want touching your education? According to the bulletin, "At the school district's request, the State Education Department will assist the school's local staff to identify major priorities, delineate problems within these priorities, identify alternative solutions, and evaluate the process and results."[76]

The intent of the state, bless its soul, is to eventually do good things. Unfortunately, state governments aren't really set up that way. In order for the state to help anything or anyone, it needs to develop a common terminology in order to assure accountability on the part of those receiving the taxpayers' money. That is exactly where the state's involvement falls apart. The concepts in effective teaching or effective schools aren't important because of the terminology used, but because of the concepts being communicated.

Once a common state terminology is developed, there then has to be training to instill this terminology into the teaching staff so that everyone is talking the same language. In-service is a good place to do that, which is one of the main reasons in-services are so deadly to the minds of many good teachers.

However, by the time this common language, this governmental 'standard' by which everyone and everything can be evaluated, is in place, the improvements the state originally wanted to initiate will be bogged down in institutional self-perpetuated doom.

In a booklet on Effective Schooling Practices: A Research Synthesis called Onward to Excellence: Making Schools More Effective, the correlates presented in the Effective Schools research

---

[76] Effective Schools Consortia Network bulletin # 16

were broken down into more easily identifiable parts which were **Classroom characteristics and practices** and **School characteristics and practices**, (there are also District Characteristics and practices but they are not included here). These are further broken down into the following. I list them here because I believe they are important.

Classroom characteristics and practices

1. **Instruction is guided by a preplanned curriculum**
   - Learning goals and objectives are developed and prioritized according to district and building guidelines, selected or approved by teachers, sequenced to facilitate student learning and organized or grouped into units or lessons.
   - Unit or lesson objectives are set in a timeline so that the calendar can be used for instructional planning.
   - Instructional resources and teaching activities are identified, matched to objectives and student developmental levels and recorded in lesson plans. Alternative resources and activities are identified, especially for priority objectives.
   - Resources and teaching activities are reviewed for content and appropriateness and are modified according to experience to increase their effectiveness in helping students learn.

In other words, plan ahead. If you know where you're going, it's easier to get there. Nothing takes the place of planning. The unplanned teacher who merely follows whims from day to day is doing nothing for the students. A larger question would be 'why are they even there?'

As far as resources go, all good teachers update these and review them constantly. If change was good anywhere in education, it's in the updating of resources, not for the sake of it, but because the current materials are outdated. That doesn't mean get rid of a book in English because it's been taught for many years. That's what classics are for. But the materials used to teach about that book may be in line

A Nation of Idiots

for reconsideration or change. Change just for the sake of change, however, is anathema to education.

Much learning can be called sequential. Students learn how to do one thing, and that in turn leads to the next, and so on. Math is a good example, although the concept is germane to all disciplines. For this reason, teachers need to know ahead of time, sequentially, what's going to happen. This becomes especially important when setting up a schedule of reinforcement necessary to push knowledge from the short-term to long-term memory.

On the other hand, none of this is meant to establish a rigid, narrow educational philosophy. The last thing we need is for education to become dogmatic. Everyone plans differently. The important thing is that they have plans.

2. **There are high expectations for student learning**
   - Teachers set high standards for learning and let students know they are all expected to meet them. Standards are set so they are both challenging and attainable.
   - Quality standards for academic work are set and maintained consistently.
   - No students are expected to fall below the level of learning needed to be successful at the next level of education.
   - Teachers expect students to do well on tests and earn good grades.

This sounds simple, but in a lot of schools it isn't done or isn't done consistently. And yet, it **is** simple. But it's also a consideration that becomes complicated by administrivia. Expectations should be written down and handed to the students, as well as sent home so the parents understand the expectations from the beginning. Have the parents sign the paper so they can't cop out later.

Many Feelgooders don't think that pushing kids towards 'artificial' expectations is good for their psyche. Just the opposite is true. Higher expectations give everyone something to shoot for, and most students respond positively. I've especially seen this in students who were considered 'special needs' and therefore considered incapable of reaching higher expectations.

Karl E. Thelen

One goal for a student of mine in my English class was to be able to write a complete sentence by Christmas. I was appalled with this since he had already written several pages for me in his journal. He was already way beyond sentences. I asked that we raise the expectations considerably. If he made them, great, but if not, then at least he stretched himself farther than he would have had we kept to only a complete sentence by Christmas. A special ed. teacher told me that this particular student was now able to study on his own and attributed it to being held to the higher expectations; the student had felt the joy of actually learning something and wanted more.

3. Students are carefully oriented to lessons

- Teachers help students get ready to learn. They explain lesson objectives in simple, everyday language and refer to them throughout lessons to maintain focus.
- Objectives may be posted or handed out to help students keep a sense of direction. Teachers check to see that objectives are understood.
- The relationship of a current lesson to previous study is described. Students are reminded of key concepts or skills previously covered.
- Students are challenged to learn, particularly at the start of a difficult lesson. Students know in advance what is expected of them and are ready to learn.

Again, knowing ahead of time saves time and increases time on task. There's nothing wrong with letting students know what you're going to do. The only time a teacher shouldn't let the students know is when the teacher doesn't know. Then it's up to the administrator to know.

Focusing on the goals, writing them down, handing them out, checking for understanding, referring back to keep on track, and reviewing after the fact; these are all the things that help students learn and that's why teachers are there. The more students know what is expected of them, the more likely they are to achieve it.

4. Instruction is clear and focused

A Nation of Idiots

- Lesson activities are previewed, clearly written and verbal directions are given, key points and instructions are repeated, student understanding is checked.
- Presentations, such as lectures or demonstrations, are designed to communicate clearly to students. Digressions are avoided.
- Students have plenty of opportunity for guided and independent practice with new concepts and skills.
- To check understanding, teachers ask clear questions and make sure all students have a chance to respond.
- Teachers select problems and other academic tasks that are well matched to lesson content so student success rate is high. Seatwork assignments also provide variety and challenge.
- Homework is assigned that students can complete successfully. It is typically in small increments and provides additional practice with content covered in class. Work is checked and students are given quick feedback.
- Parents help keep students involved in learning. Teachers let parents know that homework is important and give them tips on how to help students keep working.

There's that need to plan, again. The better prepared a teacher is, the more focused is the learning. It works time and again. The importance of parents should never be neglected, as well as the need to keep using feedback to improve the instruction.

Listening is one of the hardest ways to take in information. Teachers who understand this will repeat themselves in enough ways to get the key concepts across to the students. Add in the visuals and drawn concepts for the right brain dominant students and many more will be included in the learning.

It's also for this reason (not all students are listening at any given time) that teachers will continually check to see that the students understand what's going on. Nothing should be assumed. If the students are comfortable in a class and the teacher has presented himself early on as someone who will be patient when answering questions or explaining the work at hand, then the students will let the teacher know when they don't understand. This is also why guiding

141

Karl E. Thelen

students through a lesson helps. It keeps the focus on the lesson where it belongs. Letting students try the work on their own lets the teacher know if they have accomplished the goals.

Following that, homework, which should relate specifically to the class work, should be for practice or helping prepare for the next lesson. Too much homework, piled on at times, is only busy work and has no purpose other than to burden and bore the students. No one knows this better than the students. Some teachers don't even bother to correct the homework.

Lastly, the parents' role; if the parents are supportive of the school at home, and expect homework to be done, and done correctly and well, then the positive impact is highly visible. If the parents believe their school is doing the best job it can, then, again, the positive results are palpable. If, however, the parents knock the school, if they express dissatisfaction, if they blame all ills on the school system, recovery is almost impossible. Students play this game well, and will take every opportunity to blame their lack of effort or inability on the school, parroting their parents. The end result, of course, is a longer and rougher acclimation into the real world. This leads directly into #5 below.

5. **Learning progress is monitored closely**
    - Teachers frequently monitor student learning, both formally and informally.
    - Teachers require that students be accountable for their academic work.
    - Classroom assessments of student performance match learning objectives. Teachers know and use test development techniques to prepare valid, reliable assessment instruments.
    - Routine assessment procedures make checking student progress easier. Students hear results quickly. Reports to students are simple and clear to help them understand and correct errors. Reports are tied to learning objectives. Teachers use assessment results not only to evaluate students but also for Instructional diagnosis and to find out that teaching methods are working.

- Grading scales and mastery standards are set high to promote excellence.
- Teachers encourage parents to keep track of student progress, too.

Throughout the listing of attributes there are clear references to effective teaching. There are high expectations of the teachers as well as the students. Teachers are expected to know what they are doing and how to determine if they're actually teaching anything. These are all good things for education.

By monitoring the students' learning, something important happens. The teacher will know if they are learning. This sounds like another no-brainer, but I've sat in on many teacher-parent conferences and I've been continually appalled at how some teachers struggle to explain a student's grade, how they arrived at it or how they seem to have nothing in place to track the student's progress, or lack of it.

To be an effective teacher, any teacher should know any student's grades instantly. I've done this since 1986, when I bought my first computer. (There are now plenty of grading programs). I wasn't yet familiar with Hunter or Effective Teaching. I just thought it would be good to let students as well as myself, know how they were doing at any given time. Now the research has shown that when students know how they are doing on a frequent basis, they can make corrections more quickly, thereby improving their grade.

The monitoring doesn't have to be formal tests. I have had many students who could tell you the answer, but froze when they got to a test. Interviewing them orally in regards to the material wouldn't be considered a formal test, but it certainly achieves the goal of establishing the extent of learning.

Often in discussions the level of understanding can be quickly determined. Checking for understanding of the learning is also an important aspect of Effective Teaching. Without doing it, the teacher is merely going through the motions, waiting for June to roll around.

Holding students accountable for their work is also important. All students should know what the expectations are for doing their own work and owning it. This happens when the teacher lets the students know, through the teacher's practices, that it **is** important. When students know they aren't being held accountable, even the nicest of students will resort to copying the homework or class work, or whatever it is they have come to realize won't count for much. No one, adults included, likes busy work or doing something that is meaningless. Students need to hold their teachers accountable.

I make a pledge to my students that I will get their tests back by the next class. Most of the time I can maintain this. Often I have them ready before the class is over. I do it because it's one more workable thing that can be done to help their grades go up, which can be an indication of learning taking place.

I've heard students complain of teachers who never seem to correct their papers, or return reports. A grade at some point miraculously appears, usually around report card time. It should have appeared back when the learning was relevant and the grade may have helped motivate a student to do better. I knew one teacher, early in my career, who actually took all the term papers that had just been turned in, said that they were all trash and dropped them into the trash can. She had never even looked at them. I still see teachers like that today, not as overt, but just as oppressive.

The results teachers get should also clue them in as to whether what they are doing, and the manner in which they are doing it, is working. I've changed what I do and how I do it many times, and even as I close in on **The End**, I still work at making lessons better. Just as a test question that no one ever gets right is an indication of a bad question, a lesson that never works speaks for itself (if the teacher is listening).

Presentation is important. Most things need to be broken down into their parts so that everyone can get the whole picture. This takes practice, the heart and soul of change. This is another reason that aspiring teachers should be involved in education sooner so that they can work some of the 'practice' things out before they have their own classroom. Practice always makes you better. By retooling, reshaping, adding and subtracting on lessons to constantly make them better, especially in tying in with other learning to come, teachers can assure effectiveness in what they do. The changes aren't always large changes, sometimes they're just small course corrections. If there is to be 'change' in education, let it be here, carried out by master teachers and those who are headed in that direction.

One teacher I worked with used the same notes every year. His presentation never changed. Nothing ever changed. The joke was that the paper he had his notes on was not always legal pad yellow

A Nation of Idiots

Grades should not be candy. They should not be 'inflated' so that they become meaningless. Grades, which represent the standards of the class, should be set to promote excellence. To do that, standards must be set high enough for students to recognize them as goals, as a legitimate outlet for the effort they put in to learn what they are at school to learn. Many students **are** there to learn and are irritated by any teacher unable to help them do that. The bar should not be lowered for anyone. Everyone should be judged by the same bar, otherwise the results are meaningless, just what the process was supposed to avoid. Once the height of the bar becomes adjustable then everyone will be a winner, everyone will be above average; everyone will be an A student. Well, unfortunately, when a reality check is done, again, the 'reality' part won't help anyone who really isn't what their school said they were. Those who will run the world in a generation will need the honest to goodness skills and abilities it takes to do just that, run a world. Meaningless grades will motivate no one.

Lastly, again, mom and dad, you need to be there. You need to check up on your student. You need to ask questions, look at their work, and keep track of their grades. Hold them accountable to their work. Be accountable yourselves.

6. **When students don't understand, they are retaught**
    - New material is introduced as quickly as possible at the beginning of the year or course, with a minimum review or reteaching of previous content. Key prerequisite concepts and skills are reviewed thoroughly but quickly.
    - Teachers reteach priority lesson content until students show they've learned it.
    - Regular, focused reviews of key concepts and skills are used throughout the year to check on and strengthen student retention.

One of the reasons for checking while students are working to see if they understand the material is so that the teacher will know if they need to go back and reteach something. You don't always have to wait for a test if you keep on top of things. This is especially true when you consider that learning leads to learning, and if a student doesn't understand the current concepts, then they won't be able to understand the next concepts. Learning will stop. This is contrary to why we are there, so it must be corrected, retaught. It might also be a good time to institute one of those small course corrections and teach it differently the second time. When my students don't understand something I've explained, I'll tell them that it's because I didn't explain it well enough. Then I try it in a different vein. If that still doesn't do it I'll ask a student who does understand to explain it. That almost always does it, since they speak the same language. I have no problem going to my bullpen if I have to.

I also tell my students not to forget anything I've taught them, and then check to see that they listened throughout the year. I reserve the right to test them on anything we've had in class at anytime. And my expectation is that they will pass that test. Otherwise, as they know, bad things will happen:)

7. **Class time is used for learning**
   - Teachers follow a system of priorities for using class time and allocate time for each subject or lesson. They concentrate on using class time for learning and spend very little time on non-learning activities.
   - Teachers set and maintain a brisk pace for instruction that remains consistent with thorough learning. New objectives are introduced as quickly as possible. Clear start and stop cues help pace lessons according to specific time targets.
   - Students are encouraged to pace themselves. If they don't finish during class, they work on lessons before or after school, during lunch or in other times so they keep up with what is going on in class.

Many class days are lost to a lack of time on task by the teachers. Community members would find it hard to believe, but a lot of class time is wasted every school year by poor teachers who have no focus and therefore no plans, and have nothing to follow or point the way. Usually, these are the teachers who give homework unrelated to class work and are the ones who often don't even collect or correct it. This is one of the biggest complaints I've heard from students over the years, teachers who assign homework and then forget about it, or say it isn't important after the fact.

A Nation of Idiots

By staying on task, the students come to realize that it's important, and many will raise their own expectations to meet the teacher's. By introducing material quickly and efficiently, with all the checks for understanding in place, students also come to realize the importance of their teachers being prepared, as well as the need for their own preparation. Focusing on the task at hand and instilling its importance enhances learning over time. Again, the importance of planning in order to keep track of all students, as well as being able to provide for those who are ahead and for those who will make it, but have a different way of getting there, cannot be over stressed. You can't get where you're going if you don't know how to get there.

For those students who can do the work but just have a different pace, the responsibility to finish the work is on them. I have a spot where all unfinished work is placed until the students, on their own time, or at their own designation, come in to finish the work. This works out well on essay tests where I'd prefer they have a good answer rather than one finished by the end of class.

8. **There are smooth, efficient classroom routines**
   - Class starts quickly and purposefully, teachers have assignments or activities ready for students when they arrive. Materials and supplies are ready, too.
   - Students are required to bring the materials they need to class each day. They use assigned storage space.
   - Administrative matters are handled with quick, efficient routines that keep class disruptions to a minimum.
   - There are smooth, rapid transitions between activities throughout the class or day.

Time on Task and Classroom Management; there's that need to plan ahead and know what you're going to do. Students respect teachers who are on task and expect the students to be. Most students really would prefer a quiet, academic atmosphere to one held hostage by unruly students and a poor teacher.

In order to accomplish this classroom setting, every teacher should know before they start how the class would be run. It doesn't have to be a militaristic, martinet run classroom. All students respond to fair and reasonable expectations as to when the class will start,

Karl E. Thelen

what the students' role is and what the teacher's role is. It isn't a hard concept to communicate, but for some reason, many teachers can't do it.

The students on the fringe of bad behavior, those who wait until they see which way any situation goes before they jump in and cause a problem, are always assessing the abilities of the teacher to maintain control. They know whom they can push and whom they can't. It's an on-going game and the poor teachers are the targets, the students the losers.

A teacher who is ready for the class, with materials, goals, a means of achieving those goals, and the expectations that everyone will do as expected, will be much more successful than those who have no clue and didn't spend enough time figuring it out.

Quite often I can stop any 'disruptions' with no more than a raised eyebrow or a move towards my "Sophomore Tenderizer" that hangs on the wall behind me. Most students know within a very short time what I expect and realize I'm serious in achieving those expectations. Discipline in most instances after that can be taken care of with humor, or a simple request. It should never take any more than that. Yellers and screamers only provide a free show and may actually incur further bad behavior in order to keep the show going. Nothing takes the place of firm, but fair classroom management. It's easier to lighten up than it is to tighten up.

9. **Instructional groups formed in the classroom fit instructional needs**
   - When introducing new concepts and skills, whole group instruction, actively led by the teacher, is preferable.
   - Smaller groups are formed within the classroom as needed to make sure all students learn thoroughly. Students are placed according to individual achievement levels; underplacement is avoided.
   - Teachers review and adjust groups often, moving students when achievement levels change.

It makes sense to begin a lesson with all the students. It wouldn't make sense at this point in the learning to speak to everyone individually. Once past this initial phase, then it's easier to determine who needs what help (checking their understanding, which is best accomplished by letting them try the lesson on their own, independently, while the teacher, or aides, move about and watch the students work). Based on this information, the teacher would then know how to proceed with groupings.

10. Standards for classroom behavior are explicit
- Teachers let students know that there are high standards for behavior in the classroom.
- Classroom behavior standards are written, taught and reviewed from the beginning of the year or at the start of new courses.
- Rules, discipline procedures and consequences are planned in advance. Standards are consistent with or identical to the building code of conduct.
- Consistent, equitable discipline is applied for all students. Procedures are carried out quickly and clearly linked to students' inappropriate behavior.
- Teachers stop disruptions quickly, taking care to avoid disrupting the whole class.
- In disciplinary action, the teacher focuses on the inappropriate behavior, not the student's personality.

Firm, fair, and reasonable discipline; no one can argue with it, especially if it's well publicized. Discipline can't be avoided. Without it, nothing works. Feelgooders cringe, but good teachers are those who know from which everything flows, and that name is discipline. Students who know what to expect from the start get there faster and stay there in the presence of a master teacher.

In discipline it's important to remember that it's the actions, the behavior that needs to change. Teachers should never call any student stupid. It isn't the personality that's the focus, although that can be the reason for the behavior in the first place, but the action.

11. Personal interactions between teachers and students are positive

- Teachers pay attention to student interests, problems and accomplishments in social interactions both in and out of the classroom.
- Teachers make sure they let students know they really care.
- Students are allowed and encouraged to develop a sense of responsibility and self-reliance. Older students in particular are given opportunities to take responsibility for school-related matters and to participate in making decisions about important school issues.

My own personal interactions with teachers from kindergarten on were anything but positive. It's because of this that I have an affinity for treating students as best as I can. I'm not saying I've always been successful (especially in the early years before I had control of the reins), but it's the past that makes me try to make the present and future better.

No teacher can keep up with all the students' social interactions, interests, or accomplishments. This may be easier on the elementary level where teachers tend to have the same class all year, but is still something that needs to be consciously adhered to. However, any teacher can express an interest in every student at some time for some reason.

It doesn't take much to let students know you care. It doesn't have to be sloppy and sentimental. Birthdays are a good example. Know when your students' birthdays are. After 32 years I just started this year having my students mark their birthday on my calendar. I had always depended on students to let me know if someone was having a birthday, but I never knew everyone's, especially the real quiet ones or students who not too many people had a lot to do with. Now I get them all, finally (it's never too late).

The reason this is important to me is because I like to sing 'Happy Birthday' in class, (I get to lead) and *everyone* has to sing along, or I give them a low grade. My grading pen, as I call it, is always out and ready to grade. Needless to say, I have 100% participation, and they also, to get full credit, have to point and waggle their fingers at the birthday person whenever they say the word 'you' or their name. And students are always encouraged to put some pizzazz in the ending:)

It also doesn't take much to congratulate students when they accomplish something whether it's in sports or academics or extra curricular activities. These usually appear in notices and are readily available to anyone who wants to know.

12. Incentives and rewards for students are used to promote excellence
- Excellence is defined by objective standards, not by peer comparison. Systems are set up in the classroom for frequent and consistent rewards to students for academic achievement and excellent behavior. Rewards are appropriate to the developmental level of students.
- All students know about the rewards and what they need to do to get them.
- Rewards are chosen because they appeal to students. Rewards are related to specific student achievements. Some rewards may be presented publicly; some should be immediately presented, while others delayed to teach persistence.
- Parents are told about student successes and requested to help students keep working toward excellence.

Who doesn't like to be rewarded for something? I figure that if it works for me it'll work for anyone. And the rewards can be anything, as long as the students value it. Pizza works well for upper classmen. Fair, reasonable and attainable grades work for many. Sometimes an accomplishment can be rewarded with a certificate or a plaque. Sometimes the reward is given privately, and sometimes it's given in front of the whole school or community. The important point is that students know that there is an appreciation for their effort, that it isn't all in vain, that it's not just *busy work*. It's equally important to know that the recognition is credible, not just apiece of paper which is handed out to everyone.

Karl E. Thelen

School characteristics and practices

1. **Everyone emphasizes the importance of learning**
   - All staff has high expectations for student achievement. Expectations are for all students; students are expected to work hard toward the attainment of priority learning goals.
   - Everyone accepts that school is a place for learning.
   - When educational issues arise, student-learning considerations are the most important criteria used in decision-making.

Everyone, all staff, all students; the entire school emphasizes learning. There's nothing ambiguous about that. The fact that education is the focus eliminates any question of what the district should do when a question arises. They should do that which provides for the increasing of student learning. That may mean hiring staff over a pet project, an expenditure that is hard to explain to many taxpayers.

If anyone in the district doesn't accept that school is where learning takes place, then they should pack it in and go to Feelgood land, a favorite vacation spot for **A Nation of Idiots**, where schools exist to make everyone feel good, but little learning takes place.

Too many people try to turn the schools into teen centers, where the main purpose of the building is to provide refuge. At teen centers, the emphasis is more on 'make me feel good' rather than on 'what can I do to further myself?' Schools should never be seen as teen centers, or 'malls.'

The question arises, 'What do you do with anyone who doesn't believe in the sanctity of learning and the purpose of schools?' My answer is cruel. Fire them. You can't have high expectations during the day, but then at night, have everything fall apart because a night custodian allows students to skateboard through the school after hours. Teachers who don't help out with maintaining a safe and orderly environment and allow students to run past them in the hall should be let go however and whenever it's feasible.

2. **Strong leadership guides the instructional program**
   - Instructional leaders portray learning as the most important reason for being in school; public speeches and writings emphasize the importance and value of high achievement.

- The leader has a clear understanding of the school's mission and is able to state it in direct, concrete terms. Instructional focus is established that unifies staff. The building leadership believes that all students can learn and that the school makes the difference between success and failure.
- Building leaders know and can apply teaching and learning principles. They know research, legitimize it, and use it in problem solving. Effective teaching practices are modeled for staff as appropriate.
- Leaders set expectations for curriculum quality through the use of standards and guidelines. Alignment is checked and improved; priorities are established within the curriculum; curriculum implementation is monitored.
- Learning time is protected from disruption. Administrative matters are handled with time conserving routines that don't disrupt instructional activities. Time use priorities are established, widely communicated and enforced.
- A safe, orderly school environment is established and maintained.
- Instructional leaders check student progress frequently, relying on explicit performance data. Results are made visible. Progress standards are set and used as points of comparison. Discrepancies are used to stimulate action.
- Leaders set up systems of incentives and rewards to encourage excellence in student and teacher performance. They act as figureheads in delivering awards and highlighting the importance of excellence. Resources needed to ensure the effectiveness of instructional programs are acquired; resources are sought from many sources, including the community, as needed; allocations are made according to instructional priorities.
- School leaders establish standard procedures, which guide parent involvement. Emphasis is placed on the importance of parental support of the school's instructional efforts.
- There is frequent two-way communication with parents. Leaders make the accomplishments of students, staff and the school as a whole visible to the public.

- Instructional leaders expect all staff to meet high instructional standards. Agreement is obtained on a school-wide instructional model. Classroom visits to observe instruction are frequent; teacher supervision focuses on instructional improvement; staff development opportunities are secured and monitored.
- Leaders express an expectation and strong desire that instructional programs improve over time. Improvement strategies are organized and systematic; they are given high priority and visibility; implementation of new practices is carefully monitored, the staff is supported.
- Leaders involve staff and others in planning implementation strategies. They set and enforce expectations for participation; commitments are made and followed through with determination and consistency; Leaders rally support from the different constituencies in the school and community.

There they go and I must hurry after them, for I am their leader. That's just the opposite of what we need in education, but quite often that's exactly what we get. Administrators need to be academic leaders; they need to know what is going on in the school and what is going on in the classrooms. I mentioned this to a principal once and he became instantly angry, "I'm supposed to know everything that's going on?" I told him that wasn't just my opinion, but was part of the Effective Schools criteria. He was surprised. But a lot of administrators react basically the same way. And that shouldn't be the reaction.

Being an academic leader is a lot of work, but it's the best way to gain credibility, not only with the staff, but also with the students and their parents. Any principal who can explain the school's programs and speak knowledgeably in regards to what individual teachers do to achieve the school's goals gains the respect of those he is speaking to. It shows he cares. It shows he's a professional. It's shows his true character.

An academic leader who has the trust of his staff can help keep the school on task a lot more easily than someone who has to push and pull all the time. It makes it a lot easier to get people to help get

A Nation of Idiots

with the program if the person in charge knows what the program is. It's easier to maintain high expectations if the administrator is not only going to back you up, but is also able to explain the conceptual underpinnings that make it worthwhile. This demonstration of a common positive goal is easy to explain to students and their parents, and the sense of it then becomes easier to accept. Ah, leadership.

3. **The curriculum is based on clear goals and objectives**
   - Learning goals and objectives are clearly defined and displayed; teachers actively use building curriculum resources for instructional planning. District curriculum resources are used, when available.
   - Clear relationships among learning goals, instructional activities and student assessments are established and written down.
   - Collaborative curriculum planning and decision-making are typical. Special attention is focused on building good continuity across grade levels and courses. Teachers know where they fit in the curriculum.
   - Staff, students and community know the scope of the curriculum and the priorities within it.

There are those goals and objectives again. Knowing where you are going makes it easier to get there. The relationship between goals and the direction of the school is self-evident. Without a clear view of where you want to go, you won't get there, and often won't even realize you aren't there. On the other hand, when there are clearly defined goals **everyone** will know whether the school is headed in the right direction or not. Knowledge is power. That's the point when everyone in the school becomes capable of helping the school get there. Curricula are the goals and objectives of the individual courses. Everyone in the school should understand their importance in maintaining direction and focus. The written curriculum should be the taught curriculum, something else that doesn't happen as often as it should.

4. **Students are grouped to promote effective instruction**

Karl E. Thelen

- In required subjects and courses, students are placed in heterogeneous groups; tracks are avoided; under placement is avoided.
- Instructional aides and classroom grouping techniques are used to help keep the adult/student ratio low, especially during instruction aimed at priority objectives.

Heterogeneous grouping, where there is an equal mix of top, middle and low achieving students, can work for generalized, required courses. The idea that top students will help those more in need doesn't always work on its own. It takes the skill of a master teacher to make heterogeneous grouping work. When you have anything less, then the whole concept falls apart.

At the school I'm currently at, the grouping we do is called heterogeneous, but in reality it's nothing more than random grouping done by the computer. What is more important, from my own experience, is to give students a choice as to which classes they take, regardless of the degree of difficulty. We did this before the honors English classes at my present school were eliminated (they made some students appear to be smarter than others). Anyone could sign up for the honors class. No one was placed in it without permission. Doing it this way eliminates the specter of tracking where students are told what class they are going to be in and on what level.

In the honors class, by making it by choice, we had students who had to struggle every day just to get a C, but they were prouder of that C than they would have been with an A had they been tracked into an easier class. On the other hand, and it just has to be accepted, there were students who could have taken the honors class but chose another, easier class so they wouldn't have to work so hard.

5. **School time is used for learning**
    - School events are scheduled to avoid disruption of learning time.
    - Everyone understands time-use priorities; school communications highlight the need for time for learning; procedures are developed to maximize learning time.
    - Time use allocations are established among subjects taught and staff follows the time use guidelines.

A Nation of Idiots

- The school calendar is organized to provide maximum learning time. Prior to adoption, new instructional programs or school procedures are evaluated according to their potential impact on learning time.
- During the day, unassigned time and time spent on non-instructional activities are minimal; the school day, classes and other activities start and end on time.
- Student pullouts from regular classes are minimized, either for academic or non-academic purposes. The amount of pull out activity is monitored and corrective action taken as necessary to keep things in balance.
- Extra learning time is provided for students who need or want it; students can get extra help outside of regular school hours.

Time on task; it's so important it keeps coming up. The biggest enemy to *time on task* is 'pullouts,' those nasty interruptions whereby students leave class for sports, extracurricular activities, guidance groups, play practice, band rehearsal, doctor appointments, court appearances, discipline and shopping.

The idea that time in the classroom is important and that disruptions are to be kept to a minimum is just what education needs. Unfortunately the realities of time constraints, availability of people, travel time, and other disruptions always rise to the surface. But if everyone in the school understood the importance of *time on task*, then the job of obtaining maximum *time on task* would be easier to achieve.

The fact that there are schools who have already been capable of achieving this lessening of distractions should be encouraging for all those schools that would like to become more effective. The path is clear.

6. **Learning progress is monitored closely**
   - Test results, grade reports, attendance records and other methods are used to spot potential problems. Changes are made in instructional programs and school procedures to meet identified needs.

- Summaries of student performances are shared with all staff that then assist in developing action alternatives. Periodic reports are also made to the community.
- Assessments are coordinated; district, school and classroom efforts work together; duplication of effort is minimal. Assessments match learning objectives.
- Staff follows simple routines for collecting, summarizing and reporting student achievement information; results are related to learning objectives. Individual student records are established and updated periodically; group summaries are pulled from individual reports and reviewed over time to check for trends.

By now it should be obvious that paying attention to the results coming out of the classrooms is important. It's not on a 'need-to-know' basis. Everyone needs to know. That way, when there's a need to change or correct something, it has a better chance of getting done. It's called keeping records.

7. Discipline is firm and consistent
- A written code of conduct specifies acceptable student behavior, discipline procedures and consequences; students, parents and staff know the code; students and staff receive initial training and periodic reviews of key features.
- Discipline procedures are routine and quick to administer. Disciplinary action quickly follows infractions and is always consistent with the code; treatment is equitable for all students. Follow-up and action for absenteeism and tardiness normally occur within a day.
- Students are told why they are being disciplined, in terms of the code of conduct.
- Discipline is administered in a neutral, matter-of-fact way; the disciplinarian focuses on the student's behavior, not on personality.
- Out-of-school suspensions or expulsions are kept to a minimum; in-school suspension is used in most cases.

It's easier to lighten up than it is to tighten up. Without discipline, there is nothing. It has to be consistent because the students would know right away if it weren't. Everyone has to be in agreement, and then follow through. Consistent discipline does wonders for the atmosphere inside a school. An academic atmosphere breeds academics. A carnival atmosphere breeds the opposite. Schools need to decide which atmosphere to promote.

8. **There are high expectations for quality instruction**
    - All staff believe that students can learn regardless of their ability level and enthusiastically accept the challenge to teach them. When staff get together they often discuss instructional issues.
    - Supervision and evaluation procedures are written and intended to help teachers set and work toward professional growth goals. All staff receives feedback on performance at least annually.
    - Classroom observations are made according to guidelines developed in advance; feedback is provided quickly; emphasis is on improving instruction and boosting student achievement.
    - Staff development opportunities are provided; emphasis is on skill building; content addresses key instructional issues and priorities. In-service activities are related to and built on each other; incentives encourage participation.

If you look for it, you'll see it. As you think, you become. These are two statements that are highly philosophical, but both apply equally well to education. They are akin to being prepared, to planning the day or the week or the month. If you look for excellence, you'll start to see it. If you think in terms of excellence, you'll become it. Anything that helps staff and students see the excellence around them and strive to become excellent themselves is good. The more in education who begin to see it and think it, the sooner it will happen in all corners of the building.

9. **Incentives and rewards are used to build strong motivation**

- Excellence in achievement and behavior is recognized. Requirements for awards are clear; explicit procedures ensure consistency; evaluations are typically based on standards rather than on comparisons with peers.
- Awards are set at several different levels of performance, providing all students with opportunities for success and recognition.
- Incentives and rewards are appropriate to student developmental levels, are meaningful to recipients and are structured to build persistence of effort and intrinsic motivation.
- Teaching excellence is recognized. All staff has the opportunity to work for rewards, according to objective, explicit criteria and standards; student achievement is an important success criterion.
- Both formal and informal recognition are used; at least some rewards are made public.

Make something worthwhile and everyone will strive to achieve it. And once it's achieved, let it be known. Toot the horns; celebrate the victory, for education will have just won.

10. Parents are invited to become involved
- Parents have various options for becoming involved in schooling, especially in ways that support the instructional program.
- Procedures for involvement are clearly communicated to parents and used consistently.
- Staff members provide parents with information and techniques for helping students learn, through training sessions or handbooks, for example.

The importance of mom and dad being involved can never be over-stated. The school-home connection is an important element of survival for an effective school. An effective school will want the parents there by the school's side. Not the parents mentioned earlier, but those who care for education, not their own aggrandizement.

11. Teachers and administrators continually strive to improve instructional effectiveness

- Throughout the school there is an ongoing concern for improving instructional effectiveness. No one is complacent about student achievement; there is an expectation that educational programs will be changed so that they work better.
- School improvements are directed at clearly defined student achievement and or social behavior problems; strong agreement is developed within the school concerning the purpose of improvement efforts.
- Priority goals for improvement are set which give focus to planning and implementation. Goals that specify desired changes in achievement or social behavior are known and supported in the school community.
- The full staff is involved in planning for implementation; specific recommendations and guidelines provide the detail needed for good implementation; plans fit the local school context and conditions.
- Implementation is checked carefully and frequently; progress is noted and publicized; activities are modified as necessary to make things work better. Everyone works together to help the improvement effort succeed; staff members discuss implementation and share ideas and approaches.
- Resources are set aside to support improvement activities.
- School improvement efforts are periodically reviewed; progress is noted and the improvement focus is renewed or redirected; successes and new goals are reported.

Plan, plan, plan, implement, observe, evaluate, plan, plan, and plan some more.

12. There are pleasant conditions for learning

- Physical facilities are kept clean and made reasonably attractive; damage is repaired immediately.

Mount Abraham Union High School, in Bristol, Vermont gets the best marks for this. Starting with custodian Leonard Blaise who was

Karl E. Thelen

there when I started teaching in 1980 and continuing to the present with the current head custodian Reggie Wedge, nary a mark on the walls, broken glass or door, or whatever, goes by without being fixed immediately. When things are fixed right away, they stay fixed longer. The previous school I was at never fixed anything and so students just kept making things worse. Beyond that, nothing more need be said.

Whether a school becomes effective or not is up to that school. District mandates don't ensure compliance, nor does it assure that the programs that are implemented are going to be interpreted, or put into practice, as the progenitors envisioned. I've found Dr. Larry Lazotte's words to be true, that if it doesn't happen in both ends of the building, it won't happen at all. Individual teachers can become effective by practicing in their classrooms. But master teachers spattered throughout the building won't make an effective school.

Chapter ten

A Circle of Assessment; How to get there from here

Currently in modern public education, there are two popular methods of assessment, standardized tests and portfolios. Standardized tests, objective in nature, are the result of education's need to know how well its methods are working in the post-industrialized era. Americans want to know where their children are in relation to the neighbors' kids. The quality of education isn't important as long as the test scores are high.

Portfolios, subjective in nature, are the reaction to standardized tests and sit at the opposite most extreme end of the assessment spectrum. The quality of many portfolios isn't important as long as all the pieces are there. Neither method satisfies the need to be assessed for all children. There are large numbers of students who are not gifted in the extremes of subjectivity and objectivity, and therefore don't do well when assessed by those instruments designed to test those skills and bases of knowledge. There has to be another way to determine the true strengths of all students. A circle of assessment, because it would identify student strengths early, would provide the answer.

In its rush to please the locals, public education has allowed itself to be used in a great debate over the best way to determine what students know, a debate that misses the real point altogether. The question shouldn't be centered on whether standardized tests or portfolios best assess student ability, but on the **best way** to assess students, period. To answer such a question, and understand the concept of a circle of assessment, educators need to be well versed in many areas; current assessment tools, both standardized and portfolio style, Gardner's multiple intelligence theories, hemisphericity, learning styles, and memory research. If you know your enemy, you can better defend against it, and here the enemy is the notion that only a standardized test or a well-kept portfolio can tell us what we need to know about any student.

In order to best assess students, school districts also need to be aware of these concepts in order to promote community involvement and to be able to keep track of progress at the board level. All adults involved should be aware of learning styles, brain hemisphere preference, strengths in intelligences, how information is processed and how information goes from short-term to long-term memory. Once this is accomplished, the schools may assess the student with a 'circle of assessment,' a wide variety of tools that draw out a composite of the strengths each student has, from an early age right through their formative years. It would be on this circle of assessment that academic choices could be based, such as acceptance to college, as well as employment, or other areas where the present determining factors are either a standardized test score or an accumulation of portfolio pieces.

The schools of the future, assessing students with a circle of assessment, based on lessons designed around each student's intelligences, enhanced through use of identified learning styles, and reinforced with sound memory concepts, will propel America light years into the future in terms of the students we turn out who will be responsible for the global village for which we had helped them prepare.

Unfortunately, this is not seen in the schools of today which rely too heavily on a testing process that only allows a small number of students to truly shine, and leaves many feeling that they just don't have it. The recent call for a national test of student ability by the President and members of Congress shows the mood in America at present. We don't need true assessment, we need numbers, and preferably numbers that show where we are in relation to each other, as well as where we are in relation to everyone else in the world. Are we smart? Are we number one? And if not, how come, and how do we get there? So says the national mood. Scary? You bet. Along with the call for the national standardized test will be the portfolio advocates calling for national portfolios, keeping stride with the standardized test monkey right into the twenty-first century.

Standardized Testing; The Rush to be Average

Educators need to know and understand the strengths and weaknesses of standardized tests, how many there are and what their true value is. The main tests for high schoolers are the American College Test (ACT) and the Scholastic Aptitude Test (SAT). There are also the standardized tests taken from elementary through graduate school. Each of these tests is designed for a specific purpose, but, as many believe, there are many other skills and qualities students have that are not tested. Also of importance when talking about standardized tests are the value they do serve and how the results can be best used to improve the students' learning.

The tale of the standardized test is a long and sad one. Long in the sense that it seems to all of us baby boomers that they've always been there, following you from elementary school, through junior high and rearing up as ACT/SAT's as graduation nears, and finally holding you hostage to the Graduate Record Exam before admission to graduate school. It's sad because they don't deal every student a fair hand and choices and decisions are made on the hand you're dealt.

In 1947 Educational Testing Service (ETS), the largest, private, non-profit testing and educational research organization, began administering most of the standardized testing done in America.[77] ETS administers the SAT. Since then, the rush to rank, grade and place students has escalated beyond the capacity to prove the actual worth of all the information standardized tests give us. In fact, there is much evidence to point to the ineffectiveness and inequality of many standardized tests.

Since 1959 the (ACT), administered by American College Testing in Iowa City, Iowa, also tested students in large numbers. The ACT and the SAT have evolved into premier examples of standardized tests that are used to determine someone's future; are the students in or are they out?

The use of the two tests, according to B. Denise Hawkins, is split by geography, with larger numbers of students in the Midwest, Southeast, and Southwest taking the ACT, and the rest the SAT. Twenty-two states use the SAT, which tests students on verbal and

---

[77] Hawkins, Denise B., "A Multiple-Choice Mushroom: Schools, Colleges Rely More Than Ever on," Black Issues in Higher Education, 02-09-1995, p. 1

Karl E. Thelen

mathematical skills and reasoning, and twenty-eight states use the ACT, which is longer than the SAT and covers math, English, reading and science reasoning. In 1994, 900,000 students took the ACT, and over a million and a half take the SAT annually.

The SAT is given five times each year around the country at designated sites. There are two parts to the exam, Verbal and Mathematical. Items are best answer multiple choice type and students have three hours to complete the test. Students who read a lot and therefore, generally, have a better vocabulary have the advantage in the verbal section over those who may be as competent but have less developed verbal skill. How well someone does on the test depends less on knowledge of specific information and more on developed skills, such as the ability to use one's vocabulary well even without a strong base of knowledge. The quantitative part of the test measures the ability to deal with ideas rather than mathematical achievement.[78]

The ACT offers a group of four tests on English, mathematics, social studies, and the natural sciences. The claim for the ACT is that it can predict college success, and also includes questions that check for the ability to problem solve when it involves mathematical reasoning and being able to interpret passages. Again, students who are wide read, have a broad vocabulary and have developed critical skills in reading and thinking are at an advantage.

Traditionally, those students who haven't developed the language and mathematical skills so necessary to public education and standardized tests are those who will be told they won't do well in future schoolwork, often based on these tests. And yet, these very students, many of whom have strong spatial, artistic, bodily-kinesthetic, and personal intelligence, are right brain dominant, and have a global learning style, will turn out, in many cases, to be highly productive in society once they leave public education and find their niche in society.

Public education could enhance this process greatly by determining early these preferences and tailoring each child's course on the educational journey for maximum success. This doesn't mean schools should rush out and start providing each child with a one-on-

---

[78] Ahmann, Stanley, Glock, Marvin D., *Evaluating Pupil Growth: Principles of Tests and Measurement*, Boston, Allyn and Bacon, 1968, p. 386

A Nation of Idiots

one course of study, but rather that schools should take the teacher training time and invest the money and create the environment to match groups of students who have the same learning style, brain dominance and intelligence strengths with teachers whose teaching style complements the groups, or have classes where these concepts power the curriculum.

To give an idea of the scope of standardized testing in America, the following testing services are provided for high schools just by ETS, which administers 9 million tests a year; 1.8 million are the SAT; 1.7 million are the PSAT/National Merit Scholarship Qualifying Test; and 701,000 are AP (Advanced Placement) exams.

ETS is also responsible for the National Teachers Exam Core Battery and Pre-Professional Skills Test, the Graduate Record Exam General Test, the Test of English as a Foreign Language, and the Graduate Management Admission Test.

Along with the concern of many that standardized tests don't tell the whole story of a student's ability, are other concerns that have cropped up over the years. The question of bias is one, along with the inability of multiple-choice questions to measure students' capacities, as well as the inability to determine student attitudes and behavior, which is considered to be the "ultimate criterion for measuring student learning."[79]

Other concerns are that teachers, in order to raise test scores to prove efficacy, tend to teach to the test, focusing on only those concepts or areas of knowledge specifically targeted by the specific test. This is especially true where teacher performance is tied directly to the scores; if the students' scores don't go up, the teacher loses money. The need to show mastery or improvement in the standardized scores causes many teachers to do what they have to in order to survive.

Another concern is the very real phenomenon of "test phobia." Many bright, capable students freeze up when the stakes are high and never get the correct answers on the paper. Also, standardized tests only test for a few skills and abilities, tend to be left hemispheric in brain dominance, and only show the results of those with analytical study skills. The critics who say the tests don't test every student's

---

[79] Travis, Jon E., "Meaningful Assessment," Vol. 69, The Clearing House, 05-15-1996, p308.

ability have a case. Many students just never get the chance to show what they really know.

The strongest concerns are that the tests are biased, strongly favoring those students, as has already been mentioned, who have a strong vocabulary, read a lot, and are left brain dominant. The tests rely heavily on multiple-choice questions, which lack the ability to see the student's reasoning or how they process the information in order to make the choices they do. The tests don't measure attitude or behavior, those qualities that many consider to be more important determiners of a person's future ability and success.

Along with test phobia enters the whole concept of learning styles, which includes the best time to take an exam, which would be at different times for large populations of students. The fact that these test scores can follow you through life adds yet one last caveat to the long list against using standardized tests as a sole determining factor in anyone's life. College acceptance is a good example.

Portfolios; You Show Me Yours and I'll Show You Mine

Portfolios have been sweeping the country in the last few years and seem to be gaining speed, even though critics have been warning about the dangers of using such a subjective, and in many cases vague, means of assessing students' potential and learning. Having been on the state portfolio committee in Vermont in 1990-91 at its inception, I have first-hand experience in how the question of using portfolios originated and also, because of that process, have developed a fear of an assessment tool that only benefits a small segment of our students. However, by state law, portfolio assessment is required in Vermont.

Portfolios found their way into the American educational vocabulary in the eighties. There were many educators in favor of the subjective means of assessment that was going to revolutionize assessment, and thereby learning, when they first came on the scene. There were also those who deemed portfolios too cumbersome, too costly, and too open to the subjective whims of the (often unqualified) teachers' evaluation process.

The idea of the portfolio has a history in the visual arts where a compilation of one's work is a must. Originally it would include illustrations or samples of past performance of a designer, artist or photographer. What was placed in a portfolio was always the best of the person's efforts, the artist's 'public self.' "The public self represents the way one desires to be viewed by others-those aspects one consciously wishes to communicate to others and display to the external world-and sometimes it represents a mask worn for presentation to others."[80]

The portfolio would give prospective employers a good idea as to whether or not the applicant has the skills necessary to do the job they need done. Under these circumstances the portfolio was a good idea and made sense. However, once the educational pundits got hold of the concept, it started to become a problem to others.

One of the problems that surfaced early was the fact that portfolios required enormous investments of time on the part of the teacher, after, of course, the teacher was "trained" in scoring the very subjective contents of the academic portfolio. Training these raters of the portfolios in order to be consistent, fair and accurate requires time, effort, and a lot of money, first for the field trials that are necessary to check for validity and reliability, and then for the cost of teacher training and implementation. The standards to which all students are to be held need to be explicit.

That concern was compounded by the fact that in order for there to be common standards among individual scorers, the same criteria of judgment has to be used by everyone in the same way, something that's hard to achieve. During training as evaluators, many teachers wanted to ignore the standards and help the borderline students who were failing. Many were concerned that their decision would raise or lower a student's score, adding to the already subjective nature of the assessment tool.

When it comes to having well trained portfolio evaluators, the track record is not impressive. Inadequate training and consequent low reliability are the norm. It would take between ten and twenty-three separate portfolio tasks, all of which must be laboriously hand scored, to reach an acceptable level of meaningful results.

When the New York State Regents exam began using elements of portfolio assessment, "some teachers had 120 portfolios to score,

---

[80] Castiglione, Lawrence V., "Portfolio assessment in art and education," Vol. 97, Arts and Education Policy Review, 03-13-1996, pp2

taking 35-40 minutes each to grade."[81] The time element involved with the portfolio process can become prohibitive.

The headlong rush to get away from standardized tests by embracing the portfolio model leaves education with the same problem it had before, how to assess everyone so that their strengths are allowed to shine and be made relevant to their lives. Standardized testing showed us the strengths of those who were good readers, with strong vocabulary and math skills. The portfolio showed us the strengths of those who were arty in nature and were traditionally left out to dry as far as being labeled as smart or competent enough in public education to go on to the next educational level. There are, however, many positive qualities to portfolios as will be shown when the argument for inclusion in the circle of assessment is made. There are very different assumptions and objectives measured by norm-referenced (standardized tests) and performance based (portfolios) approaches. The two forms of assessment give different inferences from the data. There are differing underlying assumptions inherent in each.

Multiple Intelligences; The More the Merrier

The theory of multiple intelligences is important to understand since the purpose of the circle of assessment is to show the strengths of all students, and, as you will see, the various intelligences each of us possesses can be brought out in all students, especially when they become aware of the possibilities. There's something good that happens when a student realizes for the first time that they are intelligent in some way, and that this intelligence had been exhibited for years in their hobbies and strong interests outside of school. It's time for public education to take the initiative and have the foresight to involve all these students in their education and help them gain more by identifying and promoting their strong suits. Intelligences in the multiple intelligence theory have specific learning styles attached and lessons can be developed that complement those qualities.

In 1983 Howard Gardner, a Harvard professor, wrote a book called <u>Frames of Mind: The Theory of Multiple Intelligence</u>. Here Gardner made the case for seven intelligences, opposing the

---

[81] Ibid., p. 6

A Nation of Idiots

traditional belief that you were either intelligent or not, that there could be a scale to show just where you were in relation to everyone else. The original intelligences were linguistic, logical-mathematical, spatial, bodily kinesthetic, musical, interpersonal, and intrapersonal. Individuals are born with potential in all intelligences, but develop preferences, or strengths, as they mature depending on cultural contexts, as well as personal and local influences.

Linguistic intelligence deals with language, one of the more complicated tasks students have. It isn't enough just to know how to talk and write your name. Comprehension, interpretation, analytical power, and construction are all necessary components of language. One who is linguistically intelligent can write well, read well, speak well, and can use his language to his advantage.

Logical-mathematical intelligence gives the analytical side of the student. Having this intelligence in abundance allows one to see deeply into issues and problems and make educated decisions. Logical-mathematical intelligence involves calculating, analyzing and doing experiments. The learning styles are categorizing, classifying and working with abstract patterns.

Spatial intelligence allows students the ability to see things as they would be in space, how to fill up their environment. It involves drawing, building, designing and creating things. The learning styles most closely related would be working with pictures, colors and visualizing.

Bodily-kinesthetic intelligence gives the student the ability to dance and perform. Students understand and can use the mechanics of the body. Bodily-kinesthetic intelligence is when the body processes knowledge through bodily sensations which is why these students learn through touching, moving and interacting with space.

Musical intelligence is responsible for song and an appreciation of music and its affect on the soul. It involves singing, humming, and listening to music. Students with this intelligence learn best by listening to rhythms and melodies.

Interpersonal intelligence helps the student understand others, and opens a large number of doors in the areas of psychology, sociology, medicine and other areas where understanding and relating to others is important. Interpersonal intelligence is developed in people who are good at working with others. Their learning style is through sharing, comparing and cooperating with others.

Intrapersonal intelligence is the ability to understand oneself. It is this that keeps us in tune with ourselves, keeps us on the right path, and helps us know ourselves so well. This intelligence involves those who like to work alone and understand their self well. Their learning style is by doing individualized projects and self-paced instruction.

At the present, Gardner has added an eighth intelligence: naturalist intelligence. This intelligence gives everyone the ability to relate to their environment in terms of its importance to every living thing and the interconnectedness of life on earth. A possible ninth intelligence, existential intelligence (the ability to look at larger questions of one's existence), is being looked at as of this writing.

The intelligences line up with other aspects of the circle of assessment in terms of the ways people learn. For example, those who are dominant in linguistic intelligence, which includes reading, writing, storytelling, and speaking, learn best by saying, hearing and seeing words. Class work that leans toward these activities would most benefit these students.

These intelligences and their corresponding learning styles are strong arguments for losing the current attachment on both standardized tests and portfolios as determining factors for every student's success or failure. Both of these assessment tools have a place in the circle of assessment, but as equal tools with all the others, not as holy grails of assessment.

Hemisphericity; Am I In My Right Mind?

A case for a circle of assessment has to include Hemisphericity. The concept of Hemisphericity has been around since the early eighties, but only now is it catching on to the point that lessons are utilizing the concept of left and right brain functions and their corresponding learning styles and repositories for the various intelligences.

Hemisphericity will determine many preferences for the student, whether or not the student and teacher are aware of it. Preferences include the environment, cool or warm; the noise level, loud or quiet; the manner of taking in information, verbal or visual; the social aspects, working with others or alone; organized or not; and how we see and understand, globally or analytically. These qualities greatly affect a student's ability to take in and process information, and the outcome can be a student who's considered smart or not so smart. It's been shown that having an awareness of these concepts on the part of the teacher enhances student learning.

The left side of the brain is responsible for organization, the analytical side, knowing the answer, getting right to the problem and solving it. It is the no nonsense side. It works best alone. It likes bright lights when working, a quiet environment, a little on the cool side and everything needed to complete the task right there in front of it.

The right side is the creative side, the side that falls in love, the dreamy side. It is here that dance is created and song is sung. There isn't much organization on this side. It's the global side, where the big picture needs to be seen to make any sense. They'll get things done, but in their own time. The right side doesn't mind distractions while working, likes the lights down a bit, so it's comfortable. The environment should be on the warm side. It likes to work with other right brains.

Both sides of the brain are distinctive in their approach to learning, and both exhibit specific characteristics that can be identified so that students, knowing where their strengths are, can best direct their educational efforts to their advantage. Standardized testing only tests for left side knowledge, the memorizing side. Portfolios, on the other hand, only test for right side knowledge. Depending on which form of assessment is used students can look either smart or not so smart. Depending on which tool the college of their choice prefers can determine acceptance or rejection.

When the SAT's are used as a sole or main criterion, then the right-brain dominant students have less of a chance to be accepted. When the determining factor is based on a portfolio, the right-brained students, the artistic students who tend to keep portfolios anyway, have the upper hand.

It should be noted that we are not solely left brain dominant or right brain dominant. We all use our entire brain, but the majority of the time our preference dominates. A large section of the population could be called whole brain dominant since this is where approximately 60% of the people are. The extremes on either end would give us our most talented artists and more prominent scientists.

When the traits of hemisphericity and Gardner's multiple intelligences are compared to each other, more in terms of overlays rather than straight comparisons, we can see very obvious parallels. Gardner's linguistic and logical-mathematical intelligences would be akin to the left-brain dominant student under the concept of hemisphericity. Whereas those who are gifted in linguistic and logical-mathematical intelligences do well on standardized tests as well as public school in general, so, too, is it true with those who test out as left brain dominant. The other intelligences (spatial, body-kinesthetic, musical, interpersonal, intrapersonal, and naturalist) do better under the portfolio system. At the same time, they correspond directly to the right brain dominant traits of being the creative ones, the ones who become our architects, sculptors, actors, carpenters, dancers, social workers, and environmentalists.

Knowing the above will help teachers design and implement lessons that incorporate the various intelligences and hemispheric preference. The Educational Kinesiology Foundation, founded by Paul and Gail Dennison, is one such example of what can be done with the information on intelligences and left-right brain research.

The Educational Kinesiology Foundation has created a long list of activities that can help put students in the right frame of mind (the correct hemisphere) depending on the material being learned. Through their 'Brain Gym' presentations and world-wide network of educators who are promoting the concepts they advocate, the Dennisons are reaching many of the students I have mentioned who traditionally don't do well in public education. In one book that they produced on whole brain integration, it says "…Switch on to a deeper level of brain performance and a deeper appreciation of your uniqueness through an understanding of your own hemispheric dominance and how to maximize your innate potential through movement (kinesthetic)."

The Foundation is just one example of many in the field of education where these concepts of everyone having intelligences are being put into practice with positive results that can be repeated by others.

To enhance the dominant quality or intelligence inherent in each student; activities, assignments, and lessons can be tailored to those students, allowing each to shine in their strength.

Learning Styles; If The Shoe Fits, Wear It

Learning styles is another important concept that needs to be addressed, and the tie-in with multiple intelligence and hemisphericity makes one wonder why these concepts haven't been joined together before now. Each student has their own way of learning, and as it is with the hemispheres of the brain, so it is with the classifying of the different ways we take in and use information. Each style is unique to a specific preference and each preference has identifiable qualities that can be brought out and worked with to enhance learning. Some students learn best in early morning, others in late afternoon; some learn best by doing, and some by listening; some learn better from adults, and some from their peers. The circle of assessment will take into account all the various styles of learning, the student's hemispheric preferences, and the various strengths according to multiple intelligence theory.

Thanks to the work of Rita Dunn, we can recognize these learning style traits at an early age and direct each student to their most successful track of learning.

The main component of a person's learning style, according to Dunn, is the way "that he or she concentrates on, processes, internalizes, and remembers new and difficult academic information or skills. Styles often vary with age, achievement level, culture, global versus analytic processing, and gender."[82] In the learning styles concept there are twenty-three elements in five basic strands. These compose each person's environmental, emotional, sociological, physiological and psychological processing preferences.

These preferences can be identified in students by using the Learning Style Inventory (LSI) for grades 3-12. The LSI assesses individual preferences in the following areas:
1. Immediate environment-sound, light, temperature, and seating design;
2. Emotionality-motivation, persistence, responsibility/ conformity, and the need for internal or external structure;

---

[82] Shaughnessy, Michael F, "An Interview with Rita Dunn About Learning Styles," Vol. 71, The Clearing House, 01/11/1998, p. 1

3. Sociological-learning alone or in a pair, as part of a group or team, with peers, or with an adult, in a variety of ways, or in a consistent pattern;
4. Physiological-auditory, visual, tactual, kinesthetic perceptual preference, food or liquid needs, time of day energy levels and mobility needs;
5. Global or analytical processing inclinations-through correlation with sound, light, design, persistence, peer-orientation, and intake scores;

Knowing the students' preferences, specifically by using the LSI, helps the learning process by doing the following:

- Lets the student know how they prefer to learn, suggests a way to redesign the classroom to accommodate the learning styles.
- Explains which students need direction and which do not, shows the order of studying for each student and how to be successful, indicates the way the student is likely to achieve.
- Shows which students are conforming and which are not and how to deal with both.
- Indicates the best time of day when students will learn best, when their energy high is.
- Identifies students who need to snack or move around, suggest which students are analytical and which are global in their approach to learning.

When these preferences are adhered to, the students increase their ability to process information and retain it.

"A meta-analysis of forty-two experimental studies conducted with the Dunn and Dunn model between 1980 and 1990 by thirteen different institutions of higher education revealed that students whose characteristics were accommodated by educational interventions responsive to their learning styles could be expected to achieve 75 percent of a standard deviation higher than students whose styles were not accommodated. (Dunn 1995).

"In addition, practitioners throughout the United States have reported statistically higher test scores and grade point averages for students whose teachers changed from traditional teaching to learning style teaching at all levels-elementary, secondary, and college. Improved achievement was often apparent after only six weeks of learning style instruction. After one year, teachers reported significantly higher standardized achievement and aptitude test scores for students who had not scored well previously."[83]

Using assessment instruments already in place for learning styles, hemisphericity, and intelligences, we are half way to assessing the whole student and have many of the openings on the circle of assessment filled in.

Memory; The Long and Short of It

Understanding how information goes from short-term memory to long-term memory is a must for all teachers. Being aware of the various phases of memory can help teachers plan lessons accordingly. Knowing how to present material and then enhance retention, how to help students push information on so they can remember it for later use, would be much more advantageous than to continue with the status quo, allowing a large segment of our student population to leave school with much less than they should have had, and not knowing what they had all along.

Teachers need to know how people take in, transfer and store information. It's important to know that some students take in information best if they hear it, while others need to see it, and still others need to touch it. What is relevant to our everyday lives will become long-term memory, which means the skills and abilities that our education can help us focus on and develop need to be done so in the most effective manner possible. Eventually, a circle of assessment will guide teachers and students to their strengths in order to effectively enhance learning. Storing that learning for future retrieval or synthesis is important.

A person's memory affects many of the skills needed in order to do well in public education. Reading and comprehension are memory dependent. If you remember what the big words mean when you come to them in your reading, then your memory is working. If you don't have a developed memory your reading rate will be slow and your comprehension weak.

---

[83] Ibid., p. 4

Memory, then, is your thought process; how well you take in what you are learning and how well you store and retrieve what you have learned. A well-developed thought process includes a relevant knowledge base, careful observation and classification of ideas, reflection and elaboration of those ideas, self-assessment, appropriate application, and feedback from an appropriate source.[84]

According to Bereiter, use of knowledge (transfer) occurs when the student can draw from a personal experience that is relevant to the current experience. Since this transfer of knowledge is rarely spontaneous, it can be taught. This is where the teachers come in who are well versed in how and why memory works, along with the background and expertise in the previous concepts of multiple intelligences, learning styles, and hemisphericity.

It is for these reasons that a teacher needs to know the various strategies students use to take in, process, store, and retrieve information. The more a teacher knows, the more he can model for the students, and the more their learning will be enhanced. Therein lies the case for a circle of assessment.

Carol Turkington, in her book 12 Steps to a Better Memory, says that there are three stages to memory; registration, retention, and recall.[85] We first register the information as we perceive it and file it away in our short-term memory, a place that doesn't have a lot of room. Information here will be lost in a minute or so as other information comes in. Somehow, it has to be pushed on to long-term memory.

Storing this information involves making connections or associations between words, meanings, visual imagery, or other things such as smell or sounds. We remember well when the material we want to remember is related to something in our experience. Teachers can get that job done if they are prepared to do so (effective teaching theory and memory theory) and if they have the means to assess (circle of assessment) what it is they need to relate it to (intelligence or hemispheric preference) and the manner in which it will be transferred most successfully (learning style).

---

[84] Jacobson, Rebecca, "Teachers improving learning using metacognition with self-monitoring learning strategies," Vol. 118, Education, 06/22/1998, p. 579.
[85] Turkington, Carol, 12 Steps to a Better Memory, New York, Macmillan, 1996

What will it mean when the circle of assessment is in use all around the nation? Heck, the world? Well, it will mean that we finally 'got it.' We finally realized that all of our students are important (not in the Feelgood sense), and that that importance will be demonstrated in the concern public education shows in how it determines the strengths of <u>all</u> students at an early age, that they are followed through the years in their learning and maturation, and their education is designed to enhance these strengths, not deny them, and teachers are trained to do so.

Once the concepts outlined here are part of the everyday life in public education, we will be online for the twenty-first century. Teachers, knowing that a student is right brain dominant, will not assume he or she is a slow reader when they don't read as well as other students (a left brain dominant, linguistic intelligence activity), but will have tapes of the reading material available for those students to listen to while they read so that their reading speed and comprehension is increased. It will be understood how they read (globally, auditorily) so their activities will be geared for that style of learning (auditory, tactile). It will be understood why they have the preference they do (right brain dominance, bodily-kinesthetic intelligence) and that will be O.K. Labels are gone, since no one learning style, hemispheric preference, or intelligence is better, stronger, faster than any other. The playing field is leveled and students in the end are judged on their true capacities.

Standardized tests will still be around since they do have value in testing for the specific reading and math skills that left-brain dominant and mathematically and linguistically intelligent students possess. These tests start at position one in the circle of assessment. There are many of them and they can be tweaked to test for various skills and can range from minimal educationally loaded tests (measuring knowledge independent of specific instruction) to maximum educationally loaded tests (measuring educational achievement). They are by their nature a summative evaluation tool, showing what the student has accumulated over the semester or years, an evaluation that is a concluding measurement designed to evaluate an end result, the "terminal phase," according to Castiglione in

"Portfolio assessment in art and education."[86] Also, portfolios, when used to assess the right brain dominant traits, artistic, spatial, and bodily-kinesthetic intelligences, work fine. Portfolios on the circle of assessment are directly opposite standardized tests. They are formative in their evaluation style, just what is needed when planning, modifying, and adapting individualized instruction, or when data is needed that is useful for teachers.

Portfolios are at their strongest when they are used to improve student learning and not assess achievement. They belong on the circle of assessment because of their ability to show observable, concrete illustrations of what the student is able to do for actual classroom assignments, as well as show the difficulties and problems encountered during learning. Portfolios can be full of meaning when viewed in the proper context. The portfolio results constitute a strong foundation for assessing student needs, which is required before future instruction can take place.

As we move around the circle of assessment, there is a melding of the objective and the subjective. Other types of assessment to be included are performance-based tasks, which focus on the arts and athletics where performance is the end result; authentic assessment, designed to reflect the skills needed in life. This focuses on student task performance and is relevant to the student's experiences; journal or log writing can be used in assessment as a direct link between the teacher and the student, as well as a motivation for writing; interviews involve direct personal communication between the teacher, student, parents, or other teachers.

This type of assessment reveals student thinking as well as mastery and achievement. On the down side, it is time consuming. However, it is still a valuable tool for assessing students with global learning styles in order to see if they have the whole picture, which gives meaning and relevance to their understanding.

Attitude inventories can identify good and bad feelings and attitudes about school personnel and activities. Although not widely used, these inventories can be a valuable tool, which would provide substantial benefits.

---

[86] Castiglione, Lawrence V., "Portfolio assessment in art and education," Vol. 97, Arts Education Policy Review, 03-13-1996, p. 2.

Learning styles assessments have been in use for some time now and can identify the specific conditions that would provide each student the most ideal conditions by which they could enhance their learning; these forms of assessment are mostly for student summative evaluation.

The classroom assessment model, used for formative evaluation and designed to improve teaching and learning, can help teachers discover how students are learning and what instructional methods work best for those students. There are fifty assessment techniques considered simple to learn, adapt, and implement.

So, the work before educators is obvious, the tools are available; we just need to organize the work force. This is the hard part. Thanks to Rita Dunn, an assessment tool is already in place and in use to determine where the students' strengths are in terms of their personal learning style. It's now a matter of matching students' learning styles with teaching styles and rearrange the current classroom makeup to accommodate these concepts.

Thanks to Howard Gardner we can also use available instruments to determine the students' strengths in terms of intelligences and their preferences, which in turn show where the students' best chances for success are.

The teachers of the future will need to be schooled in each of the concepts. Colleges need to change their teacher programs to encompass the newest research in order to be most successful in their efforts to enhance student learning. Some old 'gatekeepers' will have to break out of their impervious cocoons of 'been there, done that.'

Communities, if they're serious about education, will have to vote in the money to pull the circle of assessment model off. Teachers need to be retrained, schools need to be rearranged in a big way, and if the community isn't behind the effort, it won't work. The students' welfare is at stake, which really means the future of America.

We can't continue as we have been, assessing, and therefore 'teaching' only with standardized testing or portfolios in mind. We need a new mind, a broader mind, encompassing much more than we do now, one where we show kids what they are capable of and then show them how to achieve it. The future is at the door, and we need teachers capable of opening it, of getting us from here to there. An all-encompassing Circle of Assessment will be the vehicle to help us do it.

Kahail Gibran wrote in The Prophet, "...He that is indeed wise (the teacher) does not bid you enter the house of his wisdom, but rather leads you to the threshold of your own mind."[87] As teachers, we have our job cut out for us. Assessing our children is most important and the students cannot be pawns in a silly game of best methods of assessment and test scores. If we can get the students to the threshold of their minds by showing them their own preferences and intelligences, we will have demonstrated wisdom. We will also be on the way to repopulating **A Nation of Idiots**.

---

[87] Jacobson, Rebecca, "Teachers improving learning using metacognition with self-monitoring learning strategies," Vol. 118, 06-22-1998, p. 579.

Chapter eleven

Things That I Do; Time to toot

I'm not the best teacher in the world. I make mistakes, back up and try again. I step on toes, I have good days and I have bad days. There are days when I think I've made the greatest of breakthroughs and there are days when I wonder why I'm there. Some days the students are friendly, other days they're not. Sometimes my colleagues make sense, and sometimes they don't. I'm sure it's that way for them, too. But one thing I can say for sure is that I'm always making an effort to follow the path laid out to become an effective teacher. It's a direction, so I keep going.

I try things that make sense at the time, but, like most things, know it takes a few times to get it the way it was originally envisioned. Practice makes you better, so I practice.

Some of the things that I do are my own creation, many are stolen ideas, borrowed from other teachers, or students. After a three-year statute of limitations, I pretend they were my ideas all along. I'm especially pleased with the ideas I've picked up from students along the way, because they quite often have more insight into what's going on and how to make the lesson more effective than I do. Sometimes we can be too close to something to see it clearly and need someone else to point out the obvious.

There's no particular order to the following list, but I'll start with day one. After twenty-three years at my present school, many students come in to my class with a healthy fear of '**Mister Mean**.' I stole the persona of Mr. Mean from Erv Heneche, who used to teach at Moriah Central HS, in Port Henry, NY. He was the original Mr. Mean, but then he retired, so I stole the character. It's a good one, and carries a lot of weight.

Karl E. Thelen

In the guise of Mr. Mean, I can get away with a lot of expectations nice teachers can't. I can expect 30 pages of reading a night and laugh when they complain. (It can't be just any kind of laugh, though. There should be some flair to it, a haunting quality. It should never be mocking, or hurtful). I can give a test, get the results and refuse to allow redo's since that only encourages sloth. I can push the students a little harder; achieve a comfortable 'level of frustration' that we all need to get motivated. Mr. Mean has high expectations.

Being Mr. Mean also makes class discipline easier since most students coming in to class have already heard what the expectations are. It takes about three years of being in a particular school for most of the students to know you as someone who has always been there. It's at that point that the most successful management plan works since, by then, the students know you and your expectations. They tend to take you more seriously now, as you're no longer the 'new' teacher. That's just something new teachers should know up front, rather than wonder, at some point, why some kids don't respond in a positive manner and, instead, treat them more like a substitute. It's akin to taking over the reins of a twenty-mule team. It just takes a while to get the hang of it.

There's even an official Mr. Mean song, which I sing to my students, and they have to listen because I have my grading pen out. It goes like this:

>I'm mister mean
>I'm the meanest teacher you've ever seen
>I'll give you an F
>And never an A
>'Cause that's the thing
>That makes my day
>Because I'm mister mean
>Ah ha ha ha ha ha ha (ah, that laugh…)

Whether every teacher has a song I'm not sure is important, but it's something to think about.

Outside my door, for the first week, and during Open House, is a large white wooden sign, with black lettering, that says '**Welcome To The Wonderful World Of English10**' (The sign was the work of a student). The sign is there for several reasons. First, I like to display

A Nation of Idiots

student work. When I get to the Museum, I'll say more. Students should know that what they do is worthy of display. In this particular instance, several years after the student who made the sign had graduated, she came back one night during Open House. As she was going past my room she saw her project and brightened up. "You still have my sign," she said. It was obvious that she was delighted. I told her I never threw anything away that was of quality work. When I retire, the sign goes with me.

Secondly, having that sign there, and obviously this is part of my own evolution, begins a subtle indoctrination into the wonders that can be achieved when you work a little for it. I will reinforce the idea that English is a wonderful world, and that many dreams can be achieved by using the language well.

Thirdly, I want to establish a **'feeling tone'** before anyone even comes in my room. Atmosphere, the way a class feels, is important. More good can happen when the students are comfortable, even if they don't know why. If the atmosphere is established ahead of time, it's easily maintained.

Students have to have a three-ring binder **notebook**. Large rings. This is the start of forcing them to stay organized. They won't do it on their own. They aren't any better than adults. In this notebook, starting with a table of contents on which every paper is listed and numbered, the students will keep everything they do; all tests, all notes, all writings, and all handouts. Among these handouts will be important papers, such as information on **Gardner's Intelligences**, **Hemisphericity**, a quote by **Oliver Wendell Holmes**, a **greeting card**, a **hemisphericity test**, a **correction sheet** and the infamous **Page 3**, which contains the expectations and a basic outline of what will be covered throughout the year. All papers are given a page number. All papers have a heading of some sort so they can be listed in the table of contents more easily and to make sure everyone is calling it by the same name so we can find it quickly.

The notebook, as it fills up, will become a working resource. Because of the notebook, I am able to work on essays for a while, have the students put the work back in their notebooks, and come back to it some other time. Very few students ever use the excuse they 'lost' it or just can't find it. I tell them that they have ten seconds to find any particular piece of paper or page that we had previously been working on. We waste very little time. This works particularly well if

I want to briefly review the key concepts before we do another speech, for example. All I have to say is "Would you turn to your speech key concepts page please," and within ten seconds everyone is there. I can then review what they need to pay attention to while doing their speech. This slight reinforcement can mean a big difference on the final result. I check the notebooks at least once every quarter and the grade is tripled because it's an on-going long-term assignment, and the triple grade indicates importance.

All students who wish to pass will keep a **journal.** First of all, writing is good for you. It cleans out the mind. If you're angry, it helps get the anger out. If you're sad, put the sadness on paper where it can't keep you down for long. Writing it away works. Confession is good for the soul. The students are told ahead of time that in Vermont, and hopefully in other states as well, it's a law that teachers are required to notify a counselor if they write about suicide or abuse of any kind. That way, if they write about it, it makes it easier to tell someone in a capacity to do something about it. It's a good law.

Secondly, journals are a historical record, documenting that particular school year for that particular student. I encourage all students to keep their journal after they leave my class, although I know many do not. Much of what we know about anyone who may be considered famous we found out through their journals. Many children kept journals on the westward migration of the pioneers, which is how we know of many of the hardships suffered by families in their punishing environment. My wife uses some of these journals in her fifth grade class to teach about the Oregon Trail and related matters. Journals are important written records.

Thirdly, I think journals are important because they give any student the opportunity, if they so choose to use it, to look back on themselves through out the year and see growth. We grow so slowly day-by-day that we rarely see it. When someone has documented something so important, its value can't be argued. Students often comment on just that; that they had gone back to the beginning of their journal and read what they wrote and couldn't believe they had changed so much.

For most people, writing seems to take a lot of effort. What takes the effort, actually, is sitting there trying to think of the perfect thing to start with. Many students, as well as adults, think that writing means starting at the beginning of something and going straight through to the end. Writing is anything but that. Good writing may start with just an ending and the writer may work backwards to the beginning. Or write the middle first, and then come up with a beginning.

That's why we do **five-minute writings**: non-stop writing exercises to clean out previous knowledge that has been compacted by a summer of fun things into brown, crusty stuff, so a beginning to their writing can be found easily. Students write without stopping, without thinking about what they are writing, for five minutes (I actually go for three on most occasions because their little hands get tired). They can't stop to erase or cross out. They can't stop to correct mistakes. These things interfere with the developing train of thought. Just keep writing. I also have them write while listening to 'white noise,' or, as one left-brain dominant student noted, "Irritating music... to help the right brainers."

Five-minute writings are designed to not only clean out the crap, but to help develop a train of thought. Once students get the hang of it and just allow what's already there to come out, they begin to see that all writing starts the same. No one starts with the 'perfect' beginning. Just start writing and fix it later. Get what you know down on paper so you can work on it. Once the idea of 'perfect' writing is eliminated, the 'flow' is easier to turn on at will.

Page 3 I'm particularly pleased with. Over the years, Page 3 has taken on almost mystical proportions. Page 3 is my list of expectations that lets the students know what we'll be covering and other expectations. It explains the notebooks, journals, and table of contents, about no hats being worn (basic common courtesy), what to bring to class each time, how much to read, and so on. It will be, obviously, the third page in their notebooks.

Whenever a student asks me something that is already listed on Page 3, I say "Read Page 3." Sometimes they'll get angry with me for not answering, and a Feelgooder would wag his finger at me and shake his head, but the students need to make the effort. Often other students in the room will answer for me and say to another student "Read Page 3." Sometimes a student will say "Mr. Thelen, oh, never mind, I know, read Page 3," and they do and answer their own question. I think it's important that much of the burden of their education is on them. Page 3 is designed to make my life easier and, in the long run, theirs too.

Karl E. Thelen

I spend a lot of time correcting tests, as all teachers do. When the tests are written answers, short or long, I not only grade the answer, I also make corrections to spelling, grammar, punctuation, usage, and so on. This takes a lot of effort. Each student is given, as part of an initial packet of things they'll need in my class, a Correction Sheet. This sheet is designed to eliminate all the errors they personally make by the end of the year. It works for those who want it to, which is usually most of the students. Whatever corrections I've made on their papers, they now have to transfer to their correction sheets. The sheet is divided across the top into Spelling, Punctuation, Grammar, Usage, and Legibility.

The first thing the student has to do is identify the paper the corrections are being taken from, whether it's a five-minute writing, or a specific essay test or whatever. This just keeps things organized, which is important for the correction sheet to work.

For each word they spelled wrong, they have to write that word, spelled correctly, once on their correction sheet. It isn't punishment; I just want them to be aware of how the word is spelled. This way they can focus on the spelling and not on finishing twenty-nine more of the same word. A lot of students just write one letter at a time, thirty times, then go on to the next letter, never learning how to spell the word. That's what happens when it's punishment.

If they made the most common error I see and didn't capitalize the beginning of a sentence, they have to write the entire rule 'Begin a sentence with a capital.' once for each time they didn't capitalize a sentence. The second most common error, at the tenth grade level, is not putting a period at the end of a sentence. For this, the rule 'Put a period at the end of a sentence.' is written once for each time they didn't put a period. I will also mark it wrong if they didn't put a period at the end of **that** sentence when they write it down.

Usage, in many respects, is straightened out. I pay special attention to those common maligned utterings such as gonna, coulda, shoulda, woulda, me and my mom, who and whom, good and well, kinda, sorta, alot and my favorite, Ioun't. It isn't long (because they get tired of putting it on the correction sheet) before most students are writing going to, could have, should have, would have, my mother and I, kind of, a lot, and I don't know. (This last one I got from my daughter. "Where are you going?" "Ioun't know").

A Nation of Idiots

Anything I can't read is considered illegible, and I can read a lot of disparate handwritings. Anything marked with a wavy line, question mark, or circled (assuming it's not a misspelled word), has to be written neatly in the legibility column.

This is a lot of work on my part and the students' but it's important work and needs to be done. I also make sure it's done right. I tell the students, and then I make sure I do it, that I will take every paper they have made corrections from, along with their corrections sheet, and go over every paper over the weekend to make sure that they did what they were supposed to. I wish every teacher did this, but I know they don't, otherwise I wouldn't be spending so much time on these simple corrections when the students are fifteen years old.

It isn't long before I see a dramatic difference in the quality of what they are writing, not only in terms of content, but the structure as well. Well-punctuated, grammatically correct writing, with proper usage is much more pleasurable to read.

Also in their notebooks they will have information on Hemisphericity. Everyone has preferences in terms of which side of the brain is used most. Each side controls different aspects of how we learn and what we do with that learning. It's already been covered so I won't dwell on it here other than to point out the difference it makes to many students to know that the reason they may seem slow within the public school system is because they are right brain dominant and public education is set up for left brain dominant people. Right brain dominant students learn differently and they need to know that. I've heard some students say, after finishing the hemisphericity test, "So, I'm not stupid, I'm just right brained."

Understanding hemisphericity helps the students know why I tend to say something I want them to know and then, to the best of my ability, show it to them at the same time. I not only say the new vocabulary words, but I show a card with the word on it, then I write the definitions on a large piece of oak tag. It's also why I'll explain the entire process of what we are doing so that the right brain dominant students, who see things globally, will understand where we are going. Once they understand where they have to get to, they are able to do the work much more successfully, since now it makes sense to them.

I give my students a list of Gardner's Intelligences (I try to update, but this field is moving fast). The reason is the same as for

Karl E. Thelen

Hemisphericity. The more they know about how they learn, and that everyone has intelligence, the more they can be more successful than they otherwise would have been. Again, there's a need to-know-basis for all students that public education was designed for only two of the intelligences, Linguistic, or Language, and Math. Unless students today are good in those two disciplines they may feel left out in a public school.

Oliver Wendell Holmes earns a place in the notebook, with his quote 'The human mind once stretched to a new idea, never goes back to its original dimension.' I tell my students that this is what I'm going to do to them. It's easy for Mr. Mean. I will stretch their minds, and no matter how they try, they'll never be able to go back to their original dimension. Feelgooders would say I'm unnecessarily scaring all the boys and girls, but I say they need to know what it is that I'm going to be doing, and I tell them exactly how I'm going to do it. Sometimes they help me do it. I will reinforce this concept of their mind expanding, mostly with new knowledge, new ideas, throughout the year.

Complementing this idea is a large banner I have hanging, and this one has been there many years, that says 'Those who think with greater meaning will want the words with which to do it.' It means that as our horizons, our concepts, our understandings grow; our vocabulary needs to expand as well in order to express those larger ideas. I hammer this theme home often, and make no bones about the fact that that's what I intend to do. Forewarned is forearmed. I **will** make them think with greater meaning, and **I** will give them the words with which to do it. I get a big kick whenever I overhear a student say, "Hey, I just thought with greater meaning."

Also in their opening packet for the notebook is a computer generated greeting card, unfolded. I tell them this is their first intelligence test in my room and that they have 30 seconds to fold it correctly. Go!

In all the years that I have been doing this, only one young lady, who became extremely flustered by the time limit, was unable to do it. I told her that due to the possibility that I hadn't given clear directions, she would have a ten-second extension. She completed the folding in that time. To my knowledge, she never suffered any long-term damage.

On the front of the card it says 'Welcome to the Wonderful World of English 10.' (Ah,ha) I explain to them why it is a wonderful world; it will help the ladies determine whom they'll marry based on their vocabulary level, and that people who can speak well, write well, and have good vocabularies are more successful in life

Inside the card are two messages. The first says "Study Steady." I consider this a powerful message, even though it is so simple. No matter what we do in life, if we do a little bit at a time, it will get done. A lot of people I've met don't seem to understand that this is how things get done, a little at a time. Waiting until the right moment to start comes along never gets the job done. I reinforce this concept throughout the year, also. If a student asks what they should do to raise their grade, my first response is, "Study steady." They don't always like that answer, but they know what it means.

The second message says, "As you think you become." I believe this concept to be very important for all mankind to know. As I tell my students, if you think positive thoughts, you'll eventually just be a positive person. If you think negative thoughts, then a negative attitude will be yours for life. If you constantly find fault in others, this is who you will become. If you strive to help others, then people will look to you for help. If you look long enough for something, eventually you'll see it.

It translates into class easily because a lot of students come in being very negative, and with very low self-esteem, believing they're stupid and unable to accomplish anything. Consequently, it's harder to motivate them than other students. If their thinking can be turned around, and we can get them going in the opposite direction, they will become positive members of society. I've seen this transformation with many students who have done nothing more in their lives than change their thinking. The instant you turn around, you're headed in the opposite direction.

On page four of the notebook is every student's Magic Vocabulary List. Vocabulary is one of the three determining factors of success in a chosen career. Master these and the future is yours. So we have magic vocabulary, the start of giving them the words with which to think with greater meaning.

I go more into detail regarding how vocabulary helps woman determine whom they will marry. It seems women tend to marry men with comparable vocabularies. So I tell my female students to raise their vocabulary levels so they'll choose someone successful.

To show the importance of vocabulary to their lives now, I take them back, back to when they were mere babes in the crib, back to when one word would get them all they wanted. "WAH!!!!!!" If they were hungry, "WAH!!!!" They were fed. If they were wet or worse, "WAH!!!!!" They were changed. If the pin is sticking them, "WAH!!!!!" (I tell them that eventually mom and dad will figure that one out). Or if they just wanted to be held. At that point in their lives, that one word filled all their needs.

I ask each class how many of them still get all their needs met by saying to dad, "WAH!" They get the point. As you get older, your vocabulary needs to expand because your needs expand and you have to be able to express those needs in an acceptable manner.

I spend time on the origin of words. I tell them about John T. Crapper, and Otto Titslinger, what they'll find along River Road, who first lived on James Place, and what used to be all along Elm Street. Words come from things already there. We don't really create words out of nothing. They almost always tell a bit of history about the place or thing they are named for. Grist Mill Road says it all. White Church Road. Town Hall Meeting Road. Who started Ford? Who runs, well, who used to run, Turner Broadcasting?

I lump all of these things under a concept I came up with many years ago called Tuna Fish. Tuna Fish means that the definition is in the word itself, you just have to look for it. For example, a three ring binder notebook is called that because it has three rings, it binds, and is a notebook. Simple enough. A spiral notebook is called that because it has a spiral for a binding and is a notebook. This eventually leads to discussions on prefixes, suffixes, and roots. Once they realize roots stay the same even though the beginnings and endings may change, they can make a more educated guess on SAT's and other vocabulary slanted tests.

After a while of massaging them with the idea that all words can be defined to some degree by the parts within, I give them their first Tuna Fish Test. The first word I start with is Pneumonoultramicroscopicsilicavolcanoconiosis. At first glance it may seem like I'm being unfair. The first human reaction is usually to say, "I can't do that," but let's have our first lesson in thinking you can so you will.

As most things need to be, words need to be broken into recognizable parts in order to decipher them. Pneumono will always have to do with the lungs; pneumonia, for example, a lung disease. Ultra always means really or a lot. Most students know that from commercials. Ultra brite toothpaste. Microscopic isn't hard for anyone. Everyone seems to know that it means really small. Silica is a little hard for many, but if you refer to Silicon Valley and what they make and what they make them from (computer chips, from sand), then students can make a pretty good guess. Volcano always means something hot. Students know it has to do with lava, which is hot. And I wind up telling them that the ending means an inflammation of something. So most of them come to a basic definition of an inflamed lung disease caused by very small pieces of hot sand. If this was one of the words on the SAT there would be four choices and the chances of getting it right on that short matching test increase greatly once you apply a little Tuna Fish to it. I call it Tuna Fish, by the way, because that's where Tuna fish comes from, a Tuna. Makes sense to me.

Twice a year students will have to do a major project where they make something based on anything they believe they have learned in my class. I depend on these projects to make me and my room look good. The project is not limited by medium. It can be a poster, a drawn picture, made from clay, or other weird art molding substances. It can be a shadow box, made from paper mache, or be a symbolic representation of some literary concept in one of the books we read. These projects have to synthesize learning. They make use of spatial and artistic intelligence. They force left-brain dominant students to use the right side of their brain more. They force students to internalize learning to a large degree. New knowledge is built upon previous knowledge.

Over the years I have come to accumulate enough projects that I can put them into various categories. There are clocks, flags, weapons, scenes from stories, items from around my room that have a practical application such as podiums and pointers, and posters depicting many of the concepts I reinforce through the year such as Gardner's Intelligences, hemisphericity, and speeches and the physiological changes they cause. There are also shadow boxes that contain a small scene inside a shoebox (when looked at through a small hole it can give the scene very striking qualities, with holes for light at strategic points), and posters, like those just mentioned, plus

Karl E. Thelen

those of all types and purposes. The point is their knowledge doesn't remain static or inapplicable to anything. Projects make them stop and confront things they have learned and reflect on them.

The accumulation of projects leads me to my room. I've had shelves built for projects, given extra credit to anyone who would build stands on which to place projects, and have considered doing other types of shelving to further the display. I pay for the shelving myself, by the way. No taxpayer's funds used. Some other teachers have begun calling my room The Museum. At first I didn't care for that designation, but the more I thought about it, the more I realized it was kind of like a museum. I have projects that go back to my second year at my current school, farther back actually because there is one poster, by a former talented student named Jan Gillam, that I've had since I taught in New York State.

I don't keep all projects. That would be impossible, but the joke is that I never throw anything away. I keep the projects that can stand the test of time. Every year some projects go just from the weight of time. Some get knocked off the shelf, some get broken through mindlessness, and some have just run their course. I also make a point to keep projects that represent books or themes that will be covered. These I can use in my presentation. They have a practical value.

I keep projects that are well made and have an obvious amount of time invested in them. I keep projects that speak to the soul of the student, usually paintings or drawings they have done exposing their natural talent. I keep projects that just tickle me for one reason or another because of some innate quality. The Museum is always open.

Another topic I consider important is daydreaming. I remember once, of many times, in sixth grade, when I was being yelled at because I wasn't paying attention. I had been guilty of daydreaming; going off to somewhere nicer than the classroom I was stuck in. My punishment, for the teacher convicted me on the spot, was to be yelled at for a very long time and be asked if I was stupid and did I have a problem following along? I, of course, at that point, had no answer, nor would I have dared one. It was best just to be stupid and be quiet about it.

Nowadays, we know that daydreaming is natural and is the best way to recharge our creative juices. Well, some of us know that, and soon all teachers should know that. Knowing it saves a lot of grief, a

A Nation of Idiots

lot of yelling, and eliminates the need to ask if someone is stupid merely because their mind wandered.

In my class this is called 'going to Bermuda,' and it's OK to go there. Bermuda is a nice place. Not the real one, but the one in your head, the one you go to when you're, heaven forbid, not paying attention. If new teachers understand that only half the class is actually listening at any given moment, they'll come up with better ways to get the information to all students.

I have a wall hanging on the ceiling, so you have to bend your head to read it, that says, "Are U in Bermuda?" I inform my students about Bermuda, explain that we all go there, that it's a pleasant place, that the amount of time you're gone could be from a second to all class, but if they've missed what I call the 'connector' information, they'll have no idea what's going on in class. This is why it's important to know if they were gone, so what's being talked about can be repeated and everyone brought up to speed. It's also important that they know the benefits of daydreaming. The only rule is that the whole class can't all go at the same time.

Another item mentioned on Page 3 is the grade sheets. These sheets will list all the grades for all the work they have done for the quarter. They are computer generated, and I send them home every two weeks. The parent has to sign it so I know they know their student's grade, and then it comes back to be given a 100. If it doesn't come back and the student is interfering with my ability to communicate with home, I'll give them a 0. Jobs not completed need to be rewarded too. It's tough educational love.

I've had many parents thank me for sending these sheets home. Many of them complain that once their child is out of the junior high, they don't hear from the teachers anymore, at least until progress report time, and by then it may be too late to successfully intervene. Parents should still be on top of their child's progress by asking the right questions at home, but that's been covered.

The grade sheets also let me know if I've made a mistake. That can be corrected immediately. Best of all, it gives the student the opportunity to make course corrections quickly, and move their grade upward.

I also make the students write in complete sentences, at all times. Complete sentences engender complete thoughts. This is the way the human mind works. Work it and it expands. If it is allowed, however, to continue to use truncated words and incomplete sentences, then this will cause a nationwide truncated thought process. It's already begun, which is why we have **A Nation of Idiots**. It's a reason why the trend towards 'fast' news, truncated headlines and text and e-mail English is having a negative, long-term effect. The ability to think clearly and in more than monosyllabic images is declining. It's also surprising how many students, at fifteen, don't know how to write a complete sentence. By reinforcing this concept, there is an accumulative affect throughout the year.

Many of the things I have been talking about fall under the categories of what I call Proximity and Absorption. I have used these two words for years to describe what I do and what I believe about students' ability to learn. In a nutshell, I believe that if a student is in proximity to me, he will absorb something of what I am teaching and learn.

This is one of the reasons for having the Museum. By keeping the well-done projects students can use them as templates to guide them in making their own. By sitting in the room, over time, many of the projects begin to have relevance, begin to make sense. I have one well-done drawing of a student's representation of Gollum from The Hobbit, sitting on a rock in the Thinker pose, with the words that say Think Deeper. We were half-way though the second semester when a student sat up a little straighter in his chair after staring at the poster, which conveniently hangs in the front of the room, and said "Hey, I get it now." He had gotten the message that the answers are quite often a little farther down. He had probably stared at that poster all year. Think Deeper.

Absorption is the counterpart to proximity. It's similar to what happened to the student above. He sat there long enough, absorbing something he didn't understand, but then, at some moment, after taking in all the other things he experiences in a day or week, came to a realization. Absorb enough of something long enough and it will ooze out your pores. If it has to do with education, that's even better. My room is set up for proximity and absorption.

Several other things that I do as a matter of course is to start on time, hand out key concepts sheets for whatever we happen to be working on so the students will know what we're going to be working on, expect them to remove their hats when they come in, maintain a

A Nation of Idiots

large cache of weapons, feed them popcorn and make bets I know I'll lose just to wind up buying pizza as payoff.

Starting on time is important from the first class. By starting on time early on, there will be much more time on task as the semester or year goes along. I lock my door at the start of class. Some teachers, especially the Feelgooders, think this is awful, that it embarrasses kids when they have to knock to come in. They should be embarrassed to interrupt a class that's already started. Once they know I'm serious, I have very few students who come in late.

Jim Ross, a master teacher in his own right, makes students who are late to his class answer the question, "What do you want?" with "I want to learn." It's the only acceptable response. If they don't want to learn he doesn't let them in. I wish I had grabbed that line first. I can rest, though, knowing that if I ever go to another school, that line is mine.

When students know you will be starting on time, they will internalize that and be ready to go much more often than had the expectation not been there. Starting class on time means you have their attention when you're ready to begin. When I am ready to begin all I say is, "If I could have your attention I'd appreciate it very much," and most times I get their attention and we're off. That doesn't have to be the signal to start as long as something lets them know you're starting, and it's consistent enough for the students to know what that signal means.

At times I've tried something my wife told me about, that another teacher she knew did and when I heard it I thought, "hey, that sounds neat." If its a really hyper day, usually when a low pressure is moving in, or we're a few days from a full moon, or they can smell vacation, I'll say "If you can hear my voice, clap your hands once." The first time I did this I was surprised at how many students clapped their hands. The other students quieted down immediately. It was a very powerful signal. I've only tried it a few times, but certainly on those rare occasions where they would dare to tempt Mr. Mean and not be quiet enough to hear my signal it will come in handy. Teachers need tools. I am a teacher; let me work.

Along with starting on time, which is all part of good planning, are the key concept sheets. I hand one out before we start something new, like a new book, or before we start speeches, or to introduce a new concept. The key concept sheets let the students know why we are doing something and what they should be getting out of it. They also keep me on track, since this is what I say I'm going to do, and all I have to do is follow the plan and do it.

I ask students to remove their hats when they come into my room as an act of common courtesy. In **A Nation of Idiots,** manners are coming up missing, and I hear a lot of people lamenting their loss.

Hats should come off in any public or religious place. That includes churches, synagogues, restaurants, schools, theaters, formal concerts, and especially my room. Students take them off because that's one of the expectations. This goes back to being Mr. Mean. They all know that this is something they're going to do, so that lessens the need for any student to become defensive over it. I think most students accept my argument about common courtesy and the need to have socially acceptable behavior so we can all get along in a democracy. Many teachers, by what goes on in their rooms, don't agree with me, but I think most of that is because they don't know how to get the kids to take their hats off without a big confrontation.

Another belief I live is that all teachers should have a large cache of weapons on hand. I realize that in this day and age, when Feelgooders would have us believe that any reference to weapons is bad, that this might be misconstrued as a call to violent action. But as educators, we can't let Media generated emotion invade our sensibilities. My weapons are all benign. They can't really hurt anyone, and the students aren't allowed to play with them. The students can take them out and look, but they can't play.

The most important weapon I have is my Sophomore Tenderizer. The Sophomore Tenderizer has a life and legend of its own. The Sophomore Tenderizer has been known to quell outbreaks merely by the teacher looking at it. So effective is the Sophomore Tenderizer that I've never really ever had to tenderize someone. But if your students believe that there's always a first time, then the power is there.

I also have a double-edged broadax. This is very intimidating, especially to junior high students who aren't sure about me yet. The ax is made of wood, by the way. I have a one sided ax, and that's the one I use when talking about Leon Trotsky being assassinated in Mexico City by an ax to the head while bathing. (I use this while we read and study <u>Animal Farm</u> by George Orwell).

A Nation of Idiots

I also have a large number of swords that have to do with either The Hobbit or another book called The Crystal Cave, by Mary Stewart. These are also for display purposes, and are too much trouble to bring out to threaten anyone with, so pretty much I stick to my Sophomore Tenderizer if I want to push the Mister Mean stuff.

The weapons that are the most fun, however, are the boffers, which are broom handles wrapped in foam padding and then wrapped tightly with duct tape. For a while there were boffers all over the school. You could get hit many times with a boffer and never feel it. I only have one left, since the others were all borrowed after school and never brought back. I'm lucky to have the weapons in this age of political correctness and zero tolerance, so I don't say too much:)

The weapons, of course, are just props, strategically placed around the room to precipitate discussion, recognition, and a connection that sparks other activity. I've seen many master teachers with props of their own.

Having props is an idea that works, and every teacher probably has the propensity to have their own 'props' whether it's an art class, physics class, or history class. Each discipline has those aspects that could be reinforced, or used to entice the students into inquiring, that speak to the discipline itself.

My good friend, Jim Ross, has been doing Colonial reenacting for over twenty years and brings British and Colonial paraphernalia to his history classes so that his students can experience history firsthand. He also started a daylong encampment on the school campus so classes can come out and ask questions of the reenactors and, again, experience first hand the sounds and smells of early America. Props can instill excitement, one of the main ingredients for learning.

The weapons aren't the only props I have and rely on on a daily basis. Certainly the most stellar is Podi, the podium from which most speeches are made. A former student named Larry Cutting made Podi in 1974. Podi has been refurbished twice, taken apart, sanded, repaired, put back together, but always she is Podi.

When standing on Podi, students are way above the audience, designed, as any good podium, to give the speaker the edge over the audience, a mesmerizing technique perfected by Adolf Hitler and Ronald Reagan, both of whom employed large podiums to address their constituents. Hitler, of course, having some mental problems, way over did it.

Karl E. Thelen

Podi is introduced in the opening remarks on day one. It is here that the respect for Podi and what she will help the students accomplish begins. I tell them the history. By now some of their parents have been up on Podi, and gone through the same adrenaline burning pain of abject fear at what is always voted the number one fear of most Americans: public speaking. And yet, ironically, public speaking is the one activity that can make you face yourself and that fear, and help you become most successful later in life. After their first speech they always come back for more.

I pass out The Twelve Rules For Living and say that they apply in my room as well, and the expectation is that we will all practice them. They are as follows:

1. If you open it, close it.
2. If you turn it on, turn it off.
3. If you unlock it, lock it up.
4. If you break it, admit it.
5. If you can't fix it, call in someone who can.
6. If you borrow it, return it.
7. If you value it, take care of it.
8. If you make a mess, clean it up.
9. If you move it, put it back.
10. If it belongs to someone else, get permission to use it.
11. If you don't know how to operate it, leave it alone.
12. If it's none of your business, don't ask questions.

I've cooked popcorn in my room for any class, or student, that wanted it for too many years to count. We take a break at certain times, usually in the middle of an 80-minute block (we're currently on a block schedule in the high school, four classes per day, two days to go through all the classes, with classes running approximately 80-85 minutes). The popcorn, although it isn't much, calms them down a little. Some days the sound of the popping seems to excite them, but most days the lulling pop pop poppity pop, along with the wafting buttery smell soothes the savage beasts.

I make bets I know I'm going to lose, but, hey, I make the $$$$$. By betting on something I know I can't do, or haven't been able to do, I show that I'm not afraid to try, to put it on the line and go for it. The bet is always for pizza. I've spent a lot of money on pizza over the years.

One standard bet is that I can balance a wooden pointer on my nose, then drop it down to my tongue, onto my chin, back to my tongue, and then back up onto my nose. I've lost a lot on this one, but one day I did manage to get it all the way back to my tongue, but putting it back up on my nose is going to take a bit more practice.

A second bet I make, and the most frequent, is that I'll be able to correct their vocabulary tests in a certain length of time, depending on how many words are on the test. I lost once because in the middle of correcting I had to take a phone call and the students wouldn't let me out of the bet. I lost by forty seconds. It took me five large pizzas to cover all bets.

The above are things I do in the first few days to prepare for the year ahead. I lay down groundwork, let everyone involved know what to expect, and then go for it. I promise those who stick with me a journey they'll remember for years, whether they want to or not. Through proximity and absorption, I will connive to teach anyone in my room. Reva Cousino, an English teacher I've work with for 23 years, used to say, "If they come in my room, I'll teach them." It was a line meant to take away some of the pressure of constant change that is rampant in education today, the nonsensical things that pop up, remnants of trying to fix our **Nation at Risk** and, now, more recently, a reaction to President George Dubya's education initiatives. In other words, don't worry about what changes people say are coming, wait and see who comes in your room. That's where teaching happens. That's where it will always happen. If they come in my room, I will teach them. The future of education depends on the quality of the individual teacher.

Karl E. Thelen

Chapter twelve

In Conclusion; It's all been said before

A lot has been said here, and yet, I've only scratched the surface. When many different forces align themselves, by accident or by plan, against something as precious as education, defending against them takes a Herculean effort. Quite honestly, since we are a nation that is all too comfortable with our technological toys and our reliance on immediate gratification, that extreme effort may not be in us.

At the moment we are **A Nation of Idiots**, but we don't have to be. The change has to be a concentrated emphasis on quality teachers, derived from apprentice programs that immerse teacher candidates in the oil of education. The solution will never be found in quick fix educational/curricular fads or inane administrivial attempts at motivation. Changing the box doesn't change what's inside it. A school run by poor administrators and staffed with unqualified teachers will never be effective.

Parents need to stop blaming the schools for their child's problems. The schools didn't force anyone to drink alcohol and create fetal alcohol syndrome. The schools didn't poison the mother's body with nicotine, and the schools didn't shake the baby when it wouldn't stop crying and cause the resulting mild to severe brain damage. The schools didn't have the children from the very beginning in order to instill values and morals and limits. So back off, mom and dad. If parents believe the school isn't challenging their child then create a challenge at home. Take responsibility for what always used to be parental responsibility. Buck up, suck it in and get your hands dirty.

Feelgoodenism needs to be weeded out of all schools, out of all daily life in America. Reality needs to pervade education. Life is tough and doesn't allow for many second chances to redo a paper.

When you fail the test of life, there often isn't any makeup or extra credit to bring the grade up. Quite often you're simply fired.

This may sound like I'm advocating a harsh, prison-gray reality in education. I'm not, I'm just for getting rid of anything that allows a student to hide behind a poor excuse for poor behavior, or is allowed to get away with harming another person or vandalizing someone's property because the child was 'misunderstood' or didn't know any better.

We need to stop coddling kids. They're tough, they're resilient, but they also pick up on the game quickly. That's why expectations for behavior and academics need to be set high. This will keep the brighter students busy enough and lessen the subtle problems they can cause when they become 'bored.' Education needs to get just beyond their frustration level.

The real problem with Feelgoodenism is that it limits students in many ways. Students who are kept from any stress that getting an education may cause them don't develop the skills needed to cope in a stress-filled society. Much of what we learn and know as adults came about because of our need to defend ourselves against the slings and arrows of life. We learn people skills when we have to confront a bully, or deal with an ever-changing list of friends. If we remove all the obstacles of life from our children they will grow up defenseless. They will grow up only to meet a State standard. They will be mediocre.

In classes, the lowering of expectations can be devastating. Without the mental stimulation that a good challenge incurs, learning will be lessened or non-existent. What if a kindergarten, teacher, a Feelgooder, said to her students, "Boys and girls, I've decided that learning the alphabet can be very stressful, so I've decided to let each of you choose just one letter to learn about. You can study your letter at your own speed. You can do projects about your letter, you can write a report about your letter, and you can share your letter with your classmates." When the student is all finished learning about their letter they will have learned a lot, about that letter. The purpose of learning the alphabet, however, is to have a base of knowledge on which to build the rest of the student's language. One letter won't quite make it, but the students will sure feel good.

School boards need to be realigned. Their basic makeup has to change so that the group that decides the direction of a school is made up of master teachers. School boards should not be political, should not be forums for anger or personal vendettas. Since this isn't going to happen anytime soon, those who are on school boards need to learn their trade, so to speak. This is not easy to do. The farther removed from education someone is, the harder it will be to understand what's really going on.

All school board members first need to understand that as an individual, they have no authority in the school at all. Only a majority vote has any authority on a school board. That would keep the one-issue hot heads corralled. That doesn't mean school board members shouldn't come in the school. They should come in often, not to interfere, but as part of their 'learning the trade.' They should visit the classrooms and stay a while in order to get the flow of what's happening. The more they're in the school the more they'll learn. They should even try their hand at teaching, feel the heart rate increase, feel the pressure of holding kids accountable, take care of the paper work for a while, learn the trade.

As for the large corporations, especially the three mentioned most here, the pharmaceutical, alcohol and tobacco industries, waiting for conscience to kick in might make all of us real old, so it looks like legislation is needed, similar to what our good neighbor to the north, Canada, has.

If education is as valuable as everyone in America says it is, then there should be no question about going all out to correct the problem, and that means that those who contribute a large share to the problem need to be responsible and help correct it. There's nothing wrong with making a profit. That's the American way. But when it interferes with or circumvents the pursuit of happiness, it isn't good.

The problem of teacher health care needs to be solved. Not by the State or Federal governments simply picking up the tab, but by forcing down the costs. If the problem is over-priced prescriptions and over-prescribed medical care, then that's where the solution has to be. It would also mean that those in education who use their health care for every minor ache and pain need a good dose of reality themselves. Everyone needs to be responsible.

The media will not be reigned in, certainly not while there are such huge profits to be made. It's up to everyone else then, to spread the word, and the best way to do that is through media literacy classes. Only if the targets of the media bombardment become aware

A Nation of Idiots

that they are targets, and know how the money-suckers manipulate them, will the scourge of the mass media be thwarted.

The special education budget has to be removed from the shoulders of the local taxpayers. With all the governmental mandates in place and the inability of many school districts to afford the increased costs without jeopardizing all other educational programs, the special needs students aren't receiving the services that they really need. The teachers and paraprofessionals who man the ranks of special education should be compensated much better than they are now. Slave wages won't attract too many for too long. And you already know who I think should help pay for it.

Effective teaching and effective schools research is there for the taking. These are not the bright ideas of an incompetent administrator or the musings of a Feelgooder. These are the things good teachers and good schools are already doing, and have been doing for a long time. That doesn't mean any school district has to parrot what another district is doing right down to the exact words and same daily schedule. It means, hey, you want to get better? Here's a way, but get your own terminology.

Whereas being an effective teacher is a personal goal, being an effective school involves many others and is a little tougher to achieve. The decision-making model of going from the bottom up, from the teachers to the board, is contrary to how most systems are set up. Too many are still top down, even if the façade of being an effective school shows the community just the opposite. It's easy to adopt the terminology and not have the concepts in place to back up the talk. This is a good reason to keep an eye on ambitious administrators. They might talk the talk, but judge them by the walk.

Testing in the United States has reached superstar proportions. All the big people want to talk about testing and make sure that all of us are at least above average. Proponents of standardized testing square off against proponents of portfolios, and both sides miss the majority in the middle.

Testing should never be used to compare to others or to institute great change. Testing results should be used to keep track only of an individual student or an individual school's progress or areas of special need. There are too many variables in education to make cut and dried decisions based on any single set of data.

Karl E. Thelen

Starting early in the student's career all those responsible in any way for that child's education should have a clear understanding of hemispheric preferences, intelligence strengths, learning styles, environmental preferences, memory, and anything else that will help match the student with the best route to success. No test should carry enough weight to derail any student in pursuit of their future. Also, the understanding that preferences change over time should be a strong leveling force on the entire process. We're looking to help students open their opportunities, not lock them into any particular future.

The way I see it, unless things change, sometime in the future, all basic skills will be eliminated, since it will have caused too much pressure to have to know how to punctuate, spell, or add and subtract. This will coincide with the master plan of all giant corporations, who only want your money, to have all transactions done electronically. Your pay goes directly into your banking account, and all payments are automatically deducted, and no one can keep track of what they should have or what they do have since they can no longer add or subtract. Then, at some predetermined point in time, one, small, electronic glitch will ripple through our advanced technology and everything will be gone. Everything, that is, except the rather comfortable lifestyle of top executives from the two remaining global media-industrial giants who will then be enjoying the fruits of **A Nation of Idiots** on a warm beach somewhere in a roped-off part of the world. They will be aided and abetted, by the way, by their good friends the mass media manipulators, who knew you still had a little left to give.

I have no doubt the above scenario will come true, unless, of course, enough people wake up and realize that the quality of education in America depends on the quality of the individual teacher. It always has and it always will. Until that time we will continue to be **A Nation of Idiots**.

Thank you for reading A Nation of Idiots. Do you have any comments on the book or experiences of your own in this Nation? The author would like to hear from you. Please visit the author's website at www.anationofidiots.com, or write to him at Kthelen@anationofidiots.com.

Karl E. Thelen

Index

A

A Circle of Assessment, *15, 163*
A Nation of Idiots, 1, *7, 10, 15, 27, 35, 49, 52, 53, 54,* 58, *62, 67, 71, 78, 93,* 94, 152, 182, 196, 198, 202, 206
AARP magazine, 48
Absentee Parents, *42*
academic atmosphere, 29, *147, 159*
academic goals, 132
academic leader, 42, 134, 135, 154
accountability, *39, 137*
ACT, 165, 166
Act 60, *12*
Acting Presidential, 67
Active participation, 119
<u>Activities at the Ready</u>, 125
Administrative leadership, 134
administrators, *1, 8, 16, 18, 24, 27, 28, 31, 32, 33, 35, 39, 92, 131, 132, 134, 135, 154, 161*
Advanced Placement, 167
advocacy group, 66
advocates, 14, 101, 114, 164
alcohol, *67, 110*
ambient light, 12, 53
American College Test, 165
American Medical Association, 49
Amway, 75, 80
Analysis, 126
Animal Farm, 198
Annual Report to Congress, 22nd, 97
Anticipatory Set, 118
AOL/Time Warner, 56
Application, 126
association principle, 89
Astra-Zeneca, 49
attendance, *19, 133, 157*
Audy, Steve, v
Authority, 72, 90, 92

B

Badgerer Parents, *44*
Bartlett, Stephen, 47
Benjamin, L. Ann, *38*
Bermuda, 195
Bertelsmann, 56
Bewkes, Jeffrey, 55
Blaise, Leonard, 161
Bodily-kinesthetic intelligence, 171
Bristol, Vermont, 161
Buddy Parents, *43*
Bureau for Education of the Handicapped, 96
Burger King, 58
Bush, George W., 116

C

Calvin and Hobbes, 65
chalkboard, 123, 127
Cherrier, Ed, v
Cialdini, Robert B., 72
circle of assessment, 163, 164, 170, 172, 175, 177, 178, 179, 180, 181
Claritin, 47, 50
Classroom characteristics and practices, 138
Clearly defined curricula, 133
Clinton, Bill, 62
Colleges, *7, 181*
Columbine High School, 84
Comedy Central, 56
Commitment, 85
Committee to Reelect the President (CRP, 77
Community Parent Resource Centers, 102
Comprehension, 125, 126, 171
Congress, 48, 49, 51, 96, 98, 99, 100, 101, 103, 105, 106, 107, 108, 109
consistency, 78, 79, 80, 81, 154, 160
Consistency, 72

consistency principle, 78
consumer advertising, 48
Contrast Principles, 73
Cooper, Jane, v
cooperative learning, 129
Corey, Mike, v
Cornell University, 76
Corporations, *10*, *52*
correction sheet, 185, 188
Cousino, Reva, v
Covering Ground, 124
Coyle, Susan L., 48
Crapper, John T., 192
Cutting, Larry, 199

D

Dangerous Drugs, 67
Deaver, Michael, 65
Decius, 87
Democratic National Committee, 77
Dennison, Paul and Gail, 174
Department of Education, *27*, *38*
Design For Effective Instruction, 123, 124
Designer drugs, 49
dignifying a wrong answer, 122
discipline, *2*, *9*, *15*, *17*, *22*, *24*, *26*, *27*, *28*, *29*, *32*, *33*, *36*, *37*, *125*, *135*, *136*, *137*, *149*, *157*, *158*, *159*, *184*, *199*
Disney, 56, 57
Doublethink, 58
Dr. Larry Lazotte, *162*
Dunn, Rita, 175

E

Early Intervention Program for Infants and Toddlers with Disabilities, 100
Edmonds, Ron, *130*
Education for all Handicapped Children Act, 95
Education of the Handicapped Act, 96, 100
Education of the Handicapped Act, P.L., 91-230, 96

Education Research Report, *38*
Education Trust study, *24*
Educational Kinesiology Foundation, 174
Educational Testing Service, 165
Effective questioning, 120, 121
Effective Schools, *6*, *14*, *24*, *31*, *32*, *130*, *131*, *132*, *137*, *154*
Effective Teaching, *6*, *14*, *118*, *130*, *143*
effective teaching techniques, *25*
Elementary and Secondary Education Act, 104
Emmons, Jason, v
emotional attachment, 60, 61, 64, 67
Enabler Parents, *43*
English teachers, *17*, *26*
Essex Industries, 107
Ethics and Human Rights Committee of the American College of Physicians, 48
ETS, 165, 167
Evaluation, 126, 127
Experts, 68

F

F.A.I.R., 55, 56
Federal Aid, *12*
Federalist Papers, *23*
Feelgood land, 152
Feelgoodenism, 2
Feelgooder, *3*, *4*, *5*, *20*, *29*, *42*, *54*, *116*, 187
Feelgooders, 1, 2, 3, 4, 14, 71, 96, 97, 104, 107, 111, 139, 149, 190, 197, 198
feeling tone', 185
field trips, *36*
Five-minute writings, 187
Fixed Action Patterns, 72
Food and Drug Administration, 50
Four Sources of Wasted Time, 124
Franklin, Ben, 69
Free Appropriate Public Education, 96

G

Galewitz, Phil, 50
Gardner, Howard, 170, *181*
General Electric, 56
Georgia, 23
Giandomenico, Lawrence L., 124
Gibran, Kahail, 182
Gillam, Jan, 194
Gollum, 196
good ol' boys, *21*
grade sheets, 37, 195
grading punisher, *19*
Graduate Management Admission Test, 167
Graduate Record Exam, 165, 167
Guided Practice, 122

H

halo effect, 86
Hartling, Elizabeth, 33
Hats, 198
Hawkins, B. Denise, 165
Haycock, Katy, *23*
HBO, 55, 56
headline hanky panky, 60
Headline News, *12*, 56
health care, *10*, *11*, *35*, *46*, *47*, *48*, *49*, *51*, *66*, *115*
hemisphericity, *25*, *123*, *163*, *175*, *177*, *178*, *185*, *189*
Hemisphericity, *15*
Heneche, Erv, 183
Higher Image, 74, 86, 89
Hitler, Adolf, 199
Hobbit, The, 196
Houston Chronicle, 50
Humiliators, *41*
Hunter, Madeline, 118

I

IDEA, 97, 98, 99, 100, 101, 102, 104, 105, 107, 109, 112
IEP's, 103, 104, 105
Independent Practice, 123
Individuals with Disabilities Education Act, 96

Influence, 72, 76, 85
in-service, 6, 11, 27, 28, 103, 134
Instability, 68
Instruction is guided by a preplanned curriculum, 138
Intellectual Parents, *43*
International Monetary Fund, 55
Interpersonal intelligence, 171
Intrapersonal intelligence, 172
isolate, focus, magnify, 60

J

Japanese, *13*
Jefferson, Thomas, 69
Jeopardy students, 121
journal, 119, 140, 180, 186
Julius Caesar, 87

K

KFC, *4*, *58*
Knowledge, 125, 126, 155

L

Lazotte, Dr. Larry, *6*, *130*
Learning Style Inventory, 175
Learning Styles, *15*, *175*
Leave No Child Behind, *12*
Lee, Nikki ☺, v
legislators, *1*, *9*, *37*, *132*
level of frustration, *6*, *184*
Liddy, G. Gordan, 77
Liking, 72, 85, 87, 88, 89
Linguistic intelligence, 171
Lipitor, 47
Litigators, *42*
loaded language, 60, 62
Logical-mathematical intelligence, 171
long-term memory, 25, 70, 139, 164, 177, 178
Lunden, Joan, 50

M

Madeline Hunter, 6
Magic Vocabulary List, 191

mandates, 13, 33, 47, 95, 96, 98, 112, 114, 162
mass marketing, *10*
mass media, *1*, *10*, *11*, *12*, *48*, *52*, *58*, *63*, *71*, *79*, *87*, *93*
Massachusetts, *23*
Massachusetts' \i, 23
Master teachers, *5*, *6*, *24*, *27*, *134*
Maxine Connor, v
McDonald's, 71
McDonalds, 58
McGovern, George, 77
Media Manipulators, 86, 88, 89
medical profession, *10*, *78*
Memory, *15*, *177*, *178*
Merck, 50
Milgram Experiment, 90
Milgram, Stanley, 90
Military Leader, 68
Military Strongman, 68
Mineville, N.Y, 107
Mitchell, John, 77
Monitoring of student progress, 133
Moriah Central HS, 183
Mount Abraham Union High School, 161
Moyers, Bill, 65
Mr. Mean, 183, 184, 190, 197, 198
Multiple Intelligences, *15*, *25*, *170*
Murdoch, Rupert, 56
Musical intelligence, 171

N

National Early Intervention Longitudinal Study, 108
National Security, 66, 68, 71
National Teachers Exam, 167
New York State Regents, 169
Nexium, 49
Nixon, Richard M., 77
Noriega, Manuel, 68
North Carolina, *24*
notebook, 123, 124, 185, 190, 191, 192

O

O'Brien, Lawrence, 77
Office of Special Education Programs, 107
Opportunities for student responsibility and participation, 135
Order and Discipline, 136
Oregon, *23*
Orwell, George, 58
Orwell, George, 198

P

Page 3, 185, 187, 195
Panama, 68
Parent and community involvement, 135
Parent Training and Information Centers, 101
parents, *1*, *7*, *8*, *9*, *14*, *16*, *17*, *33*, *36*, *37*, *38*, *39*, *40*, *41*, *42*, *45*, *59*, *79*, *95*, *96*, *97*, *100*, *101*, *102*, *104*, *107*, *109*, *114*, *132*, *135*, *139*, *141*, *142*, *143*, *153*, *154*, *155*, *158*, *160*, *180*, *195*, *200*
Patient Parents, *42*
PBS, 65
Perceptual Contrast, 73, 74, 77
pharmaceutical companies, *10*, *46*, *49*, *50*, *51*, *56*
Phillips, David, 84
Planning Process, 130, 132
Pneumonoultramicroscopicsilicavolc anoconiosis., 192
Podi, 199, 200
polls, 60, 66
popcorn, 197, 200
Port Henry, NY, 183
portfolio, 15, 117, 118, 163, 164, 168, 169, 170, 173, 174, 180
portfolio assessments, *15*
Portfolios, 163, 168, 180
Positive school climate, 131
Praxis I, *23*
Praxis II, *23*

Pre-Elementary Educational Longitudinal Study, 108
Press-Republican, 47
projects, 21, 81, 107, 109, 172, 193, 194, 196
PSAT/National Merit Scholarship Qualifying Test, 167
punishers, *19*

R

Radical, 69
Reagan,, 199
Reagan, Ronald, 65
Reciprocation, 72, 75
reciprocity rule, 75, 76, 77
Regan Study, 76
Regan, Dennis, 76
rejection-then retreat, 76, 77
remedial courses, *7*
Rewards and incentives, 136
Rita Dunn, 14
Ross, Jim, v, 199
rubrics, *40*
rule of reciprocity, 75

S

Sargent, June, v
SAT, 11, *12*, 165, 166, 167. See Scholastic Aptitude Test
Scarcity, 72, 92
Schering-Plough, 50
Scholastic Aptitude Test, 165
School atmosphere, 131
School board members, *8*, *35*
School characteristics and practices, 138, 152
screamers, *20*
Screamers, *40*
Seagram, 56
Senior Administrative Official, 69
Senior privileges, *29*
severely handicapped, 106, 107, 115
Shakespeare, 87
Similar Others, 85, 89
Social Proof, 72, 82, 83, 84, 85
Sony, 56

Sophomore Tenderizer, 148, 198, 199
sound bites, 60
source journalism, 66
special education, *3*, *9*, *13*, *36*, *47*, *95*, *97*, *99*, *100*, *103*, *105*, *108*, *109*, *110*, *112*, *114*, *115*
Special Education Czar, 102
Special Interests, 70
special-education, 47
Stability, 68
Staff development, 134, 159
standardized test, 11, 12, 16, 113, 164, 165
standardized tests, *15*, *163*, *165*, *166*, *167*, *168*, *170*, *172*, *174*, *180*
standards, 3, 13, 43, 103, 110, 113, 117, 118, 139, 143, 145, 149, 151, 153, 154, 160, 169
State and Local Implementation of IDEA, 109
State Improvement Grants, 104
State University of New York at Plattsburgh, 124
Statistics, 66
Stewarts, *5*
Stewert, Mary, 199
Study of Personnel Needs in Special Education, 109
Subway, 58
Swearers, *41*
Synthesis, 126, 127, 137
systems change grants, 107

T

Table Pounders, *41*
target market, 48
taxpayers, *1*, *9*, *11*, *13*, *36*, *47*, *51*, *69*, *95*, *96*, *115*, *137*, *152*
teacher quality, *24*
teacher testing, 22
Teacher/Staff effectiveness, 133
Technical Assistance Alliance, 102
Terrorism, 69
Test of English as a Foreign Language, 167

testing, *14, 15, 23, 114, 164, 167, 170, 173, 179, 181*
Texas, *23*
The Crystal Cave, 199
the enabler, *20*
The key to manipulation, 60
the morgue, 60
The Museum, 194
The Nation, 48, 49
The **National Longitudinal Transition Study**, 108, 109
The Prophet, 182
The Public Mind, 65
The Senate Committee on Labor and Human Resources, 103
The **Special Education Elementary Longitudinal Study**, 109
The **Special Education Expenditure Project**, 109
Thelen, Mary, v
Thelen, Shane A., v
Thelen, Virginia, v
Thompson, Allie, v
Thompson, Meredith, v
time on task, *24, 140, 146, 157, 197*
Title I, 104
Titslinger, Otto, 192
tobacco industry, 110
Trigger Features, 72
Trotsky, Leon, 198
Tuna Fish, 192, 193
Tupperware, 75, 85
Turkington, Carol, 178
Twelve Rules For Living, 200

U

United States, *1, 97*

University of California at San Diego, 84
Unreliable Sources, 54, 60, 62, 64, 66

V

Vermont, *12, 97, 117, 161, 168, 186*
Viacom, 56
Viagra, 47
Victim Parents, *43*
Vioxx, 47
von Goethe, Johann, 83

W

wallpapering, 60
Walmart, *5, 58*
Warner Brothers, 56
Washington, George, 69
Watergate, 77
Wayne, John, 59
Weapons of Influence, 72
Wedge, Reggie, 162
Welcome to the Wonderful World of English, 191
Wendy's, 58
Werther effect, 83, 84
Whiners, *40*
with-it-ness, 120
World Bank, 55

Y

yellers, *20*
Yellers and screamers, 148

Z

Zocor, 47

Bibliography

Ahmann, Stanley J., Marvin D. Glock. <u>Evaluating Pupil Growth: Principles of Tests and Measurement</u>, Boston, Ally and Bacon, 1968.

"A Nation at Risk." *Department of Education*. (April 1983).

A Nation Still At Risk: An Education Manifesto." Center for Education Reform. (April 30, 1998), 1-9
http://edreform.com/pubs/manifest.htm

Anderson, Judith. "Who's in Charge? Teacher Views on Control Over School Policy and Classroom Practices." *Education Research Report*. (August 1994), 1-5

—— "Who Runs the School? The Principal's View." *Education Research Report*. (May 1993), 1-6

Annual Report to Congress on the Implementation of the Individuals with disabilities Education Act (IDEA), 22nd. U.S. Department of Education. (2000).

Barnes, Fred. "Can You Trust Those Polls?" *Readers Digest*. (July 1995), 49-54

Barry, Patricia. "Ads, promotions drive up costs: Drugmakers spend billions reaching consumers, doc." *The Nation*. (March 2002), 3, 17-18.

Bartlett, Stephen. "Cuts in store for Peru." *Press-Republican*. (March 29, 2002), A3

Bradley, Ann. "Test Questions." Education Week. (12/9/1998).
http://www.edweek.com/ew/vol-18/15mass.h18

Carpenter, C. Dale-Ray, Marissa S. "Portfolio Assessment: Opportunities and Challenge." *Intervention in School and Clinic.* (September 1, 1995), 34.

Castiglione, Lawrence V. "Portfolio assessment in art and education." Vol. 97. *Arts Education Policy Review.* (03-13-1996), 2.

Chaika, Gloria. "Testing Teachers Makes Teachers Testy." *Education World.* (9/26/2000).
http://www.educationworld.com/a_issues/issues128.shtml

Cialdini, Robert B. PH. D. Influence. New York: William Morrow and Company, 1984.

Collins, James. "Special Report/How to make a better student." *Time.* (10-19-1998), 94-95.

Coyle, Susan L. Ph. D. "Physician-Industry Relations Part I: Individual Physicians." *Annals of Internal Medicine.* (March 5, 2002).

Crenson, Matt. "Americans' manners leave much to be desired." *Press Republican.* (April 3, 2002), 2A.

Curwin, Richard, Allen N. Meadler. "Zero Tolerance for Zero Tolerance." *Kappan Professional Journal.* Vol. 81. (October 1999), 119-120.
http://www.pdkintl.org/kappan/kcur9910.htm

Delisio, Ellen R. "Boards, Superintendents Should Collaborate More." Education World. (October 13, 2000). http://www.educationworld.com/a_admin/admin193.shtml/

Dunn, Diane W., Ellen R. Delisio. "Common Elements of Effective Schools." (3/11/02).

Dunn, Rita. How to Implement and Supervise a Learning Style Program. Association for Supervision and Curriculum Development. April 1996.

Ediger, Marlow. "Measuring how much students have learned." Vol. 118. *Education*. (03-22-1998), 406.

"Enhancing the efficacy of split thirty-second television commercials: an encoding variable application" *Journal of Advertising*. (3/26/99).

Galewitz, Phil. "Pharmaceutical companies add celebrity to ad formula." *Houston Chronicle*. (March 7, 1999), 2

Gardner, Howard. "An intelligent way to progress." *Independent*. (03-19-1998), E4-E5.

—— "Multiple Intelligences." *Basic Books*, February 1990.

—— The Disciplined Mind. Penguin USA. September 2000.

Giandomenico, Lawrence and Lawrence Shulman. Working With Teachers Effectively Springfield, Charles C. Thomas, 1991.

—— "Design for Effective Instruction" notebook. *Center for Teacher Education* SUNY Plattsburgh, NY.

Glenn, Robert E. "Admirable Teaching Traits." Education World. (February 4, 2002).
http://www.edcationworld.com/a_curr/curr387.shtml

Gray, James H. Viens. Julie T. "The theory of multiple intelligences." Vol. 74. *National Forum*. (01-01-1994). 22.

Hawkins, Denise B. "A Multiple-Choice Mushroom: School, Colleges Rely More than Ever On." *Black Issues In Higher Education*. (02-09-1995).

Haycock, Katy. "Good Teaching Matters." *Thinking K-16*. (summer 1998), 1-4

Hertling, Elizabeth. Retaining Principals." ERIC Digest number 147. (April 2000).

Jacobson, Rebecca. "Teachers improving learning using metacognition with self-monitoring learning strategies." Vol. 118. *Education*. (06-22-1998), 579.

Kilbourne, Jean. "Killing us Softly 3." video

Kunen, James S. "Education: The test of their lives exit exam may whip America's schools into shape, but some good kids pay a heavy price." *Time*. (06-16-1997), 62+.

Lee, Martin, Norman Soloman. Unreliable Sources. Carol Publishing Group, 1992.

Little, Joan. "Intelligences Theory Applied in Local Schools." *St. Louis Post-Dispatch*. (11-20-1994), 01D.

McChesney, Robert. *"The Global Media Giants."* FAIR. (Nov/Dec 1997) http://www.fair.org/extra/9711/gmg.html

Moyers, Bill. "The Appearance of News." *PBS Documentary Series "The Public Mind."*

"Onward to Excellence: Making Schools More Effective." Effective Schooling Practices: A Research/Synthesis. *Northwest Regional Educational Laboratory*. (April 1984). 1-20

Palmer, Sue. "Time to Teach." *Education World*. (4/26/2002).

Pardini, Priscilla. "Special Education: Promises and Problems." www.rethinkingschool.org. (Spring 2002), 1-10

Peterson, David. "Evaluating Principals." *ERIC Digest* Series Number 60. (1991).

"Retaining Principals." *ERIC Digest* Number 147.

Rodriguez, Nancy C. "Cheating teacher skews school's test scores." Eagle-Tribune. (July 22, 1999), A2.

Rosenshire, Barak V. "Synthesis of Research on Explicit Teaching." *Educational Leadership*. (April 1986). 60-69.

Shabazz, Malik. "The Bandwagon: Some Schools Lessen Weight of Standardized Test Scores." *Black Issues In Higher Education*. (02-09-1995

Shaughnessy, Michael F. "An interview with Rita Dunn about learning styles," Vol. 71, *The Clearing House*. (01-11-1998), 141.

Shobris, John G. "The Anatomy of Intelligence." *Heldref Publications*. (12-07-1995).

Special Education Inclusion." *Teaching and Learning*: Special Education Series. (June 1996).
http://www.weac.org/resources/june/96/speced.htm

Starr, Linda. "Stop Tolerating Zero Tolerance." *Education World*. (4/16/2002).
http://www.education-world.com/a_issues/issues303.shtml

—— "Too Many elephants." *Education World*. (4/23/2002).

Toch, Thomas, Betsy Wagner. "Schools for Scandal." *U.S. News & World Report*. (05-12-1997), 41+

Topp, Greg. "Schools scramble to meet new law." Press Republican. (September 2, 2002), A9

Travis, Jon E. "Meaningful assessment." Vol. 69. *The Clearing House*. (05-15-1996), 308.

Turkington, Carol. 12 Steps to a Better Memory. New York, Macmillan, 1996.

Wallace, Ray. "Formative and summative evaluation at ground zero. (Forms and functions of formative assessment)." Vol. 71. *The Clearing House*. (11-21-1997), 119.

Karl E. Thelen

Emus and Emu Oil

Emus, from the Ratite family, are the second largest flightless bird in the world. Emu oil has been found to have considerable medicinal uses. Emu oil is used for:

- Burns
- Bites
- Arthritis
- Acne
- Muscle pain
- Psoriasis
- Eczema
- Dry skin
- Wounds and scarring

Emu oil contains the three essential fatty acids, linoleic, linolenic and oleic acid. These essential fatty acids are responsible for a wide variety of health-related connections within the body. They are 'essential' to your health. Only fish oil contains comparable amounts of these essential fatty acids.

Emu oil has also been found helpful in lowering cholesterol, cutting deposits that lead to coronary artery disease, and contributing to a general feeling of well being.

Products available include:

- Pure emu oil
- Emu oil soap
- Cryo-gel (cold)
- Power Rub (hot)
- Power Rub Plus (hot)
- Lip balm
- Hand and body lotion
- Gel caps for arthritis and internal health
- Hair shampoo
- Conditioner
- Tooth and gum gel

A Nation of Idiots

If you are experiencing pain and would like to try emu oil products from Meadowood Homestead Emu Ranch, write to us, the Four Emugos, at:

>Meadowood Homestead Emu Ranch
>228 Bartlett Pond Road
>Mineville, NY 12956
>
>Or e-mail us at emupreneur@aol.com

We'll send a product and price list. Thank you for buying **A Nation of Idiots**.

Karl E. Thelen

About the Author

The author has taught high school English for the past thirty-three years. He has a masters degree in administration and supervision, spent seven years on a school board, and, along with his wife of thirty-four years, Mary, raised five kids.

The author has taught public speaking for thirty-three years, layout and design as a yearbook advisor for twenty-two years and media literacy for the past eleven years. His insight into the manipulation by the media allows him to lay much of the blame where it belongs for **A Nation of Idiots**.

The author, along with his wife, brother and sister-in-law have been raising emus for the past six years at their Meadowood Homestead Emu Ranch in Mineville, NY.

Printed in the United States
1187200003B/274-294